Hybrid CONSTITUTIONS

Hybrid CONSTITUTIONS

Challenging Legacies of
Law, Privilege, and Culture
in Colonial America

VICKI HSUEH

Duke University Press
Durham and London 2010

© 2010 Duke University Press

All rights reserved

Printed in the United States of America on acid-free paper ∞

Designed by Heather Hensley

Typeset in Minion Pro by Achorn International, Inc.

Library of Congress Cataloging-in-Publication Data appear
on the last printed page of this book.

Duke University Press gratefully acknowledges the support
of Western Washington University, which provided funds
toward the production of this book.

CONTENTS

ACKNOWLEDGMENTS

This project began with a seminar paper, developed into a thesis, and eventually became a book. Throughout all of these stages, I have received the help, encouragement, support, and generosity of many colleagues, friends, and family. It is a privilege to have such debts.

This book would not have been possible without funding and research opportunities provided by Western Washington University, Oberlin College, Johns Hopkins University, the John Carter Brown Library, the American Antiquarian Society, and the Huntington Library. Special thanks to Norman Fiering at the John Carter Brown, Caroline Sloat at the American Antiquarian Society, Robert Ritchie at the Huntington Library, and Frances Ferguson at Johns Hopkins for their generous support.

Western Washington University (w w u) has been a wonderful place for scholarship and teaching. I thank Ron Kleinknecht, Sara Weir, and the Office of Research and Sponsored Programs for providing research grants, leave time, and publishing assistance crucial for the completion of the book. My colleagues in the Department of Political Science have been a continual source of warmth, encouragement, and camaraderie. I feel fortunate indeed to be part of such a generous community and to have colleagues whom I happily call friends. I credit a large portion of my easy acclimatization to w w u to Joan Blackwell and Debbi Engebretson, who have both helped me navigate the department and the university with their kind wisdom and advice. My students are a continuing source of challenge, satisfaction, and humor.

Friends in the Pacific Northwest and in more far-flung parts have sustained me over the years with their love of reading, writing, lively conversation, stomping outdoors, and delectable food and drink. My thanks and gratitude to Amir Abedi, Rachel Ablow, Olga Akselrod, Jeff Alexander, Bidisha Biswas, Blanche Bybee, Ha-Kyung Choi, Becky Donnino and Kevin Smith, Ruth Harper, Michelle Hornof, Cynthia Horne, Jean Kim, Sarah Knight, Marc Johnson, Stormy Medler, Chandra Mitchell, Emma and Chad Norman, Niall O'Murchu, Kimberly Peters, Shawne Sanders, Paul Saurette, Jennifer Seltz, Lisa Siraganian, Kathy Trevenen, and Kathryn and Adam Resnick for their support, encouragement, and friendship.

During the past couple of years, I have presented chapters and excerpts from this book to various audiences. The following scholars were kind enough to read those early drafts, and I am exceedingly grateful to them for their comments, advice, and criticism: Richard Boyd, Cornelia Dayton, Monique Deveaux, Jason Frank, David Hall, Tim Harris, Laura Janara, Sonia Kruks, James Muldoon, Davide Panagia, J. G. A. Pocock, Mark Reinhardt, John Tambornino, James Tully, Harlan Wilson, and Natalie Zacek. I am particularly indebted to Barbara Arneil, Judith Butler, Marianne Constable, Bonnie Honig, Jacob Levy, Jill Locke, Laurie Naranch, Torrey Shanks, Verity Smith, Sarah Song, Mark Warren, and Iris Marion Young for valuable discussions during the later stages of manuscript revision, which honed and sharpened my thinking on the dynamics of constitutionalism and colonialism.

This study first took form at Johns Hopkins University, and many people there helped me to develop the earliest version of the project. My deep thanks to Amanda Anderson, Felicity Callard, William Connolly, Jennifer Culbert, Theo Davis, Frances Ferguson, Richard Flathman, Eduardo González, Siba Grovogui, Sarah Hill, Ruth Leys, Ruth Mack, David Marshall, John Marshall, Anthony Pagden, Rina Palumbo, Shilpa Prasad, Patrick Provost-Smith, Kam Shapiro, Gabrielle Spiegel, Nancy Struever, Anoush Terjanian, and Amit Yahav-Brown.

One person deserves special, heartfelt, and, in many ways, inexpressible thanks: Kirstie McClure. Her unflagging encouragement not only spurred the study from the first, but also sustained its development throughout its many incarnations. I remain inspired by her acuity, care, and tacit knowledge.

It was a special pleasure to work with Courtney Berger at Duke University Press. Her enthusiasm and support were remarkable, and I am grateful for her time, consideration, and wisdom in guiding me through this process. Mark Mastromarino and Susan Deeks were generous with their support and guidance in the final stages of the book. Last but absolutely not least, the two anonymous readers for Duke University Press were uncommonly generous with their insightful, detailed, and comprehensive comments. Their contributions were invaluable, and I learned much from their different and complementary perspectives. All subsequent errors, of course, are my own.

I dedicate this book to my family. They are the most idiosyncratic, incorrigible, hilarious, and wise people I know. They live their lives with joy, generosity, bravery, humor, and intelligence—they are my inspiration and have my love and affection always.

Earlier versions of sections of Chapter 3 were originally published in: "Unsettling Colonies: Locke, 'Atlantis' and New World Knowledges," *History of Political Thought* 29 (2008): 295–319; "Cultivating and Challenging the Common: Lockean Property, Indigenous Traditionalisms, and the Problem of Exclusion," *Contemporary Political* Theory 5 (2006): 193–214; "Giving Orders: Theory and Practice in the *Fundamental Constitutions of Carolina*," *Journal of the History of Ideas* 63 (2002): 425–46.

HYBRID CONSTITUTIONALISMS

Unsettling the Empire of Uniformity

1

The relationship[s] between desire, power, and interest are more complex than we ordinarily think, and it is not necessarily those who exercise power who have an interest in its execution; nor is it always possible for those with vested interests to exercise power.

—MICHEL FOUCAULT, *LANGUAGE, COUNTER-MEMORY, PRACTICE*

There is scarce any form of government known, that does not prevail in some of our plantations.

—EDMUND BURKE AND WILSON BURKE, *AN ACCOUNT OF THE EUROPEAN SETTLEMENTS IN AMERICA*

Since the advent of English exploration in the Americas in the sixteenth century, the English tried in numerous ways to legitimize their ventures, drawing widely on the various period discourses of conquest, discovery, and improvement. But when English proprietors began to settle colonies in the Americas during the early seventeenth century, their constitutions represented a new and influential development in English colonization and constitutionalism. "From Canada to the Caribbean," as the legal historian Mary Sarah Bilder observes, "proprietors settled and governed a far larger area than the corporation colonies."[1] And in contrast to prior English settlements, proprietors were among the first to be granted charters that conveyed a quasi-sovereign status to their colonizing ventures. As the legal theorist Christopher Tomlins explains, the most influential form of English colonization in the pre-Revolutionary period was proprietary, as "English colonizing became an exercise in the delegation of authority to landed proprietors."[2] Charters to proprietary settlement, in their most autonomous forms, included the feudal privileges given to the palatine counties of Chester and Durham after the Norman Conquest—the powers to establish self-rule, grant manors, build churches, tax, judge, punish, and wage war.[3] Other charters, more restricted in their privileges, conferred manorial rights to proprietors such as William Penn; he received the rights of manors of Windsor, political jurisdiction over free tenants, and the power to sell land.

Most distinctive of these many privileges, proprietors were able to draw on and transform the wide array of legal and political instruments in use in England. As Bilder explains, "What is striking about the early colonial period, however, is the centrality of the practice (and hence the problem) of the delegation of authority and the recurrence of developments that created dual authorities and then embraced their inherent tensions. To put it simply, for the first century and a half, English governance in America was *imperium in imperio*."[4] Yet for the proprietary colonies, as I will argue in this book, this was no simple appropriation. English constitutionalism in the early modern period, as Walter Bagehot famously observed, was "full of every species of incidental defect." Certainly Bagehot valued it as "a simple efficient part which, on occasion, and when wanted, *can* work more simply and easily, and better, than any instrument of government that has yet been tried," but he also noted its intricacy: "It contains likewise historical, complex, august, theatrical parts, which it has inherited from a long past—which *take* the multitude—which guide by an insensible but an omnipotent influence the associations of its subjects."[5] For English constitutionalism, as the historian David Konig further clarifies, was highly variegated, "a patchwork of regional and even subregional legal diversity. Laws of descent varied by and within region, for example, deriving from custom as well as from common law. Although feudal tenures were the norm for the gentry, many exceptions existed."[6] Also complicating the situation, English boroughs were differently shaped by charters obtained "at different times and under different circumstances from different monarchs, giving to each of them a different range of special privileges and varying degrees of autonomy that produced different local rules."[7] As a result, there were still many backwaters in England where mainstream legal developments had not made their imprint.

What did all this mean for English proprietary colonies in the seventeenth century? As I will argue in this book, proprietary constitutionalism developed out of a mixed condition of privilege and scarcity, freedom and dependence. The grant to proprietary settlement was not an unequivocal sign of the Crown's favor but, instead, a self-conscious recognition of both the ambitions and hesitations of colonial power. While charters were given typically to men who had served the Crown in the Privy Council or in foreign service, they could also function as an instrument of displacement, transferring potentially irritating or troublesome individuals or groups to territories overseas. In addition, although proprietors were in principle beholden to the Crown, they were often motivated by independent ambitions; indeed, these often diverged not only from the interests of other English colonies but also from those of settlers *within* the prospective colony. Last, proprietary settlements often received limited economic and political support from the Crown, which was wary of excess cost and responsibility; accordingly, proprietary interest in profit and expansion required careful evaluation of debt, risk, and defense.

These myriad pressures, I argue, were reflected in the accretion of legal and political instruments—proclamations, orders, instructions, statutes, and frames, among others—that comprised proprietary constitutionalism. For while proprietors had access to the range of English political and legal instruments according to the terms of their charters, in practice the constitutions created often diverged greatly from the example in England because, to name only some of the difficulties, the settlements had too few settlers, insufficient courts and assemblies, and inadequate enforcement. What proprietors did was to variously cobble together constitutions out of the available resources listed by the charter to meet the needs of settlement. These constitutions were not single, inclusive documents struck off at one particular definitive moment—a form more commonly associated with the modern American constitution. Rather, they were what we might call *hybrid* assemblages of law that drew together governance from an already mixed source. Moreover, as we will see, these constitutions were not stable; they were frequently adapted and altered based on responses from a variety of actors on the ground, who included not just proprietors, administrators, and governors, but also farmers, traders, indigenes, and other European settlers.

Hybrid Constitutions traces the historical development and theoretical implications of proprietary constitutionalism by examining the colonial foundings of Maryland, Carolina, and Pennsylvania. In many ways, the aims of this study are quite formal. I am interested in the specific forms of law and political power developed by proprietors, governors, and settlers in the early modern period, and I am particularly drawn to the elements of hybridity that emerged in the colonies. How, for instance, were charter privileges employed in the task of constitution making? In what ways did proprietary colonies draw on and rearrange English constitutional forms? What roles did constitutions, treaties, executive instructions, proclamations, and other governmental instruments play? To what extent were these legal and political processes embraced, adapted, and challenged by colonists and other settlers in the territories?

To address these questions in detail, this book pays special attention not simply to constitutionalism as such, but also to the processes of *founding*—the generation and development of colony and constitution as an entwined process. With this focus, the book attends to the original mixed roots of proprietary constitutionalism in English law and then traces the displacement, recombination, and adaptation of the law as it was formulated in the colonies. Proprietary constitutionalism, as we will see, did not demonstrate the stable transfer of law and politics from a stable domestic center to unsettled colonial peripheries. Rather, what emerged were forms of governance assembled, often in hodgepodge fashion, out of an array of political and legal instruments. These constitutions were particular, regional, adaptive, and irregular. They were marked by pomposity and paternalism, and yet they were also characterized by apprehension and wariness of unknown conditions.

My interest also goes beyond merely describing the formal features of proprietary constitutionalism, for what was particularly distinctive about the period were the myriad *effects* of hybridity on colonial and political practice. In the proprietary colonies, complex mixtures of civic humanist, republican, and feudal forms were aimed at servicing a variety of colonial ambitions, such as crafting conceptions of colonial polity that were meant to attract settlers and support, and to develop independent communities that were distinct but nonetheless still nominally loyal to Crown privileges. At the same time, these constitutions offered conceptions of colonial polity that developed and shifted over time because they were often modified by temporary laws, executive orders, and various revisions. They were also more contradictory in their various aspirations and effects. For example, in Maryland the confident claims of the charter were not realized immediately; instead, these chartered claims operated *rhetorically* in multiple ways. The Maryland charter promoted the prospects of settlement to investors and established nominal ideas of the colony as a polity to recruit prospective settlers. This performative quality recalled the conceptions of law and polis proffered in *The Human Condition*, where as Hannah Arendt notes: "The law of the city-state was neither the content of political action (the idea that political activity is primarily legislating, though Roman in origin, is essentially modern and found its greatest expression in Kant's political philosophy) nor was it a catalogue of prohibitions, resting, as all modern laws still do, upon the Thou Shalt Nots of the Decalogue. It was quite literally a wall, without which there might have been an agglomeration of houses, a town (*asty*), but not a city, a political community." The notion that "inclosure was political" reflected an elemental understanding of the law as an instrument of prudence.[8] Still, the charter's early portrayals of colonization were quickly adjusted and transformed by the proprietor's executive *Instructions* and the Maryland Assembly's numerous proclamations, acts, and orders. In a complication to Arendt's conception, in the proprietary settlements these constitutional "walls" were built over and over again with a variety of different texts—charters, instructions, proclamations, ordinances, constitutions, and treaties. What emerges not just in Maryland's constitution, but also in the other proprietary constitutions examined in this study, are forms of hybridity that include not merely formal mixtures of law, but also mixed qualities of temporality, rhetoric, and culture, and it is these qualities that help us in turn to conceptualize colonial power, polity, and identity in new and distinctive ways.

What this book explores, in consequence, are constitutions spurred by colonial ambitions that develop in the midst of rapid change, limited resources, and contrary and inconsistent circumstances. In this way, these proprietary constitutions represent the ("on the ground") working out of political theory in response to the ambitions and contingencies of colonization. Such work is certainly relevant for understanding the attributes of English colonial power in the early modern period. But cast more broadly, such work also helps us to reconsider colonialism and constitutionalism as *grounded practices* that rely as much on legal and political precedent as on more tacit and circumspect tactics of discretion, adaptation, and negotiation.

These constitutions, with their dual sovereignties, mixed array of political and legal instruments, and unruly populations, demonstrate less a purposeful march to modernity and uniformity than something much more ambiguous and unwieldy. In particular, the example of the proprietary colonies offers a way to respond critically to some of the most compelling recent works in political theory, where English colonial expansion in the Americas during the seventeenth century has become a weighty issue.[9] Most notably, critics such as Bhikhu Parekh, Iris Marion Young, and James Tully link the elements of homogeneity, exclusion, and coercion in modern constitutional forms to the entangled development of English colonialism and constitutionalism in the early modern period. Parekh, for example, looks to the colonial record to argue the imperialist aspects of a host of canonical texts, such as John Locke's *Two Treatises of Government*.[10] Through a different approach, Young focuses on the treaties between colonists and indigenes in the colonial and Revolutionary periods and connects the restrictive elements of liberalism to the long history of "conflict between Indians and colonists."[11]

Among the most comprehensive and widely cited of recent criticism is Tully's *Strange Multiplicity: Constitutionalism in an Age of Diversity*, based on his Seeley lectures delivered at Cambridge in 1994.[12] In a historical and critical survey of four hundred years of European and non-European constitutionalism, Tully discusses the current prevailing language of "modern constitutionalism."[13] This discourse, he contends, developed many of its most assimilative and exclusionary features toward cultural diversity through its designs to justify English settlement of the Americas in the seventeenth century. More specifically, *Strange Multiplicity* depicts the colonial emergence of modern constitutionalism in terms of an "empire of uniformity," stressing its imperial features and its tendencies toward cultural homogeneity.[14] "Modern constitutionalism," in Tully's survey, encompasses seven features. Most notable among them, it holds "concepts of popular sovereignty which eliminate cultural diversity as a constitutive aspect of politics"; characterizes itself in terms of "a society of equal individuals who exist at a 'modern' level of historical development"; is "defined in contrast to an ancient or historically earlier constitution"; and "rests on the 'stages' or 'progressive' view of human history, which the classic theorists produced in order to map, rank and thereby comprehend the great cultural diversity encountered by Europeans in the imperial age."[15] This "competing tradition of rights, virtues and manners," Tully argues, was initially established in contrast to the "customs of non-European societies at 'earlier' and 'lower' stages of historical development" and in dispossession of the territory and sovereignty of "Aboriginal nations."[16] In its emergence, according to Tully, modern constitutionalism did not simply reject indigenous and non-European culture outright. More subtly, it viewed culture as either bounded or able to be transcended. European institutions, manners, and traditions are upheld as superior forms of rationality and advancement, and peoples of traditional or non-European societies are cast as underdeveloped, primitive, and pre-modern.[17]

For Tully and others, the language of modern constitutionalism—despite its vexed colonial emergence—has come to be not simply familiar and conventional but, indeed, the standard of impartial treatment for cultural diversity. "The invasion of America, usurpation of Aboriginal nations, theft of the continent, imposition of European economic and political systems, and the steadfast resistance of the Aboriginal peoples," Tully laments, have become "replaced with the captivating picture of the inevitable and benign progress of modern constitutionalism."[18] Especially in the face of ongoing dilemmas centered on cultural identity and recognition, we need, in Tully and others' estimation, to reevaluate the triumphal sentiments that cast constitutionalist development as a march of progress.

Modern critics have given much needed attention to colonialism's ambitions and coercions. The normative thrust of their critiques enables more global considerations of the dilemmas of conquest, especially as they pertain to broader conceptualizations of legitimacy, rights, and justice. So, too, have they been valuable in focusing on the numerous ways in which indigenous rights and cultures have been excluded and delegitimized in the historical development of constitutionalism. Ironically, though, while much contemporary theory seeks to unearth the instrumental and coercive forces helping to form modern constitutionalism, its reliance on macro-historical narratives of colonialism and more formal accounts of constitutionalism often thwarts this ambition. First, contemporary theory's emphasis on describing long-term effects often encourages interpretations that emphasize the stadial, hierarchical features of Enlightenment imperialism. Second, the more formal treatment of constitutionalism tends to deemphasize the multiple, particular ways in which early modern constitutionalism was not only conceptualized but *practiced*. These accounts thus at times seem to solidify and lengthen the conceptual and historical power of modern constitutionalism, making it difficult to apprehend the vicissitudes of English colonial power.

To be sure, Tully and others tackle an extremely wide purview—one that ranges from the sixteenth century to the twenty-first century—and with such ambitious accounts it is neither unreasonable nor unsurprising that more minor details drop from view. At the same time, when the field of examination is cast so broadly, modern criticism may be unable to attend to the details and nuances regarding the creation and implementation of colonial constitutional forms. Perhaps most consequential in this regard, contemporary theory, in its strong focus on tracking the rise of modern constitutionalism, often skirts discussion of the many contingencies, contestations, and failures of colonialism. As I suggest in this book, the prevailing approach, while productive in a number of ways, runs the risk of reinscribing, even if negatively and inadvertently, the triumphalist narrative of the modern constitutional form.

This study adopts an approach different from much of contemporary political thought—an examination that is both smaller in scale and more explicitly contextual in approach. Instead of tackling a wide swath of constitutional development over the centuries, *Hybrid Constitutions* focuses on a specific, highly relevant period of colonial and constitutional development: the founding of the seventeenth-century English proprietary colonies. Yet while *Hybrid Constitutions* seeks to actively engage contemporary theory concerned with the legacy of colonialism, this book is deliberately not a response in kind. The bulk of my analysis is local rather than global, and it is limited in its historical scope. It examines the founding periods of three Anglo-American proprietary colonies in the seventeenth century and emphasizes practice (on the ground) rather than the long-term effects of colonial interactions from the early modern period to the present. With its focus on proprietary founding, it seeks in part to address an element of English colonialism largely unaddressed by political theory and one that was a formative element of English colonialism and constitutionalism. In that way, the book's more local and genealogical focus seeks to extend, supplement, and at times amend contemporary assessments. Distinctively, selfish ambition and grandiose ideals were deeply co-mingled in the proprietary colonies, and the process of creating polity involved the constant remaking of a tradition that was itself irregular and patchwork at its origins. Equally, in these examples of founding, we can see an aspect of appropriation that can too easily drop from view—namely, the persistent mixture of cruelty and accommodation that help to forward colonial ambitions.

The Terms of Hybridity

Three different, at times overlapping, forms of hybridity take center stage in this study. The first form of hybridity is *political/legal* in nature. Central to this hybridity was the proprietary charter; although strongly shaped by the feudal imaginary of the palatinate of Durham, it was also intrinsically open-ended with respect to the specific forms of law employed in the colony. The Crown granted proprietors an express power to make and publish the laws with the "assent advice and approbation of the freemen," but "provided nevertheless, that the same laws be consonant to reason, and be not repugnant or contrary, but (as near as conveniently may be) agreeable to the laws, customes, statutes, and rights of this our kingdom of England."[19] Indeed, while the proprietor's license to create such laws was a unique privilege, it did not entail or require the production of a systematic internal consistency. Even within its own terms, the category of "laws, customes, statutes, and rights" would have been a mixed, irregular assemblage in England. Customary law recalled decisions made by judges in local jurisdictions, while statute laws were written code designated in contradistinction to the unwritten common law. Rights, in addition, could reference a host of protections, not all of which were commensurate with each other. Especially pertinent here, as J. G. A. Pocock and others illustrate, is the fact that the revivals of both the ancient constitutionalist forms of the common law and republicanism in England were themselves creations of the seventeenth century.[20] Compounding the ambiguity, the charters made no specific provision for which form of law should take precedence.[21] The primary restriction was of a negative tone—namely, that the law must not be "repugnant."[22]

This assemblage reflected the various traditions of law and politics in England. It also reflected, as Daniel Hulsebosch argues, the ways in which

English understandings of the constitution were multiform and unsystematized. As Hulsebosch notes, "Although no single document captured all English constitutionalism, there was an evolving canon of great documents. *Magna Carta* (1215), the *Petition of Right* (1628), and the *Bill of Right* (1689), for example, were on everyone's list, while the Levellers' *Agreement of the People* (1648) was on few. These documents were not exhaustive. Commentary in treatises, essays, and judicial reports fleshed out their significance, as did oral tradition. Beyond the documents and the commentary were the institutions that interpreted and applied them, the practical conventions that gave constitutions life. Collectively, these documents, ideas, and practices formed the empire's constitutional culture."[23] In that respect, the English constitution was *polyvocal*, as were proprietary constitutions, in which various media—charters, constitutions, fundamental rules, executive orders, and assembly statutes—played a role in founding a constitutional order. Some constitutional elements were fully fleshed out and refined, such as the Pennsylvania colony's *Frame of Government*, but others, such as the Maryland Assembly's many statutes, were more ambiguous and unformed—they were temporary, often of limited application, and subject to change.

These qualities suggest a marked change of emphasis to the imperial inflection Tully and others lend to the emergence of modern constitutionalism in the seventeenth century. In different ways, the legal instrument of the proprietary charter helped diffuse political tensions from the gentry, merchants, and political and religious dissidents, only to displace and recharge them in new, but no less turbulent, peripheries. What emerged was not exactly an imperial monolith but, instead, a delegated, dispersed, and entangled series of various proprietary enterprises whose loyalty to each other and the Crown was far from secure. This was due in large part to the fact that proprietary founding was subject to authority that was *polyvalent*. As we will see, although proprietors and colonists were supposed to give formal deference to the Crown, in reality the monarchy had little oversight over the day-to-day activities in the colonies. Further complicating the dynamics of authority, the proprietors themselves were often absent or distant from their settlements; they delegated tasks of negotiation and mediation to colonists and settlers on the ground. In that sense, to paraphrase Istvan Hont's description of the neo-Machiavellian English commonwealths, proprietary governance was not structured solely in terms of a bipolar world of rulers and ruled. Instead, a host of lesser agents—governors, lieutenants, and a wide variety of colonists and settlers—were highly active in participation, mediation, and negotiation.[24] As a consequence, in this setting we can reimagine colonial power along different lines. The center and the margins were both in flux, and on the colonial ground, proprietor and colonists used their constitutions self-consciously (and not always effectively) to respond to conditions of instability and insecurity. Although these proprietary communities did contribute to the expansion of the empire, they also were neither direct expressions of Crown interest nor directly managed by royal administration.

The second form of hybridity this book examines is *temporal*, and it is to a degree an outgrowth of the political and legal mixtures in proprietary constitutionalism, which in many ways harked back to older conceptions of constitution. As Jack P. Greene comments, the English constitution was "conceived of as an accumulation of customary practices, long-standing legal procedures and principles, and basic individual rights that had slowly taken shape over the centuries not just in the courts and legislative chambers in the capital but also in the various administrative and judicial institutions in the local communities, an accumulation of concepts and practices, moreover, that expressed the fundamental rules by which the polity was "constituted" and on which it operated."[25] Composed of a variety of written and unwritten instruments, these proprietary constitutions were quite unlike our more modern conceptions of constitutions, in which founding orders were enshrined in a single document and inaugurated at a single moment. Consider, for example, Rousseau's famous conception in which the social compact serves as the device that creates "an act of association" and "immediately produces an artificial and collective body, made up of as many members as there are voices in the assembly, and receiving from this same act its unity, its collective personality, its life and its will."[26] By contrast, proprietary constitutions were more attenuated; their creation involved multiple revisions, adaptations, and even revocations. Moreover, unlike Locke's more pragmatic conception of "civil society" in which a new body politic was established in contrast to a pre-modern past, these proprietary constitutions were neither fully ancient nor wholly modern.[27] In particular, varieties of civic humanism, republicanism, and feudal and common law appear in the proprietary constitutions in fragmented and adapted ways. Due to Pocock's influential account, much has been made of the republican influence on American ideas in the eighteenth century.[28] But until recently, less attention has been paid to the popularity of republican and civic humanist discourse in the seventeenth century. Yet as a number of important studies now note, James Harrington's ideas were at the height of their popularity in the middle of the seventeenth century, and many of the writers who influenced Harrington—Cicero, Machiavelli, and Tacitus, among others—were important in the first half of the seventeenth century and cited frequently in English advice and conduct books. As Markku Peltonen, Mark Goldie, Patrick Collinson, and Quentin Skinner, among others, illustrate, republican discourse was ubiquitous in the Tudor and early Stuart period well before the Civil War. This discourse, as Skinner notes, neither precluded monarchical power nor raison d'état; instead, the civic humanist version of republicanism often mixed popular *and* monarchical rule. In addition, as Goldie and Peltonen depict, the civic humanist and republican conceptions described by seventeenth-century writers such as Bacon, Harrington, and others were often civic in spirit but not at all urban.[29] In this way, the proprietary constitution appears as a form of political theory that mixes ancient and modern ideas in complex ways. The mixtures, moreover, reflect the vicissitudes of power and privilege as proprietors equipped largely with the at times incongruent welter of English law sought to acquire and manage power, property, and peoples in tenuous circumstances. These qualities were not only influential in the early modern period, but they also, as I will argue in the final chapter of this work, can be seen in some of the Revolutionary and nineteenth-century American forms of democratic practice, popular participation, and legal rights.

Equally important, this temporal mixing of ancient and modern did not apply only to political languages. It also included the representation of *colonial space*. Colonial investors, in particular, became interested in promoting overseas settlements as a result of reading travel accounts, letters, and missionary diaries. In turn, new colonial ventures were themselves imagined and apprehended as creations of print materials—charters, promotional materials, and pamphlets—that were to motivate and energize investors and colonists to the activity of colonization. For example, Andrew Fitzmaurice notes the use of civic humanist and republican rhetoric in early modern English colonial materials, pointing out that these promotional pamphlets were not simply recitations of facts. They were, according to Fitzmaurice, "a form of action and believed to perform fundamental acts in the foundation and conservation of a commonwealth."[30] In a way, then, the circulation of these printed pamphlets and promotional materials modernized the rhetorical process by which the trope of the commonwealth was employed as a means to persuade or dissuade. At the same time, as David Hall observes, the charters and constitutions of these proprietary settlements participated in older practices of rhetoric. They were read aloud in public, and these performances symbolized the sovereignty of the king's representatives and served a critical function in creating a corporate identity for the settlers. As Hall notes, "At the outset of colonization, the single most important category of document was the royal charter and its equivalent, a commission from a proprietor or chartered company declaring the sovereignty of the King's representatives and affirming their right to land. The performance of these texts in open-air ceremonies was a distinctive feature of colonization."[31] Still, as we will see, the performance of the charter did not preclude agitation from or discontent among colonists or among those who already occupied the territory. The charter may have helped clear the ground for a theater of actions, but it certainly did not vouchsafe the stability of the settlement.

Proprietary founding, to that degree, seemed to occupy a middle ground between the modern and pre-modern, what Benedict Anderson describes as the period when "sacral monarchy began its slow decline in Western Europe."[32] If proprietary ventures were an expression of an older age—most notably, of the monarchical privilege to delegate territory to favored subjects—they were also in part creations of a newly developing print age. Modernity, in Anderson's account, is characterized by a mode of apprehending the world in which "simultaneity is, as it were, transverse, cross-time, marked not by prefiguring and fulfillment, but by temporal coincidence, and measured by clock and calendar."[33] The new print media of the late eighteenth century and nineteenth century facilitated this "simultaneous" mode of apprehension. In the case of the English-speaking colonies and the Spanish American satellites, as Anderson explains, "Newspapers serve modern man as a substitute for morning prayers. . . . It is performed in silent privacy, in the lair of the skull. Yet each communicant is well aware that the ceremony he performs is being replicated simultaneously by thousands (or millions) of others of whose existence he is confident, yet of whose identity he has not the slightest notion."[34] By contrast, as I argue in Chapters 2 and 3, the transmission and circulation of seventeenth-century English colonial print materials was far more limited and selective. Transatlantic transmission of texts did allow proprietors, investors, and administrators to project conceptions of founding to distant settlers, yet these representations were neither simultaneous nor uniformly distributed in reach or reception. There was, in fact, often dissonance between the metropole and periphery. For example, as became obvious in Maryland and Carolina, the proprietary colony embraced political and legal features of palatine power that were outdated and even decried in England. Thus, this delegation of legal and political power did not come without costs to the Crown and its ability to oversee colonial behavior.

The final form of hybridity that this book addresses is *cultural*. Founding called for the mediation of differences in power and influence within local indigenous American tribes and among English colonists of Quaker, Catholic, and Protestant backgrounds. Proprietors ordered colonists to engage in various practices of mediation to help secure stability and profit. These included the application of *discretion* by colonists of diverse religious and cultural backgrounds; informal practices of *adaptation* by colonists to adopt language and agricultural skills; and *negotiation* of treaties for land and trade between colonial administrators and indigene elites. I track each of these practices in the subsequent chapters and argue that, while discretion, adaptation, and negotiation were primarily cultural in nature, they also extended to political and legal considerations.

These features of cultural hybridity are aspects of English colonialism and Atlantic studies that have gained significant attention from historians, ethnographers, and literary critics. Recent work in these fields has not only reconsidered the processes by which the English settled colonies in the Americas during the early modern period, but also substantially reevaluated the confrontation between the English and indigenes at the time of colonization. James Axtell depicts these relations as "cultural contact," where "one culture may predominate and teach more than it learns . . . [but] the educational process is always mutual."[35] Culture thus seems, in its changeability, fluid, unstable, or shifting. These portrayals are accurate in a sense: They help to conceptualize the porosity of the category of the "colonial," making it impossible to treat it as a fully closed identity strictly opposed to the "primitive" or the "savage." But what we can see in proprietary founding as well is that the negotiation of culture is based largely in *locale*, in the unpredictable, tacit ways in which knowledge is gleaned from context.

This is a different, less modern conception of culture, for in the proprietary settlements, as we will see in Chapters 3 and 4, the negotiation of culture was instrumental. Following its etymological roots (*neg-otium*, meaning business or, literally, the opposite of leisure), negotiation was the mediation of public *business* as much as the general *busy-ness* of colonial settlement.[36] In addition, negotiation, particularly with respect to cultural knowledge, served as a proprietary mode of brokering local power— power to trade, to farm, to hold land, to settle. Proprietary founding was in many ways a function of negotiating—not conquering or eliminating— cultural diversity. In the dynamics of negotiation, the openness to others on the ground is a responsiveness to the locality of living. It is not, strictly speaking, a negotiation of cultural identity in our more current sense— where practices, customs, and sensibilities delineate specific group, ethnic, or even civilizational membership. Rather, in the colonies the culture to be negotiated seems closer to culture's etymological roots in cultivation, growth, or *cultura*.[37] On the one hand, negotiation is *agri-cultural* in its attention to the practices, habits, and knowledge relevant to cultivating the soil: tillage, husbandry, farming. But negotiation also explores culture in a deeper, less prosaic sense—"The culture of their bodies," as Hobbes wrote of the Lacedaemonians, the modalities of living and survival in a place and a time.[38]

This proprietary version of cultural hybridity was thus not unalloyed but, to a large degree, an explicitly colonial strategy of acquisition and coercion. Although the irregular web of relations on the ground kept colonists and indigenous peoples from strict opposition, dealings between the two were certainly not uniformly harmonious. Instead, relations between colonists and indigenes needed to be negotiated in their particularities: They were shaped and affected by inter- and intra-colony interests, inter- and intra-tribal concerns, and changes in various local French, Spanish, and other European settlements. In that respect, cultural negotiation did bring together diverse peoples in an intimate reciprocity to learn each other's languages and skills, and if those peoples did seem to demonstrate a willingness to establish working relationships, this willingness was generally only of limited duration. From the proprietary perspective, negotiations could be characterized as a process akin to what Jacques Derrida describes as "shuttling": "always working in the mobility between several positions, stations, places, between which a shuttle is needed."[39] Shuttling was, in that way, a tactic, although not a guarantee, for opening up colonial opportunities.

Obvious examples can be found, as I discuss in Chapter 3, in the contrasting colonial relations toward local indigenous tribes and African slaves. Carolina colonists did in fact gather navigation and agricultural skills from local indigenes and from African slaves brought in from the Caribbean, but the legal and actual treatment of local tribes and slaves often varied widely. Even more subtle examples crop up, as well. For instance, as I argue in Chapter 4, in the treaty negotiations conducted in and around the Pennsylvania territories, cultural negotiation was a way to navigate and open diplomatic options in the complex of alliances, enmities, and engagements on the ground. However, what later colonists would describe as "nogeaucating Maters" were also instruments of power in complex ways. Treaty negotiation allowed William Penn to evade Crown oversight, and dominant tribes, such as the Iroquois and Lenape, were able to use treaties to marginalize Algonquians and Susquehannocks.[40]

In addition, although the major portion of this study is historically narrow and regionally specific in scope, I do suggest in the final chapter some of the ways in which this examination of the English proprietary colonies can be situated within a larger, comparative perspective. Indeed, cultural hybridity was unique to neither the proprietary colonies nor English colonization more broadly. Numerous colonial settlements other than the English proprietary settlements demonstrated cross-cultural negotiation. Historians such as Karen Kupperman and Richard White famously document the cultural forms of hybridity present in Dutch New Netherlands and French Canada, respectively. Similarly, colonial practices of indigenous language learning, treaty making, and cross-cultural toleration occurred in other English colonies, such as much examined Virginia and Massachusetts, and in the wider range of European settlements, such as New Sweden, New Netherlands, and the *pays d'en haut*, to name only a few.[41] Empire and law alike were shaped by processes of negotiation between participants who were very often treated as equals in practice, if not necessarily in theory.

An interpretative clarification might be useful here: This study does not attempt to reconstruct indigenous and native perspectives, in part because the task of reconstruction is beyond the scope of a work of this size. More important, many of the available sources on the proprietary colonies— charters, constitutions, executive instructions, letters and memoranda, and pamphlets—were written from a colonial perspective, and the task of reconstructing an indigenous voice from such texts is fraught with difficulty. Historians and ethnographers have long confronted the challenging prospect of characterizing indigenous perspectives from the period of English colonization in the Americas. The bulk of extant sources on the Mid-Atlantic and Chesapeake region in the seventeenth century and eighteenth century are European (that is, mercantile, missionary, and travel accounts from English, Dutch, French, German, and Swedish sources). Such materials call for cautious interpretation because they were written by or rely on information from individuals with various colonial, economic, military, and religious interests. Extant accounts were often imprecise and at times deliberately misleading in their attribution of various Iroquois, Algonquian, Lenape, Susquehannock, and Conoy tribal interests and relations.[42]

In this work, I draw on a variety of contemporary ethno-historical studies to provide provisional assessment of the interests and forms of power attributable to indigenous tribes and actors. However, I position my assessments as conditional at best and made only with the ambition of clarifying the colonial perspective. My aim is not to create an "authentic" indigenous perspective; nor do I wish to claim anything determinative with respect to claims about indigenous politics or community in the period. [43] Given the available materials (primarily English and affected by bias, omission, and inaccuracy) and the scope of the book, I focus on the various *colonial* renderings of "native" information, knowledge, and politics, and I look to trace tendencies and patterns in the colonial treatment and perception of indigenous actions while remaining open to variations in and among various native tribes. In that way, my focus on the colonial perspective is informed by and indebted to Homi Bhabha's conception of the colonial text's "hybridity," in which the native voice is ambivalently contained in colonial texts. "Hybridity," Bhabha finds, "is a problematic of colonial representation and individuation that reverses the effects of the colonialist disavowal, so that other 'denied' knowledges enter upon the dominant discourse and estrange the basis of its authority—its rules of recognition."[44] Certainly the presence of hybridity in the hegemonic discourse alone does not constitute an adequate response to colonialism's coercions; nor is mere recognition of hybridity a sufficient equivalent to indigenous understanding. Still, hybridity can do some constructive work in reconceptualizing colonial and constitutional structures not as oppositional to an indigenous position cast as primitive, traditional, and pre-modern but, instead, as creations more mixed and even conflicted in their political, temporal, and cultural orientations.

The Politics of Context

By pursuing a more dynamic, practice-oriented account of constitutionalism and colonialism in this work, I am interested not solely in describing the operations of the proprietary charter or the creation of new settlements, although certainly that is a substantial element of the study. I am also critically interested in the historicized relation between words and action in establishing constitutions and the ways in which political theory can regard that process. Many elements in this work, accordingly, are indebted to the seminal work of Quentin Skinner. Skinner, of course, is interested in the complex relationship between theory and practice, and he is deeply concerned with changes to political concepts and language over time. As he observes, "It is easy to become bewitched into believing that the ways of thinking about [our normative concepts] bequeathed to us by the mainstream of our intellectual traditions must be the ways of thinking about them."[45] In response, he advises that "the history of philosophy, and perhaps especially of moral, social, and political philosophy, is there to prevent us from becoming too readily bewitched . . . to appreciate how far the values embodied in our present way of life, and our present ways of thinking about those values, reflect a series of choices made at different times between different possible worlds. This awareness can help to liberate us from the grip of any one hegemonic account of those values and how they should be interpreted and understood."[46] My approach strongly shares Skinner's skepticism, particularly his emphasis on dismantling the hold of hegemonic discourses through contextual interpretations. In this way, too, my reading of proprietary foundings embraces much of Pocock's approach to political language—its idioms, rhetorical moves, specialized vocabularies and grammars—to consider how a tradition changes over time and place. I also owe much to Pocock's work in expanding our understandings of the political-legal paradigms of civic humanism, common law, and republicanism to include attention to material conditions and to elements of custom and manners.[47]

At the same time, my study differs from both Skinner's philosophical emphasis and Pocock's account of tradition in a number of ways. Skinner tends to focus largely on what he refers to as "major texts," and the illocutionary and perlocutionary effects that he examines are primarily matters of intellectual responsiveness as readers take up, adapt, challenge, or dismiss any particular set of inherited and expressed claims. In this fashion, Skinner both reconstructs and assesses sets of political and philosophical conversations that take place over time, valuably tracing the ways concepts are deeply embedded in and produced by historically specific social, economic, and cultural contexts. Thus, his work tends to be oriented toward an intellectual context constituted by dialogue and exchange between a relatively narrow set of writers and readers.[48]

By contrast, in the proprietary settlements that I will consider, constitutions were modified, adapted, manipulated, and ignored by a diverse and even unruly set of respondents. For example, as I will argue in Chapter 2, the prospective charter was a copperplate legal form, a starting point to solicit investors, intimidate other competing settlements, and recruit new colonists. The subsequent actions and practices involved in founding were associated with the charter but were by no means strictly dependent on the terms set out in the original patent. Stated intentions were often confused, manipulated, or ignored—and objectives were reshaped and undercut as multiple audiences with different expectations and orientations to the project of founding took up and utilized the charter. More to the point, as we will see, these changes to charters, orders, and constitutions did not represent *failures of constitutionalism*. Proprietors and elites were quite cognizant that the precise requirements of governing orders could not be fulfilled, given the limited number of settlers and supplies. However, even in their unfulfilled state, the orders could still facilitate the processes of governance, because the charters and constitutions could function as rhetorical instruments that sought to carve out the space where a political community might emerge.

As we will see, the proprietary constitutions blur strict separations between theory and practice, where theory is either incidental to "real" events on the ground or practice is superfluous to the concepts and ideas central to theory. Instead, the mode of theory and practice that emerges out of the examples of proprietary founding is one in which theory is not the template for practice, and practice is not completely antithetical to theory. Rather, in a more rhetorical fashion, theoretical proposals serve as central acts in founding, while actions are suffused with theoretical nuance, a condition that resonates with Foucault's and Deleuze's observation that "theory does not express, translate, or serve to apply practice; it is practice. But it is local and regional . . . and not totalizing."[49]

Tracing this kind of dynamic shifts the conceptual frame and denatures some of our familiar assumptions about the categories of political theory and practice. In that sense, the hybridity that I track here also does not easily conform to Pocock's comprehensive and wide-ranging conception of an ideological tradition transmitted and transformed over time and place. Indeed, the strategies of reading and interpretation I adopt in this work are tinged, in many ways, by the very features of discretion, adaptation, and negotiation that I seek to examine. My readings of the charters, executive instructions, and memoranda prioritize situational knowledge and flexibility as tactics to negotiate deeply contested terrains. My interpretations are also *discretionary* in that they arise out of partisan interest, a desire to operate outside prescribed order, and a conflicted self-consciousness about the instrumental and subjective elements of interpretation as a political process.

Each of the three central chapters of this book focuses on close readings of the proprietary charters, constitutions, instructions, and memoranda—the kinds of historical and political texts often bypassed by more normative accounts. Close readings of proprietary founding offer unique views on the effects and ambitions of governance and law. They also provide some insight into the complex and contested qualities of colonial relations, including encounters and negotiations among the English, as well as relations between English and indigenous agents. Above all, my interpretations are heavily shaped by two areas of scholarship. The first is the now abundant historical and legal literature on the seventeenth-century English American proprietary colonies and Atlantic colonization, especially the works on colonial law by Mary Sarah Bilder, Daniel Hulsebosch, Christopher Tomlins, David Konig, and Jack P. Greene. The second is the detailed research on civic humanist and republican discourses in the early modern period, particularly from Quentin Skinner, Andrew Fitzmaurice, Annabel Brett, David Armitage, and Markku Peltonen. These works are especially effective in emphasizing the distinctive instability that affected both center and periphery in early modern England.[50]

In many ways, the picture of constitutionalism examined in this work is not an image of a singular power extending its force to the edges of the colonial dominions. Instead, hybrid constitutionalisms appear in the flows of power and insecurity at both the center and the periphery—particularly as settlement disperses power into the hands of heterogeneous, diverse actors. Such delegations did service the Crown and the cause of colonial expansion, but the latitude of the proprietary charters also suggests a pertinent shift in the historical interpretation that political theory adopts. The Crown did not strictly command colonial enterprises as much as set them up for indirect management.

My primary concern in this work, then, is with opening up multiple conceptual and historical registers to understand the complexities of colonialism and constitutionalism. Thus, the title of this work emphasizes *hybrid constitutions* as multiple—and differentiated—objects of inquiry. Although the chapters are roughly chronological in their order, this book does not look to develop a teleological account. I treat constitutionalism and colonialism not as formal concepts developing progressively from the sixteenth century to the present but, rather, as historicized systems of meaning that are dynamic—repeatedly interpreted, contested, and transformed in their local practice. Even the last founding examined in this study, that of the colony of Pennsylvania, illustrates not the "end" of hybrid constitutionalism but simply one of many possible versions of its reconfiguration. By envisioning these forms of constitutionalism and colonialism as local and particular creations, we might begin to pull apart at the teleological conceptualizations applied to the colonial past.

Above all, my appraisal is not meant to be salutary. The task of pluralizing and contextualizing early modern colonialism is a way to critically engage not only contemporary theory's concern with colonialism but also its concurrent ambition to recover hidden and alternative forms of constitutionalism. Much of contemporary theory seeks, along with its critiques of the edifice of "modern constitutionalism," to recuperate the forms of cultural adjudication suppressed in the wake of colonialism: the traditions of indigenous peoples, treaty conventions, and the multiform, irregular ancient constitutionalist forms of common law and civic humanist adjudication. Primarily, theorists have sought to canvass the colonial past for historical moments of cultural negotiation—intercultural dialogue, co-operation, and action—for two key reasons: first, to loosen the hold of the prevailing narrative that treats colonial settlement only as a process of indigenous subjugation; and second, to stimulate new conceptions of just cultural recognition. For example, Young focuses on the history of Mid-Atlantic treaty practices in the late seventeenth century and early eighteenth; these treaties generated new models of cultural adjudication that, as she further clarifies, were capable of "affirming colonial North America as a terrain of interaction, constructing American subjectivity as ambiguous, and fashioning a relational understanding of government jurisdictions."[51] In a comparable vein, William Connolly looks to the "history of interactions between settlers and indigenous peoples" to "think more creatively" about how "indigenous peoples have forged counter-identities within settler societies" and, conversely, how "descendants of settlers" can adapt their traditions to connect to indigenous practices.[52] Tully, in a more comprehensive account, suggests that we reappraise "entire areas of the broader language of constitutionalism—such as the common law, earlier varieties of whiggism and civic humanism—which provide the means of recognizing and accommodating cultural diversity."[53] These more situated, mediated, and dialogic modes of understanding and recognizing culture, he suggests, may allow us to better adjudicate the diverse claims to recognition posed by our "post-imperial age of cultural diversity."[54]

Accordingly, with its more streamlined focus on the proprietary context, *Hybrid Constitutions* looks to clarify already familiar aspects of colonialism and constitutionalism and to engage more unexpected features, such as subtle forms of power and privilege. Historical narratives influence our political knowledge precisely by bringing understandings to the table that shift the present's relationship to a complex and equivocal past.

The book builds its historicized conception of hybridity in the proprietary constitutions through the three central chapters. Chapter 2, " 'Not Repugnant or Contrary': Law, Discretion, and Colonial Founding in Maryland," describes the historical, juridical, and religious implications of Maryland's initial charter and its invocation of palatine authority. The charter projected an authoritative image of the colony that drew on a welter of feudal and civic humanist references, but this vision of settlement was also relevantly hybrid and open-ended in political terms because

Maryland was limited only by the provision that the combination not be "repugnant." What emerged as most relevant in proprietary determinations of law and rule on the ground was "discretion," what Renaissance writers described as *discrimination* in making judgments and decisions. This discretion, as described in colonial correspondence and the proprietor's executive instructions, was particularly attuned to local contexts on the ground. It proved to be a central component not only in shaping the colonists as decision makers but also in administering internal and external differences of culture, religion, and politics.

Chapter 3, "Giving Orders: Theory and Practice in the *Fundamental Constitutions of Carolina*," more fully tackles hybridity not simply as a feature of politics, but also as a temporal and cultural issue. This section provides an account of how the Carolina constitutions functioned differentially as a political imaginary and as a practical tool for founding on the ground. Employing the writings of John Locke, James Harrington, and Niccolò Machiavelli, I interpret the Carolina orders as a civic humanist republican vision of polity mixed with utopian and paternalistic elements. This constitutional vision, although authoritative and rigid in some elements, also treated the prospect of founding as contingent and potentially subject to dissolution. As I suggest, the movement of the *Fundamental Constitutions* from formal proposal to governing order on the ground illustrates some of the flexible and adaptive elements of hybrid constitutionalism. Although the *Fundamental Constitutions* was never implemented in full in the Carolinas, the Lords Proprietors created temporary constitutions modeled on its features, and they encouraged colonists to pursue "prudence" and "discretion" in their adaptation of language and skills from local indigenes.

Chapter 4, "Under Negotiation: Treaty Power and Hybrid Constitutionalism in Pennsylvania," moves beyond a focus on charters and constitutions to look at alternative instruments, such as treaties, as elements of hybrid constitutionalism. I suggest that the many treaties negotiated by the proprietor William Penn with the Lenapes and Susquehannocks were responses to both the growing administration of colonial polities by the Privy Council in England and the potential factionalism posed by diverse groups on the ground in the colony itself. These treaties were sources of flexibility and mediation between diverse groups, yet they were also instruments of power that differentially served participants. For Penn in particular, the negotiation of formal treaties was a way to reserve power to himself as proprietor.

The final chapter, "Negotiating Culture: Plurality and Power in Hybrid Constitutionalism," places the proprietary examples of hybrid constitutionalism within a broader geographical, chronological, and theoretical framework, discussing subsequent and current dilemmas of constitutionalism and cultural recognition. I discuss how hybridity can be conceptualized as a critical concept that allows us not only to reconceptualize the historical terrain of constitutionalism and colonialism in early America, bringing much needed attention to elements of colonial dependence, but also to reconsider contemporary dilemmas of adjudication in Australia, New Zealand, and the United States.

Hybrid Constitutions looks to convey the multiplicity of colonial and constitutional forms circulating in a central period of English colonization, focusing especially on the complexities of practice as a way both to examine and to challenge colonial ideology. In addition, I examine the economic, social, and cultural implications of feudal law, republican, common law, and civic humanist ideals as they were employed and adapted in the processes of founding. This brings to light elements of English insecurity and instability often overlooked. It also highlights the central importance of indigenous knowledge and skills to English colonial settlement—aspects often bypassed in the broader narratives of triumphalist and anti-triumphalist accounts. As a secondary outcome, this work also sheds new light on several major English political thinkers—ranging from John Locke and James Harrington to William Penn—whose ideas were influential to the period's proprietary settlements. By drawing on colonial historiography, law, and cultural studies of political and cultural interaction, *Hybrid Constitutions* addresses a crucial but hitherto neglected issue that affects political debates on the history of constitutionalism and multiculturalism.

"NOT REPUGNANT OR CONTRARY"

Law, Discretion, and Colonial Founding in Maryland

2

Charters are Donations of the Sovereign; and not Lawes, but exemptions from the Law . . . the phrase of a Charter is *Dedi*, *Concessi*, I have Given, I have Granted.

—THOMAS HOBBES, 1651

The most democratic laws were therefore voted in a rivalry among the men whose interests they bruised the most. In this manner the upper classes did not excite popular passions against them; but they themselves hastened the triumph of the new order. Thus a singular thing! One saw the democratic impulse more irresistible in States where aristocracy had the deepest roots. The State of Maryland, which had been founded by great lords, proclaimed universal suffrage first and introduced into its entire government the most democratic forms.

—ALEXIS DE TOCQUEVILLE, *DEMOCRACY IN AMERICA*

In 1632, Cecilius Calvert, the second Baron Baltimore, received a proprietary charter for the largest tract of land in the Americas that the Crown had ever conveyed to the responsibility of a single person.[1] Unmatched not only in its geographical size, the particular type of jurisdiction the charter conferred on its holder—a palatine authority—permitted Calvert to function in effect as a virtual king within the colony of Maryland. The grant allowed Calvert "the ample Rights, Jurisdictions, Privileges, Prerogatives, Royalties, Liberties, Immunities, and royal Rights, and temporal Franchises" that had been "exercised, used, and enjoyed, as any Bishop of Durham, within the Bishoprick or County Palatine of Durham, in our Kingdom of England, ever heretofore hath had, held, used, or enjoyed, or of right could, or ought to have, hold, use, or enjoy."[2] In doing so, Calvert received the most extensive grant of prerogatives given to an English colonial proprietor at the time. The new Lord Proprietor thus possessed powers to make laws, judge and punish offenders, grant land and titles, license trade, raise armies and fortifications, and wage war. The only formal restriction was that Calvert would owe his king a yearly donation—two Indian arrowheads from the Americas and a fifth of any found gold and silver. This payment was largely a token of loyalty, of "saving always the Faith and Allegiance and Sovereign Dominion due to Us, our Heirs, and Successors,"[3] although potentially it could be substantial.

Yet in many ways, Lord Calvert's newly granted charter with its liberality of privileges was a sign of the colony's uncertain prospects, for the territory included in the 1632 Maryland charter was already occupied by a number of tribes: coastal and northern Piscataways; southern Yoacomacoes, Nanticokes, Pocomokes, Assateagues, and Patuxents; and to the west and north, Susquehannocks.[4] Non-indigenous settlers in the region included English adventurers (from Virginia and Florida) and Dutch and French settlers who had been involved in missionary work and the fur and goods trade since the 1600s.[5] In addition, parts of the prospective Maryland territory had been granted previously to both the Council of New England and the Virginia Company, and controversies over title to land would persist long after the 1632 charter had been conveyed to Calvert. In particular, the Virginians protested the size and scope of the Maryland grant, arguing that the new Lord Proprietor's entitlements illegitimately overtook previous claims by English settlers such as William Claiborne, a former member of the Council of Virginia, who had established a trading post on Kent Island.[6]

What a closer examination of the charter and Maryland's founding reveals is one of the critical features in hybrid constitutionalism—namely, an awareness and flexibility that was conceptualized in terms of *discretion*. Among the multiple meanings of charter in this period was a "written document delivered by the sovereign," "granting pardon," and "creating or incorporating a borough, university, company, or other corporation."[7] By the 1650s, Thomas Hobbes had described how the charter carved out a space for a juridical form outside a sovereign realm that neither bound its subject to a specific law nor enjoined it to one strict command.[8]

This chapter examines the conditions of founding in the first years of the colony of Maryland, and it focuses primarily on the early Maryland charter and the memoranda, executive orders, and correspondence that documented the colony's start. By situating the charter's ostensible claims of prerogative in the context of the practical challenges of proprietary settlement, I argue that the Maryland charter was not a *coup de force*; nor did it create a uniform plan for rule. Instead, it offered a wide scope of privileges that encompassed a range of legal and political possibilities that at times were incongruent. The charter referenced a mixed and unsettled set of English legal forms, which included statute law, common law, feudal law, and ancient constitutional principles. Proprietors and new colonists could assemble and combine various legal and political forms as long as they were "consonant to reason and not repugnant," and there was often little systematicity or uniformity to the mass of instructions, ordinances, and laws that were to emerge as Maryland's early governance. What this amounted to was a constitutionalism *in process*, where proprietors and colonists not only proposed but also frequently re-purposed the law for subjective and local interests.

In particular, as we will see next, this constitutionalism was not a consequence of inexorable imperial power. Instead, it reflected the limitations of the Crown in granting proprietary privileges, for what the Crown did was to delegate and transfer authority to proprietors and colonial actors on the ground who were to use *discretion* to cobble together serviceable governance in response to local and particular needs. This is a conception of constitutionalism that is oriented to colonial expansion and exploitation, but does not stress uniformity or even imposition. In Maryland, governance developed by slow accretion as charter, executive instructions, proclamations, and ordinances accumulated and were altered over time; these laws stressed *insertion* into regional conditions. They varied from region to region, and they were subject to change and modification depending on circumstances. Highly local, participatory, and rooted in multiple sovereignties, this was in many ways as much a constitutionalism *in process* as it was a constitutionalism of *insertion*. These elements are not simply of historical interest, suggesting the details and intricate features of long-past polities. More pressingly, they prompt us to reassess our normative understanding of the development of constitutionalism, especially as it pertains to the processes and ambitions of colonial power. Some of the subtler aspects of colonial power and constitutional practice come into view through a more finely grained view of founding, and such features can help us unsettle conceptualizations of empire and constitutionalism by reconfiguring the scale and scope of our historical imaginary.

Chartered Options

Lavish in its style and mode of declaration, the Maryland charter at first establishes an impression of mastery and confidence, proclaiming with its opening lines: "Our well beloved and right trusty Subject Caecilius Calvert, Baron Baltimore, in our Kingdom of Ireland, Son and Heir of George Calvert, Knight, late Baron Baltimore, in our said Kingdom of Ireland, treading in the steps of his Father, being animated with a laudable, and pious Zeal for extending the Christian Religion, and also the Territories of our Empire."[9] The charter situates itself as a gift of the sovereign Charles I, a grant "humbly besought" by Lord Calvert, while it delineates its intention to "transport . . . a numerous Colony of the English Nation" that was to encompass every element—forms of "all Islands and Inlets" and "Soil, Plains, Woods, Marshes, Lakes, Rivers, Bays, and Straits"—west of the Virginia border, "in a Country hitherto uncultivated, in the Parts of America, and partly occupied by Savages, having no knowledge of the Divine Being."[10]

The sentiments of the charter stood in strong contrast with actual conditions on the ground, which were marked by conflict of various kinds. Initially, the territory for Maryland had been allocated to the senior Lord George Calvert, the first Baron Baltimore, as a gesture of preference by the Crown. The senior Calvert had been a favored adviser to Charles I and had participated in numerous overseas ventures for the Crown, although these also included a contentious military occupation in Ireland and the failed settlement at Avalon in the Newfoundland territories. When the senior Calvert died in 1632, responsibility for Maryland fell to Cecilius Calvert, his less experienced son.[11] While the senior Lord Calvert had obtained the title to the Avalon territories with little outside opposition, Charles I's similar grant to the younger Lord Calvert was deeply contested by many in England and the Americas as evidence of Catholic sympathies. Vociferously anti-Popish lords and Virginian colonists protested both the size and scope of the prospect of a Catholic settlement in the Americas. Even the title of the colony, "Mari-land," in honor of Queen Henrietta Maria, daughter of King Henry IV, was viewed as circumspect, given Charles I's promises to allow the queen to attend mass at court and to suspend penal laws against English Roman Catholics.[12]

Especially in light of its courtly and trans-Atlantic context, the Maryland charter can be understood as a complex legal and political creation that assembled a vast array of prerogatives and privileges to better support the prospect of founding. Some of these features were quite standard. Similar to a number of English patents, such as the 1603 charter for the Virginia Company, the Maryland charter indicated that land was to be held not *in capite* but, instead, in free and common socage. This arrangement accorded Calvert fewer obligations and more privileges; land held in free and common socage was not burdened with military service, and it could be freely bought and sold as long as the new landholder continued to honor his donation to the king.[13]

Similar was the Maryland charter's use of a chorographical discourse, a technique frequently employed in English charters of the early seventeenth century and Spanish papal bulls of the sixteenth century. The charter systematically provided a survey of the territory that documented climate, agriculture, and plant life. With references to titled features, such as "Watkin's Point," "the river Wigloo, on the West," and the "Bay of Delaware on the North," the charter created a detailed impression of the territory, which subsequently could be used in advertisements and pamphlets.[14] As the promotional tract *A Relation of Maryland* indicated, Calvert promised the nearly 140 passengers on the first ships to Maryland, the *Ark* and the *Dove*, clearly established land holdings in Maryland. He offered every man between sixteen and fifty who recruited five men "to transport thither" a proportion of 1,000 acres of English measure, "which shall be erected into a Manor and be conveyed to him, his heirs, and assigns for ever, with all such royalties and privileges, as are usually belonging to Manors in England."[15]

Yet unlike many other English patents, the Maryland charter assembled an especially motley mix of feudal, common law, and civic humanist referents to characterize its colonial dominion. For a territory that had been claimed and *not* sustained by numerous parties, this was no small matter. The territory included in the 1632 Maryland charter had initially been granted in parts to both the Council of New England and the Virginia

Company; in fact, disputes over the territorial boundaries of the colony remained in force until the eighteenth century.[16] What the new charter needed to do was to portray the Maryland venture as sufficiently rendered so that investors and colonists would sign on to the prospective colony; it also needed to project a polity distinctively different in legal and political terms from prior ventures and settlements.

First, according to the terms of the charter, the colony was established as a proprietary rather than a joint-stock venture, because a proprietary holding, as David Jordan has suggested, offered "the greatest possible sovereignty and flexibility in governing a colony."[17] Second, while the charter granted extensive prerogatives to its Lord Proprietor, it "also extended to the settlers" a critical responsibility "for the good and happy Government of the said Province."[18] These features, according to Jordan, signaled the Calverts' longstanding commitment to "the cherished rights and privileges of what J. G. A. Pocock summarizes as 'the ancient constitution, with the central place of Parliament in that arrangement.'"[19] The reference to "good and happy Government" also indicated the proprietor's interest in political and legal flexibility: the ancient constitution was not to be the sole or even primary model for Calvert's colony. As Jordan notes, "Their new settlement could provide neither the social structure nor the other conditions necessary to sustain the current political system of England and the role that Parliament played in that polity."[20]

Instead, the charter turned to an unusual model of polity notable for its flexibility and lifted anachronistically from the feudal history of England: the palatinate of Durham from the 1300s. Contained in the conclusion of the third paragraph of the charter, the power of the palatinate offered a potent analogy for the proprietor's privileges and is worth quoting at length:

> Furthermore the Patronages, and Advowsons of all Churches which (with the increasing Worship and Religion of Christ) within the said Region, Islands, Islets, and Limits aforesaid, hereafter shall happen to be built, together with License and Faculty of erecting and founding Churches, Chapels, and Places of Worship, in convenient and suitable places, within the Premises, and of causing the same to be dedicated and consecrated according to the Ecclesiastical Laws of our Kingdom of England, with *all, and singular such, and as ample Rights, Jurisdic-*

tions, Privileges, Prerogatives, Royalties, Liberties, Immunities, and royal Rights, and temporal Franchises whatsoever, as well by Sea as by Land, within the Region, Islands, Islets, and Limits aforesaid, to be had, exercised, used, and enjoyed, as any Bishop of Durham, within the Bishoprick or County Palatine of Durham, in our Kingdom of England, ever heretofore hath had, held, used, or enjoyed, or of right could, or ought to have, hold, use, or enjoy.[21]

Vice-regal in its ability to found houses of worship, laws, and manors, the palatinate recalled various historical aspects of the tenure of Durham until its incorporation: the land grant made by medieval English kings in return for the service of military knights; the deputation of virtually sovereign powers by the Crown to be exercised by local authorities; and the military and juridical liberties bestowed on lords occupying frontier positions.[22] The palatinate was in fact still in operation in the seventeenth century, although with substantially curtailed privileges. As Anthony Pagden explains, "Although much reduced in power since 1535, Durham itself remained a palatinate until 1836. The bishop had, in effect, powers very similar to those of the Spanish viceroys."[23]

The charter's inclusion of this model from pre-Tudor England was not incidental. The senior Calvert had governed the contentious provinces of Ireland, and English policy in the territories strongly emphasized the creation of feudal estates for wealthy English grandees.[24] Drawing from his Irish experiences, Calvert petitioned to use the feudal example of the palatinate in his charter for the 1623 colony of Avalon in the Newfoundland territories, although the Avalon settlement foundered from the beginning and ultimately failed. Despite that outcome, the senior Calvert once again sought palatine privileges for the Maryland charter, and he was involved in lengthy negotiations with the Crown over retaining those terms "in his subsequent plans for Maryland."[25]

A number of earlier English charters offered investors and colonists forms of land tenure that were feudal in nature, but Maryland's reference to the palatinate was rather different—at once more evocative of the Lord Proprietor's authority and more ambivalent with respect to the territorial conditions of the new polity. On first consideration, the model of the palatinate helped to bolster the charter's assertion of jurisdiction, and it refined the description of the land that was to be bought, sold, and divided. This effect appeared in the affirmative language following the charter's initial reference to the palatinate:

> Now, That the aforesaid Region, thus by us granted and described, may be eminently distinguished above all other Regions of that Territory, and decorated with more ample Titles, Know Ye, that We, of our more especial Grace, certain knowledge, and mere Motion, have thought fit that the said Region and Islands be erected into a Province, as out of the Plenitude of our royal Power and Prerogative, We do, for our Heirs and Successors, erect and incorporate the same into a Province, and nominate the same Maryland, by which Name We will that it shall from henceforth be called.[26]

The proprietary charter's claim to "dignify" the territory with "larger titles" helped enhance the proprietor's power and depict the territory as place of occupancy, populated with a multitude of different peoples, activities, and values. Namely, Lord Calvert was given the liberty to wage war, raise taxes, and judge and punish offenders—all powers useful in defending and protecting the colony. Just as suggestively, with its references to the palatinate, the charter conveyed an image of the kind of "society required for such development to be sustained"; more specifically, this was a manorial settlement, complete with its social order of barons, freeholders, and servants and its judicial system of courts manor and courts baron.[27] As David Jordan aptly describes, it was "a finely graded society," and it provided popular power as a support to proprietary privilege.[28] The inclusion of the Durham precedent ideally suited the purposes of the Calverts. They wanted to provide for the voice of the people in the political life of the colony through a popular assembly but were still hesitant to have any expression of popular will restrict the proprietary authority. The charter thus created a representation of colonization befitting a proprietary venture that equally mixed political and economic interests.

Yet it was precisely the palatine model that also suggested the potentially fraught status of the prospective settlement. The reference to the palatinate of Durham may have helped to flesh out the terms of the forthcoming colony, offering settlers a minimal corporate identity and bestowing on the proprietor of the prospective settlement the power to raise churches, grant land, and wage war. These resources, however, were as much a privilege as a warning. The very provisions enabling the proprietors to create laws, sell land, create churches, and wage war resulted from Durham's historical status as a border settlement under siege, a place requiring fortification and defensive measures.[29] In this way, the Avalon settlement was a telling example, for it was the first settlement with palatine privileges granted to Calvert and nonetheless failed. This combination of privilege and insecurity was summed up in Cecilius Calvert's subsequent comment, in 1652, that these powers "may not be convenient for any one man to have in England yet they are necessary for any (whether one man or a Company) that undertakes a Plantation, in so remote and wild a place as Maryland."[30]

The charter's reference to the palatinate thus reveals colonial authority as a *power both created and undercut* by its position at the limits. For instance, the charter cautioned that the new settlement would need "remedy" to "sudden accidents" that "may frequently happen."[31] The "Multitude of People resorting thither" may cause "Rebellion, sudden Tumult, or Sedition."[32] More dramatically, the charter warned of the risks posed by "the Incursions of Savages, or of other Enemies, Pirates, and Ravagers" who posed the threat of "War" or "Death"[33] Characterized in this way, colonial authority was not an unqualified and superior force imposed from above. Rather—and more messily—it arose as a response to a series of potential outside and internal threats: "Rebellion, sudden Tumult, or Sedition" as well as "Incursions of Savages, or of other Enemies, Pirates, and Ravagers."[34]

This combined quality of ambition and insecurity emerged most clearly in the charter's reference to colonial law. As the charter proclaimed:

> Know Ye therefore further, that We, for us, our Heirs and Successors, do grant unto the said now Baron, (in whose Fidelity, Prudence, Justice, and provident Circumspection of Mind, We repose the greatest Confidence) and to his Heirs, for the good and happy Government of the said Province, free, full, and absolute Power, by the Tenor of these Presents, to Ordain, Make, and Enact Laws, of what Kind soever, *according to their sound Discretions* whether relating to the Public State of the said Province, or the private Utility of Individuals, of and with the Advice, Assent, and Approbation of the Free-Men of the same Province, or the greater Part of them, or of their Delegates or Deputies, whom We will shall be called together for the framing of Laws, when, and as often as Need shall require.[35]

This passage requires a little careful unpacking. On first examination, it appears that in granting its proprietor a liberty to make law, the charter simply allowed him a generous scope of privileges. However, closer examination does not reveal either the secure transfer of a settled English polity to the New World or a stable constitutionalist ground.

More specifically, the charter listed *three* different types of law, and it is not clear from the charter's terms which form took precedence. First, there was the proprietor's "free, full, and absolute Power" to "Ordain, Make, and Enact Laws, of what Kind soever."[36] As such, the proprietor was empowered in the palatine terms of the charter to act as a quasi-sovereign authoritative in his whims. But this power was offset by the second type of law that could be created in Maryland: the authority of the proprietor or "Magistrates and Officers" to establish "Ordinances" in "emergent Occasion."[37] The listing of emergency powers was commonplace in English colonial orders, such as *Ordinances for Virginia* (1621) and Sir Robert Heath's *Patent* (1629).[38] The final type of law established by the charter delegated considerable power and judgment to the colonists themselves. According to the charter, the law was to be judged by "Individuals" with their "sound Discretions," and the "Advice, Assent, and Approbation" of "Free-Men," or "the greater Part of them, or of their Delegates or Deputies, whom We will shall be called together for the framing of Laws, when, and as often as Need shall require."[39] In fact, the charter did not expressly give the power to make law to the colonists. Instead, it granted them the ability to offer *determining judgment*. This condition, in Jordan's estimation, offers evidence of Calvert's interest in establishing an assembly of colonists that was similar to a colonial Parliament—a nascent democratic model, conforming to Calvert's ancient constitutionalist sympathies and giving the people active voice in the political life of the colony.[40]

This constitutionalism, composed of the assemblage of multiple forms and traditions, was set in motion by the charter, but it was also largely in the form of *potential*, not full enumeration. The charter's attention to prospective events was embodied in its call for *discretion*. In the charter's terms, the realm of Maryland's founding necessitated particular "Individuals" working in their "private Utility" to use "sound Discretion" to respond to what is unpredictable, such as threats of piracy, mutiny, and rebellion.[41] For example, in providing a number of possible scenarios and conditions, the charter confronted its reader not with a formal rule or general principle but with a *context* for judgments.

Parsed by its ancient Latin extraction from the verbs *discretio* and *discernere*—meaning to distinguish, distinct, or separate—discretion was not solely a matter of treating any particular subject or situation with delicacy; it also entailed observation and a dynamic recruitment of facts.[42] Discretion thus implied attention to context, especially knowledge of local conditions and dynamics that could be ascertained only by participants on the ground. This was not, in consequence, the evaluation of a *static* situation but, instead, a context *in flux* in which any number of disturbances could arise.

Indeed, it seemed likely that discretion would be needed. As the charter stated, the laws needed only to "be not repugnant or contrary, but (so far as conveniently may be) agreeable to the Laws, Statutes, Customs, and Rights of this Our Kingdom of England." More specifically, the charter's judgment was that *either* the "said Lawes" of the Proprietor *or* the "Ordinances" of the proprietor, "magistrates," and "officers" were suitable as long as they were "consonant to Reason and be not repugnant nor contrary."[43] But this designation provided no fixed constitutionalist ground. As many historians have observed, English law of the period was far from systematic.[44] The legal landscape was highly variegated in England, shaped by diversity in "geography, society, religion, and political organization," as David Konig notes.[45] These orders of hybridity were further compounded by historical hybridity, as "functional variation and political rivalries within the English" resulted in the uneven and highly variable practice of the law in the courts.[46]

Thus, in Maryland the charter's specific reference to a concatenation of English "Laws, Statutes, Customs, and Rights" opened the way for wide variability and irregularity, because even the standard legal forms cited in the charter ran the risk of incongruity. Customary law, for example, was the tradition of decisions determined by local judges, fusing parts of Anglo-Saxon and feudal law in deference to local custom and preoccupation with land. Statute law, by contrast, provided fixed, written declarations reforming old and new rights, procedures, and laws.

Numerous English letters patent—for proprietary, charter, and Crown colonies—expressed an open-ended flexibility to the law, as I discussed in

Chapter 1. The 1609 Virginia charter permitted the laws to be "as near as conveniently may be agreeable." Later charters from Virginia (1611) and Massachusetts Bay (1629) employed a negative restriction, outlining that the laws of the charter "be not contrar[y] or repugnant." But the Maryland charter was one of the early few that emerged by the late 1620s and 1630s employing *both* affirmative and negative locutions.[47] As Mary Sarah Bilder argues, this ambivalent legal construction was central to setting the terms of a largely unwritten imperial constitution.[48] Drawing on the legal practices of lawyers, judges, and litigants in Rhode Island (statute debates, private cases), Bilder suggests that "repugnancy" was a key element in creating a dynamic legal culture that reveled in the tension and drama of negotiating authorities in the colonies and metropole. This situation was no less true in the proprietary colonies. "Like the corporation," Bilder observes, "governance under the proprietary produced a version of *imperium in imperio*—but in this case the development of multiple authorities."[49] As a consequence, "repugnancy" was dealt with by dual authorities, and the charter's mention of discretion was a signal that proprietors and colonists needed to negotiate legal and political culture carefully.

Given the open-ended and flexible terms of the Maryland charter, the constitutionalism conjured by the document was not a uniform legal edifice imposed by the Crown on submissive peripheries. It was instead a set of options bounded only by affirmative and negative guidelines—namely, that they were "consonant to Reason" and "not repugnant or contrary, but (so far as conveniently may be) agreeable."[50] Thus, even in principle alone, the standard set by the charters—namely, that the law was to be "agreeable and not repugnant"—provided a contradictory message of cautious privilege. Repugnancy set the limit of strangeness that the proposed legal order should not exceed; it was not an endorsement as such. And repugnancy as a standard reflected the proprietor's self-understanding that English law alone would not be sufficient for the exigencies of colonization. First, the charter did not distinguish when or where proprietary law or ordinance law took precedent. Second, and equally ambiguous, the charter's concatenation of these English "Lawes, Statutes, Customes, and Rights" was a motley assemblage, neither particularly agreeable in their differing traditions nor clear in the way the four forms arranged themselves in terms of importance. Meanwhile, the minimal restriction the charter placed—that

Calvert's laws and the ordinances be only "not repugnant or contrary . . . but (so far as conveniently may be) agreeable"—signaled the possible incongruity of the laws.[51]

This incongruity—this willingness to allow *imperio in imperium*— reveals the larger complications of proprietary founding. While the Crown formally authorized the colony, it had neither the resources nor interest to provide militia, infrastructure, and provisions to far-flung settlements. The problem of distance was one common to the English colonies, and English colonial administrators in the early seventeenth century regularly dealt with delayed communications and limited powers of enforcement.[52] As such, delegation of power to proprietors and settlers allowed the Crown to limit its responsibility and debt. Yet in doing so, the Crown also relinquished control and oversight over the colony's daily activities. The situation became even more complicated as an array of high- and low-level colonial administrators, traders, farmers, craftsmen, and others vied for authority and influence in the colonies. Intra-colonial conflicts frequently broke out. English settlements also contended with each other on issues of trade and territory, despite their shared Crown allegiance.

As a plan for a polity projected in imaginary terms before settlement has taken place, the charter calls to mind Michel de Certeau's theorization of plans written in "*repetitio rerum*." Through the distributive power and performative force of its "story," the charter raised a political "imaginary" that linked together both the power of a map and an itinerary to provide a nominal beginning in uncertain circumstances.[53] The charter's projection of an ambition operated as a provisional point of departure. In the specificity of its imaginary, the charter—even with its ambiguities—provided a useful narrative opening for colony, what we might also describe as a configuration of position from which to recruit colonists, enlist supplies, and promote materials. Moreover, the charter established the early conditions of possibility and intelligibility for organizing systems of meaning—indeed, the very systems of meaning that allowed the charters to be subsequently contested, changed, and modified.

Stemming from the charter, what emerged on the ground was a form of constitutionalism that was interactive, local, and participatory. It developed, as we will see, not with a single, authorizing text but, instead, with the cobbling together of a multitude of diverse documents—charter,

orders, proclamations, statutes, and acts—created by various people of differing knowledge, stature, and influence.

Governance and Discretion

Maryland's constitutionalism was in many ways typical of the early modern English period, when, as Bilder suggests, a plurality of written and
unwritten charters, laws, constitutions, orders, instructions, statutes, and
proclamations composed the "constitution." "The formula," she observes,
"appeared in letters patent and charters, as well as in royal instructions,
commissions, internal delegations of authority, gubernatorial correspondence, colonial laws, court proceedings, and appeals to the Privy Council.
The precise language varied, as did the various types of colonial lawmaking that were contemplated: laws, statutes, ordinances, constitutions, acts,
orders, bylaws, rules, methods, directions, instructions, as well as court
proceedings, procedures, and penalties."[54]

But from more modern eyes, the constitutionalism at work in Maryland appears unusual, mediated as it was through multiple documents,
composed of a wide array of legal and political forms, and open to altera-
tion. And from the first, temporary orders supplemented the charter. In
1633, Calvert was detained in England and could not accompany the first
two ships, the *Ark* and the *Dove*, to the Americas. In his place, he composed an extensive annotated list of fifteen orders to be executed by his
brother, Leonard Calvert.[55] The *Instructions* roughly addressed two central
concerns: first, relationships among the Maryland Catholics and Protestants at sea and on land, with particular attention to the emergence of any
possible sympathies of the Maryland Protestants to the Virginia colony;
and second, the set of actions and oaths required once the colonists arrived in the Maryland territories. These included finding a territory suitable for trade with Virginia and "Savages" (18) and the "conversion" (20)
of local indigenous tribes. Both concerns pointed to one particular issue:
creating a level of minimal stability in the colony's infancy.

This was no minor concern, for the prospect of founding a colonial
palatinate proved less than irresistible for many of the investors Lord
Calvert sought. As Alan Taylor explains, "Contrary to Lord Baltimore's
hopes, relatively few Catholics emigrated to Maryland. Instead, most of
his colonists were Protestants, primarily relocating Virginians. Many were
especially radical Protestants, known as Puritans and Quakers, wearied

by Virginia's sporadic efforts to enforce adherence to the official Church of England. Eager to attract settlers of any Christian faith, the proprietor adopted an especially generous headright system that granted one hundred acres for every adult (free or servant) transported."[56] The first colonists recruited included only seventeen Catholic investors, three Jesuit missionaries and their servants and assistants, and more than one hundred skilled and unskilled Protestant laborers and indentured servants. Even among this small crew, relations were far from harmonious. Before the *Ark* and the *Dove* left the docks at Gravesend in early winter of 1633, critics spread rumors of a popish plot that threatened to create divisive relations among the Catholic elites, Jesuit missionaries, and predominant number of Protestant laborers and servants. "My adversaries," Calvert wrote to the Earl of Stafford, "endeavored to overthrow my business at the Council Board, after they had informed by several means some of the Lords of the Council that I intended to carry over nuns into Spain, and soldiers to serve that King, which I believe your Lordship will laugh at."[57] Less laughable, however, were the interventions of the king's officers, who detained the *Ark* and the *Dove* at Gravesend and administered an oath to all passengers, declaring "that the Pope, neither of himself, nor by any authority by the Church or See of Rome, or by any other means with any other, hath any power or authority to depose the King, or to dispose of any of his Majesty's kingdoms or dominions."[58]

But not all of the original Maryland settlers submitted. Father Andrew White and the other Jesuit missionaries joined the *Ark* and the *Dove* later, at the Isle of Wight, and evaded taking the oath.[59] The Jesuits' refusal to take the oath prompted distrust from the Protestant settlers, while Catholics elites, most of the seventeen "Gentlemen Adventurers," viewed their evasion as theatrical and feared that the situation would promote Maryland Protestants' sympathies with the counter-claims of the Virginia colony. Calvert, concerned about these burgeoning tensions, encouraged Catholic colonists to suppress their objections and quarrels with Protestants lest they spread word of Catholic repression to Virginia or English Protestants. "For that end," he warned in the *Instructions*, "they cause all Acts of Roman Catholic Religion to be done as privately as may be, and that they instruct all the Roman Catholics to be silent upon all occasions of discourse concerning matters of Religion . . . this to be observed at Land as well as at Sea" (16).

These *Instructions*, like the Maryland charter and the later ordinances and proclamations, were a part of Maryland's "constitution." The *Instructions* were notable, first, because they promoted toleration between settlers and with indigenes. This toleration was not a blanket directive to treat all spiritual creeds as equivalent. Rather, toleration was an immediate tactic to respond to potential sources of contestation, especially as they might arise between elites and lower-class settlers both prior to arrival in Maryland and in the early months of settlement. For example, the *Instructions* cautioned Calvert's representatives, Leonard Calvert, Jerome Hawley, and Thomas Cornwallis, to "preserve unity and peace amongst all the passengers on Ship-board" and to "suffer no scandal nor offence to be given to any of the Protestants, whereby any just complaint may hereafter be made, by them, in Virginia or in England" (16).

Second, toleration heavily relied on an attitude of discretion, as Calvert's *Instructions* to his administrators made clear. Colonists were to be encouraged to "learn" about possible "private plots of his Lordships adversaries in England" by scrutinizing the other colonists without creating animosity or resentment (16–17). Calvert ordered his representatives to have the colonists "learn, if they can, the names of all such, their speech, where and when they spoke them, and to whom; The places, if they had any, of their consultations, the Instruments they used and the like; to gather what proofs they can of them; and to set them down particularly and clearly in the writing with all the Circumstances; together with their opinions of the truth and validity of them according to the condition of the persons" (17).

As previously noted, in the charter's call for discretion, colonists were situated in the position of readers, examining possible problems in light of their context and situation. There was, to that extent, a broadly Aristotelian element in the charter's call for colonists to develop a capacity to make judgments and to engage in action, and even to supersede the law.[60] But the discretion called for in the *Instructions* seemed to reinforce the charter's description and to suggest an even more pragmatic quality. Discretion arose as part of Calvert's more general strategy to manage distant settlers and to provide some direction and authority to a settlement already split in a number of ways.[61] It was a mode of action that mixed vigilance and caution in attending to local issues, and it was not really a comprehensive ethic but, instead, a partial and particular tactic to avoid destructive conflict.

These features—caution, vigilance, and partiality—were part of what we might describe as the *tacticality of discretion*, and they appear more vividly in the rest of Calvert's *Instructions*, which turned to the activities that colonists undertook once the ships arrived in the new territories. When the two boats came ashore on March 25, the colonists set up a large cross, planted the English standard, and held a worship service and read the charter. Such acts, as I noted in the previous chapter, were a customary practice of English colonial ventures.[62] The proprietor's representatives on the early ships traveling to Maryland carried copies of the Maryland charter, and Calvert's representatives at the colony's early settlement in St. Mary's read the charter aloud (although only a portion of the embarking colonists—namely, the elites and Jesuits—would have read the charter before settlement).[63] As Patricia Seed explains, the recitation of English charters by colonial leaders on disembarkation was a performative act that joined the legal face of the charter with a public act of claiming.[64]

However, as the early records of the colony indicated, possession was not settled simply by the oral performance of the charter. More prosaically, settlers spent the bulk of their time adapting to their new environment. Before settlers could produce political institutions and commercial crops for export, they had to clear and plant the land, set up temporary shelters, and cultivate adequate stores of food. To do all this, as Calvert noted in his *Instructions*, colonists needed to establish toleration and relative peace among themselves and to develop a *situated understanding* of the terrain.

For Calvert, the recruitment of a knowledgeable guide was as much a matter of developing a sense of those "things" useful in making a selection of "place" (17), as it was an issue of recognizing those characteristics important to avoid, such as those places already under watch by "the command of any fort" (21). Therefore, the task to "make choice of a place" (17) required making decisions about the possibility of growing staples in land "to be healthful and fruitful" (17), as well as an informed sense of who or what was to be "convenient" (18) for any number of future actions, such as "trades," "planting," and other "business" (21, 23, 23).

Of particular importance was Calvert's suggestion in the *Instructions* that the acquisition of this knowledge could come from finding "any" one to facilitate the gathering of economic, agricultural, and political information. As the Jesuit priest Father Andrew White recorded in his account

A Relation of Maryland, the vague "any" referred to by Calvert in the *Instructions* was in fact a member of the Piscataways. White explained:

> Him our Governor sent ashore to invite the Werowance to a parley, who thereupon came with him aboard privately, where he was courteously entertained, and after some parley being demanded by the Governor, whether he would be content that he and his people should set down in his Country, in case he should find a place convenient for him, his answer was, "that he would not bid him go, neither would he bid him stay, but that he might use his own discretion."[65]

Here, discretion was expressed in informal acts not simply of toleration, but also of negotiation, translation, and general exchange with local indigenes. To some extent, these kinds of practices were a staple in the early modern English colonies. For example, the pamphlets of the Virginia Company, as Andrew Fitzmaurice discusses, commended tactical relationships with local indigenes.[66] Similarly, Colin Calloway finds that relations between colonists and Indians in the English settlements of the Northeast were structured by exchange, negotiation, and dependence.[67] In Maryland, Calvert's instruction to the colonists to find a local guide (read, indigenes) was an example of the tacticality of discretion particularly oriented toward insertion into a complex set of relationships on the ground.[68] After all, when George Calvert, the senior Lord Baltimore, obtained a royal charter to the large block of territory north and east of Potomac River, he claimed territory already occupied by various interested parties. In the 1620s and early 1630s, the Chesapeake and its tributaries offered ready access to a considerable number of Indian groups with furs and beaver pelts. Furthermore, the French were heavily involved with trade in Canada, and the Dutch possessed a fur-trading network with Indian groups along Delaware Bay. During the same period, Virginians also sought to gain a stronger foothold in the trade network, and eventually a heavy competition arose between Maryland and the Virginia colony over trade in beaver pelts along the eastern shore.[69]

In this context, founding was a practice not of imposition but insertion; developing relations with local indigenes "to take with them" (17) was a way for Maryland colonists to navigate unpredictable circumstances, as White noted in his longer tract, *A Relation in Maryland* (also printed in Latin as *Relatio Itineris in Marylandiam* [1634]). According to White, Maryland colonists relied heavily on translators familiar with local languages to gain access to land and to supplies. For instance, White described "one Captain Henry Fleet" who negotiated an informal treaty with the Piscataways that reflected these dependences:

> To make his entry peaceable and safe, he thought fit to present the Werowance and the Wisoes of the Town with some English Cloth (such as is used in trade with the Indians) Axes, Hoes, and Knives, which they accepted very kindly, and freely gave consent that he and his company should dwell in one part of their Town, and reserved the other for themselves; and those Indians that dwelt in that part of the Town, which was allotted for the English, freely left them their houses, and some corn that they had begun to plant.[70]

For proprietary colonists, these associations were instrumental because learning local knowledges provided the possibility—part of the "groundwork," as it were—for founding. They were also useful in creating colonial advantage. For example, as White wrote, "Captain Henry Fleet an English-man, who had lived many years among the Indians, and by that manner spoke the Country language very well, and was much esteemed of by the native."[71] Most of the Englishmen familiar with local indigenes were primarily traders, who, as Helen C. Rountree and Thomas E. Davidson comment, "had good reason to respect the native culture and language and, later, to try to protect the native people from being overrun."[72] Learning native languages, though essential, was not a widely practiced skill, as Rountree and Davidson also explain: "Most of the Englishmen who lived in the Chesapeake region during the seventeenth century never acquired even a superficial knowledge of Indian languages or cultures. Such knowledge was the key to successful trading, for anyone who did not have it was unlikely to be able to develop or maintain a network of trading partners among the Indians."[73]

These practices illustrate the ways in which constitutionalism can include open-ended and flexible elements; they also reveal a different side of colonialism, focused on insertion—insinuating the colony in and around the constellation of relations already in place. These tactics, moreover, do not appear to be based in any fundamental appreciation of religious or ethnic differences. At the same time, total exclusion or elimination of those who already inhabited the region is not the goal, either. What takes center stage instead is a more relative, more limited set of ambitions—incorporation into crowded and claimed territory, achievement of useful local knowledge, and mitigation of colonial stress and conflict.

In fact, while discretionary practices may not have established strictly oppositional relationships between colonists and indigenes, they certainly did not eliminate or alleviate conflict or crisis between the many actors in the colony, such as the Susquehannocks, Nanticokes, Wicomiss, Jesuits, Maryland farmers, and Virginia traders. One telling instance was the fur trade in the Chesapeake, which was substantial in the late 1630s and early 1640s, especially the trade of beaver for cloth. Calvert tried to make a profit from furs by licensing private traders for 10 percent of gains from each trading voyage, and he and subsequent proprietors offered treaties and informal protections to the tribes until the 1680s to secure trading partners.[74] However, Maryland farmers and craftsmen often protested treaty proposals, and they mobilized in the Maryland Assembly to protest Indian trade and traffic.

Meanwhile, the Maryland elites who aligned with Calvert sought to strengthen their ties with particular tribes, such as the Susquehannocks, Nanticokes, and Wicomiss, groups central to the fur trade and resistant to Iroquois rule. Calvert, too, had his own agenda, seeking to restrain the Jesuits and the Maryland farmers largely because he feared that the Nanticokes, the largest and most powerful Indian tribe on Maryland's eastern shore, would exclude the colony from the fur trade.[75] The Nanticokes were heavily involved in the fur trade and had an indirect link with the Iroquois, the chief enemies of the Susquehannocks and allies of Maryland; the Nanticokes also held the territory between the Maryland colony and the Delaware or Lenni Lenape Indians—and these astute negotiators traded with the English on the Chesapeake and with the Dutch. "It is clear," Rountree and Davidson conclude, "that by the 1640s, at least, the native people were sophisticated consumers who knew what they wanted and would not settle for second best. If one set of European traders would not offer a particular category of goods, the furs would simply be sold elsewhere."[76]

This state of affairs was a version of what Calloway calls a "cultural kaleidoscope," in which crisscrossing relationships between English colonists, indigenes, and other European settlers are at once necessary for English colonial settlement and a risk to its security.[77] Relationships made across these cultural differences both negotiated the fluidity of power shifting across a variety of fronts in the Americas and changed those webs of power in ways that could not be predicted prior to interactions. In the most notable examples, indigenes served as intermediaries to squabbles between various English settlers. For instance, Captain Toby Young wrote in 1635 to Sir Toby Matthew that "William Claiborne" on Kent Island had "labored to procure the Indians to supplant" the Maryland colonists "by informing them that they were Spaniards and that they had a purpose to destroy them and take their Country from them. That the Indians had a purpose to have attempted it, had they not been dissuaded by one Captain Fleet, who had in former times lived amongst them, and is now in good credit with them." Conversely, Claiborne also accused the Marylanders of using networks of alliance with the Piscataways and Susquehannocks to underseat his stronghold. "[Claiborne] alleged," Captain Toby Young wrote, "that my Lords company had accused him to the Governor of Virginia for animating, practicing, and conspiring with the Indians to supplant and cut them off: that the Governor had appointed certain commissioners of this Colony to join with certain other Commissioners of my Lords Colony to examine the truth of that accusation and that upon their information he purposed to proceed herein according to Justice."[78]

Proprietary constitutionalism in Maryland was, in that sense, deeply local and responsive to conditions on the ground. Law in the proprietary settlements was not a matter of imperial fiat but, rather, an hybrid amalgam created by elites and settlers who variously drew on instructions, orders, proclamations, statutes, and other acts. Especially distinctive in Calvert's call for discretion in the *Instructions* was its exposure of the limits of proprietary power. Yet in its particularity and responsiveness, this constitutionalism was no less colonial in ambition. If not a simple and direct form of top-down authority, discretion heavily mixed colonial and paternal interest and it was far from free of colonial ambitions, interests, and desires. As we will see next, the acts, orders, statutes, and instructions created by the colonists, particularly in the Maryland Assembly, reflected both the growing discretionary powers of the colonists and the various struggles for power between elites, laborers, explorers, missionaries, and others.

To Do Justice: Law in Process

As the charter states, Lord Baltimore was enabled by a pluralized sovereign, "Us, our Heirs and Successors," to "Ordain, Make, and Enact Laws, of what Kind soever, according to their sound Discretions whether relating to

the Public State of the said Province, or the private Utility of Individuals."
Nonetheless, the law of the Lord Proprietor was still subject not only to the
colonists' "sound Discretions" but also to the "Advice, Assent, and Approbation of the Free-Men of the same Province, or the greater Part of them,
or of their Delegates or Deputies, whom We will shall be called together
for the framing of Laws, when, and as often as Need shall require."[79]

This revising corollary in the charter—understanding the central
role of the Maryland Assembly to provide "advise, assent, and approbation"—serves as key evidence for modern historical arguments that claim
Maryland's central place as an early form of democratic expression in the
New World. "Representative government in Maryland," according to Jordan, "owes its origin and legitimacy to this clause of the Calverts' charter which made their province the first permanent English colony on the
North American continent to provide from its founding for an assembly of
resident freeman."[80] Namely, while the charter encompassed the palatine
lord's ability to wage war, raise taxes, and create tenure, it still preserved the
rights and interests of members of the colony to judge the laws. To be sure,
the charter initially made no overt declaration of the Maryland Assembly's
power to make legislation. But, in the early years of the colony's settlement,
the colonists quickly drew on their implied powers of "advise assent and
approbation" to challenge Calvert on the sufficiency of his proposed laws
and to suggest their own irregular array of legislation. What emerged was
proprietary constitutionalism as a grasping, improvisational form.

In particular, in 1637 Calvert instructed his governor to call a legislature and present a code of laws sent out from England for acceptance by
the Maryland Assembly. Led by Assistant Governor Thomas Cornwallis,
the Maryland Assembly that convened in January 1637/8 (the first meeting
with a written record) rejected Calvert's submitted laws as not necessarily
"wholesome laws and ordinances."[81] As the governor was to write to Calvert in 1638, "The body of laws you sent over by Mr. Lewger I endeavored to
have had passed by the assembly at Maryland but could not effect it, there
was so many things unsuitable to the peoples' good and no way conducing
to your profit. . . . Others have been passed in the same assembly and now
sent unto you which I am persuaded will appear unto you to provide both
for your honor and profit as much as those you sent us did."[82]

Challenged by both his representatives and the majority of members
of the assembly, Calvert eventually wrote back to his governor granting

his assent to laws enacted by the provincial legislature, provided they were "not contrary to the laws, statutes, and customs of England."[83] These events demonstrated a notable shift in emphasis. In the early days of the Maryland colony's founding, discretion served as a modus operandi suggested by the proprietor—one that was useful in ameliorating religious and other social tensions between the new colonists and among indigenous and other European settlers. Discretion also appeared as a tactic of founding, potentially lessening Calvert's need to provide excessive supplies and resources to the colonists. However, as the colony became more settled, the Maryland Assembly in particular sought to expand its discretionary powers and to act without the sanctioned approval of the proprietor. Most obviously, after the Maryland Assembly's rejection of Lord Calvert's proposed laws in 1638, the second recorded elected assembly, in February–March 1638/9, passed *An Act for the liberties of the people*, once more invoking the terms of the charter as privileges to be held by the assembly itself:

> Be it Enacted By the Lord Proprietary of this Province of and with the advice and approbation of the freemen of the same that all the Inhabitants of this Province being Christians (Slaves excepted) Shall have and enjoy all such rights liberties immunities privileges and free customs within this Province as any natural born subject of England hath or ought to have or enjoy in the Realm of England *by force or virtue of the common law or Statute Law of England (saving in such Cases as the same are or may be altered or changed by the Laws and ordinances of this Province).*[84]

By rejecting Calvert's laws and sending their own laws to him, the Maryland Assembly asserted its ability to make, alter, and change "the Laws and ordinances of this Province." This change was perhaps surprising, but not entirely unfounded. A provision for a legislature was a feature that the senior Calvert had consciously sought to include into his 1623 charter for Avalon and, as Jordan clarifies, Calvert "carefully retained that commitment in his subsequent plans for Maryland."[85] But if Calvert initially viewed the legislature as a desirable venue to encourage the participatory efforts of the colonists, the assembly—diverse in composition and highly active—quickly became not just an oppositional force to proprietary rule but a contentious site for intra-colonial power struggles.

In the early years of the settlement, there was a constant flow of new-comers, and the assembly's relatively liberal entry requirement ensured that the legislature included diverse constituents and interests, although it was still far from representative. The assembly was largely composed of elites, freemen, and those non-landholding members of the colony who had petitioned to participate. However, women, slaves, and indentured servants were not permitted to take part, and Jesuit priests opted out of direct political involvement in the assembly for reasons pertaining to their personal religious commitments (especially not to take oaths) and not their direct exclusion by the government.[86] Because of this demographic composition, the assembly's legislative decisions were heavily influenced by deep-seated contestations between elites and freemen, especially since the passing of acts by the assembly required a majority vote. The most numerous portion of the legislature consisted of men of modest means, former servants who were predominantly Protestants, but the Catholic gentry and Calvert's representatives, although limited in number, sought at every turn to mobilize their influence and sway the balance of power in their interest.

One of the most prominent features of the laws that emerged from the assembly was that they were heterogeneous, differential, and subject to constant change. They variously took form as statutes, acts, and procla-mations, and they often served only as temporary responses to exigent events—such as particularities of trade, rumors by William Claiborne, and relations with local indigenous tribes—and not a uniform or permanent body of rule.[87] First, as David Hall describes, sessions of the Maryland General Assembly enacted *statute laws*, which were "commonly printed as broadsides in order to facilitate the process of distribution."[88] The tran-scription and reproduction of these laws often contained omissions, mis-takes, and various other errors. Second, this proliferation of statutes was supplemented by assembly *proclamations*, which could be rendered in multiple forms—orally, in writing, and in print. Proclamations, Hall ex-plains, "embodied the monarch's speech, or spoken will. Transposed into written text, the proclamation was an elaborate artifact bearing not only the royal seal and appropriate signatures but also decorative lettering."[89] Because proclamations took various forms, they could be disseminated to and altered for diverse publics.

Last, the assembly was active in creating temporary *acts* to respond to exigent circumstances. In a notable case, the assembly legislated in an *Act Touching Indians* to permit "no promiscuous liberty of trade with the Indians" in 1638, a decision particularly swayed by the leadership of Captain Cornwallis, the assistant to the governor of Maryland, who sought his own stronghold on trade.[90] Yet this act was not uniformly accepted. A number of colonists resented the proprietary government's restrictions on their independent ability to trade. Some, such as Thomas Copley, sought to expand their autonomy to negotiate with local Indians and thus complained to Lord Calvert about the leadership's emphasis on trade rather than on the basic rudiments of food. As Copley wrote to Lord Calvert, in April 1638, "In our own persons and with such as are needful to assist us, we may freely go, abide and live among the Savages, without any license to be had here from the Governor, or any other." Furthermore, in his letter to Calvert, Copley raised concerns about the colony's potential demise from such restrictions to trade. "I desire likewise from your lordship a free Grant to buy corn of the Indians without asking leave here, for indeed It will be a great pressure to eat our bread at their courtesy, who as yet I have found but very little courteous. Certainly which the chief of this Colony thus wholly neglect planting, and think on nothing but on a peddling trade certainly in the Colony, they will still make a scarcity of bread, and in that scarcity if we shall not be able to help ourselves nor the Colony without their leave, that make the want, many great difficulties may follow."[91] Meanwhile, although he pushed through the restrictions on trade in the Maryland Assembly, Captain Cornwallis remained unsatisfied. Facing resistance by many Marylanders, Cornwallis threatened outright to desert the colony unless he received more supplies. As Cornwallis warned Lord Calvert in April 1638, "If therefore your Lordship nor your Country will afford me no other way to support the great Expenses that I have been and daily am at for my Subsistence here, but what I must fetch out of the Ground by Planting this Stinking weed in America, I must desert the Place and business, which I confess I shall been loath to do, so Cordial A Lover am I of them both, yet if I am forced to it by discourteous Injuries I shall not weep at parting nor despair to find heaven as near to other parts as Maryland."[92]

With these acts, the Maryland Assembly illustrated the various contests over power being brokered in the colony. If the acts provided some settlement to disagreement among the colonists, it was partial, for the repeated meetings of the assembly provided a place in which legislation and influence changed over time. For instance, as laws proliferated in the colony, the Maryland Assembly "responded to the ever-growing pile of statutes by periodically repealing all existing laws, only to reenact in the same session a nearly identical set."[93] Moreover, statutes, proclamations, instructions, and other legal matter were produced by scribes, as Hall explains, and copies were rarely identical: "It was common knowledge that handwritten texts could easily be altered by the simple insertion or deletion of words. . . . Errors inevitably occurred as a consequence of the process of making copies."[94] Proprietors and colonists faced the challenge, as Hall puts it, of "keeping up with the laws that were current, and differentiating these from older laws that were 'temporary' (as certain English statutes, like those authorizing grants of money, usually were), repealed, revised, or superseded was no easy business."[95] The various versions of the law also could and did fuel debate and dispute, especially where conflict between Crown, proprietary, and settler authority was already brewing. "This process of review, which frequently resulted in laws being suspended or revoked, made for a persistent confusion that was exacerbated by the recurrent struggle for power between royal or proprietary governors and local assemblies."[96]

As I suggested earlier, the privileges to make law did not form a unitary or consistent body of constitutionalism: The laws to be made only needed to be "consonant to Reason, and be not repugnant or contrary, but (so far as conveniently may be) agreeable to the Laws, Statutes, Customs, and Rights of this Our Kingdom of England."[97] Rather, Maryland's "constitution" was in process—changing laws and orders that were already derived from a highly irregular source. This irregularity was often a source of colonial contestation. While the assembly had an astonishing knowledge of current parliamentary procedures and powers, it was also in constant debate about the validity and order of law. For example, as Jordan notes, members of the colony disputed whether and when common law or statute law would be appropriate, and others pondered whether local circumstance might require some "unique statutes."[98] To further complicate the mix, the colony also possessed local magistrates who issued judgments on the basis of common law and English statutes. These magistrates often were not formally trained in the law, and they enacted a workaday pragmatism in their judgments. They relied on both the regional needs of colonists and selective examination of collections of English statutes and handbooks containing legal forms and procedures.[99] The colonies sought to align themselves with England in their reliance on English tradition, but they also privileged measures of local autonomy, as was evident when Maryland judges and assembly members turned to history, English statutes, and treatises of jurisprudence.[100]

This open-endedness was rooted in the charter's call for discretion as to the specific organization of rule, a discretion that could also be conceptualized as a version of what Cass Sunstein has described as "incompletely theorized agreements," or areas of silence in the constitution that allow for later amendment and expansion.[101] But where Sunstein is focused on the ways these constitutional silences can work to harmonize and unify deliberative democracies, my focus on discretion in Maryland has illustrated some of the ways in which areas of "incomplete theorizing" assisted and supported colonial ambitions through a constitutionalism that was expedient, locally particular, and improvisational. In contrast to Sunstein's account, Maryland's constitutionalism reflects an earlier, more unsettled period where ambitions for community were inextricable from grasping and instrumental desires for colonial insertion.

Indeed, while a number of historians have looked at Maryland and the pre-Revolutionary colonies more generally as early examples of American democracy and participatory politics, the account that I offer here demonstrates some of the instrumental and, at times, contradictory features of early founding. For example, one of Maryland's most vaunted features, religious toleration, was, when situated in context, less an ideal than an element of discretion and a tactic for preventing colonial factions. Even more obviously, republican values take on different nuances in the context of Maryland. While the colonists were conceived in the charter's terms as subjects to a pre-Tudor feudal lord in border territory, they were also encouraged to be active and participatory in ways complementary to the Roman conception of citizen actors who vigorously contribute to the political life of their community. Recent scholarship by Markku Peltonen, Andrew Fitzmaurice, David Konig, and many others stresses how absolutism, the ancient constitution, and contractarian theories commingled with resistance theories and republican ideas in early modern England. In particular, Peltonen contends that humanist thought played a significant role prior to the Civil War and Interregnum, challenging J. G. A. Pocock's longstanding interpretation that republican and civic humanist themes could come to light only after the collapse of older modes of thought. Pocock, most notably, highlights the decline of English humanism in the mid-sixteenth century and argues that the medieval vocabulary of *jurisdiction* and *gubernaculum*, the theory of the ancient constitution, the doctrine of elect nation, and the tradition of natural jurisprudence prevented "Englishmen from conceiving themselves as active, participating citizens and of the commonwealth as a genuine republic."[102] By contrast, Peltonen explains that republican notions were prominent in the period prior to the English Civil War, and he further finds that republican and civic humanist themes coexisted with older doctrines. This humanism was not a detailed plan or dry schematic but more supple and fluid in its overlap with other doctrines.[103] While many have emphasized the pervasiveness of the monarchical republic, constitutionalism in Maryland was even more fecund and wide-ranging in its hybrid adaptations, drawing on common law, feudal law, and other practices of legal and political governance.[104]

The Maryland colony was certainly not the virtuous commonwealth described by Cicero and idealized by the civic humanists. It was instead quite amorphous, stretched and extended by the economic, religious, and social interests of the proprietor and diverse settlers. Yet even in failure, the utilization of these republican and civic humanist motifs suggests how much they influenced the colonial imaginary. As Andrew Fitzmaurice has suggested, in the American colonies the monarchical republic was present and influential, even if the reality was often a marked departure from the ideal. As he contends, "It is clear from many accounts of colonial corruption that the monarchical republic survived plantation because even if civic participation had dramatically decayed it remained the standard by which social and political behavior was judged through a broad cross-section of social orders."[105]

A more focused attention to the conditions of colonial founding in Maryland is not intended to account for the entwined relationship between constitutionalism and colonialism in the Americas *in toto*. But the more localized example allows different features of constitutional and colonial power to emerge. In the Maryland charter and the colony's early governance, we can see various elements of hybridity at work in early modern English constitutionalism and colonialism. Cautioned to be discreet, colonists participated in creating a heterogeneous political and legal culture of statutes, executive orders, temporary acts, and proclamations. This assemblage of law represented not the superiority of colonial power, but rather its uneven and contested terms.

To Read the Past

Many contemporary political theorists tend to treat the relationship between the English center and colonial periphery as a trajectory in which a stable, authoritative center projects its constitutionalist power over peripheral territories, both colonial and indigenous. In fact, even for those who seek to rehabilitate pre-"modern" constitutionalist traditions, the presumption that the entwined development of early modern English colonialism and constitutionalism was inexorable, uniform, and repressive becomes a useful foil. For example, as Jacob Levy notes, the theorist James Tully characterizes "'modern' constitutionalism" as "an intellectual tradition [that is] relentlessly rationalistic, assimilationist, individualistic, and hostile to ethnocultural difference of the sort that would be needed to ground, e.g., indigenous peoples' rights that predated and survived the constitutional moment."[106] Yet as I suggest, this conceptualization insufficiently addresses the conflicts over power and privilege that appear at the English center *and* the ways in which such conflicts were displaced and reconfigured through the processes of overseas English Atlantic settlement. As I have shown, constitutionalism in England was far from uniform, and its "native" hybridity was further emphasized and enhanced as English constitutionalism was differently and diversely modified, adapted, and created in the proprietary settlements overseas.

These constitutions did help facilitate the insertion of colonists into already occupied territories and to gain traction on the ground. But the proprietary delegation of power also attenuated connections both between the Crown and periphery and between the many English colonial settlements in the Americas. In that way, Maryland's proprietary constitutionalism, shaped as it was by dual sovereignties and by a hybridity spurred by the English constitution, seemed to have a double movement, in which local colonial power was enhanced and centralized Crown authority over the peripheral settlements was thwarted.

After the 1640s, the colony continued to experience turbulent struggles over power. Rumors of conspiracy among provincial indigenes and Catholics set Protestants in an uproar. Virginians such as William Claiborne and Richard Ingle incited unrest among Protestants in 1645 by intimating that the leadership of Maryland bore the specter of imperial Catholicism and arbitrary rule. By 1649 and the early 1650s, Protestant freemen in Maryland were citing the example of Parliament to defend the assembly against arbitrary adjournment by the governor. In 1652, the Protestant majority of the assembly, roused by Claiborne and Ingle, raised insurrections and revolutions against the Catholic leadership, overthrowing Calvert's deputies in 1654 and in effect achieving a suspension of proprietary rule until 1657. Protestants from Maryland and Virginia filed petitions to Cromwell in 1653 and 1655 and waged a fierce pamphlet war with petitions titled, "Virginia and Maryland, or the Lord Baltemore's Printed Case Uncased and Unanswered" and "Babylon's Fall in Maryland."[107] Even after the restoration of the proprietary government, unrest persisted through the 1670s and 1680s. As Lord Culpeper of Virginia wrote to the Lords of Trade in 1681, "Maryland is now in torment, and not only troubled with our disease, poverty, but in very great danger of falling in pieces; whether it be that old Lord Baltimore's politic maxims are not pursued or that they are unsuited to this age."[108] In the period between 1692 and 1715, William and Mary established royal government in Maryland, only to have the colony return to proprietary leadership when Lord Baltimore's Protestant son gained the title of proprietor.[109] The reestablished proprietors, however, came to hold little power, as Bilder explains, because eventually "proprietor ascendancy was eroded by the growth in the assembly's lawmaking authority and the Crown's desire for direct governance."[110] Still, despite these challenges, many subsequent English colonies sought the proprietary privileges that Maryland had exercised in its early years and, as we will see in Chapter 3, the proprietary model became the dominant model in seventeenth-century English America.

The next chapters focus not solely on proprietary charters, but on the formal and informal governing orders possible in the proprietary settlements. As I will show by looking at the founding of the Carolina colony, one of the largest proprietary ventures in the seventeenth century and a colony famously associated with the theorist John Locke, proprietary constitutionalism relied not simply on the open-ended terms of the charter but also, and crucially, on the powers of rhetoric, imagination, and adaptation.

Theory and Practice in the *Fundamental Constitutions of Carolina*

3

Unhappy, on the contrary, is that republic, which, not having at the beginning fallen into the hands of a sagacious and skillful legislator, is herself
obliged to reform her laws. More unhappy still is that republic which from
the first has diverged from a good constitution.
—NICCOLÒ MACHIAVELLI, *DISCOURSES*

While contemporary political thought does not generally
focus much attention on the proprietary colonies, the
colony of Carolina is a notable exception. In particular, theorists
have turned to the *Fundamental Constitutions* and John Locke's
involvement with the Carolina proprietary association as evidence to buttress critical interpretations of the *Two Treatises of
Government* (1690) and its conceptualization of land, labor, and
property.[1] In a key example, Bhikhu Parekh undergirds his account of Locke's colonial agenda in the *Two Treatises* with reference to Locke's practical participation:

> Locke's interest was not entirely intellectual. His patron the
> Earl of Shaftesbury had strong financial interests in the New
> World and, in the words of Locke's distinguished biographer
> Maurice Cranston, shared Locke's "zeal for commercial im-
> perialism . . . and the possibilities it offered for personal and
> national enrichment." Locke was also secretary to the Lords of
> Proprietors of Carolina (1668–75) and to the Council of Trade
> and Plantations (1673–76). In both these capacities Locke

played an important part in formulating colonial policies. He was in no doubt that English colonization of North America was fully justified, and provided its most articulate and influential philosophical defense.[2]

Accounts such as Parekh's highlight some of the colonialist biases of the *Two Treatises*, and they rightly note the effect of Locke's treatise on eighteenth-century and nineteenth-century audiences. Indeed, it is now virtually axiomatic to regard the canonical *Two Treatises of Government* as a justification for colonial subjugation, where Locke's invocation to "plant in some inland places in America" is seen as a call for territorial appropriation and cultural assimilation.[3] As David Armitage comments, "John Locke has become a crucial link in the historical chain joining liberalism with colonialism."[4]

Yet the *Fundamental Constitutions*, so often referenced by modern critics of Locke, was in many ways a very different text than the *Two Treatises*. As Christopher Tomlins points out, the colony that was envisaged by the *Fundamental Constitution* was complex and intricate, variously mixing feudal, republican, and authoritarian elements: "The *Constitutions* stands as by far the most elaborated statement of English proprietorial colonization's legalized projection of authority onto an expanse of mainland territory."[5] Moreover, the *Fundamental Constitutions* and the *Two Treatises* were very differently authored and received. The first was a text of governance, created by a proprietary body, and the second was initially an anonymous treatise largely composed during a period of exile.

As I suggest in this chapter, the *Fundamental Constitutions*, when situated in the context of proprietary politics, reveals a conception of constitutionalism and colonialism that does not adhere to a liberal or even a contractarian model. Instead, its historical roots extended more broadly and deeply into civic humanism, republicanism, and paternalism. And even though the *Fundamental Constitutions* was fastidious and elaborate, it was still, as we will see, only one of many texts that made up the colony's "constitution."

In addition, by focusing on the *Fundamental Constitutions* and the early years of the Carolina colony, we can detail the conceptual and historical dimensions of the second feature of hybrid constitutionalism: *adaptation*.[6] As in Maryland, a proprietary charter authorized the founding of the Carolina colony, granting its Lords Proprietors the wide range of privileges given to the "Bishop of Durham."[7] Carolina, too, pledged its loyalty to the Crown. Most important of all, like Maryland, Carolina was freed from direct Crown administration and enjoyed a virtually co-equal sovereignty with the Crown, which allowed it to draw freely from political languages in circulation during the period. The Carolina charter, if not fully harmonious in its array of "ordinances," "laws and constitutions," and "statutes of this our kingdom of England," nevertheless offered a wide field from which colonial governance could be crafted, "provided nevertheless, That the said laws be consonant to reason, and as near as may be conveniently, agreeable to the laws and customs of this our realm of England."[8]

But the Carolina colony turned proprietary privilege in a direction slightly different from that of Maryland. Where Maryland was largely governed at first by informal instructions, acts, statutes, and proclamations, Carolina's eight Lords Proprietors created an elaborate governing document, the *Fundamental Constitutions of Carolina* (1669) for the new settlement. As the document's solicitous preamble confidently affirmed, the province was indeed favored with "all the royalties, properties, jurisdictions, and privileges of a county palatine, as large and ample as the county palatine of Durham."[9] The more than one hundred numbered articles that subsequently concluded the original missive detailed the exact laws and structures established by its eight Lords Proprietors for Carolina's "agreeable" and "better" settlement.[10] These features, as I will argue, can be read as an adaptation of the civic republican forms popular in the period.[11] As we will see next, the creation and reception of the *Fundamental Constitutions* reveals aspects of colonialism and governance that complicate—and perhaps even undercut—the presumed modernity of English constitutional forms and colonial power. In addition, the *Fundamental Constitutions*, when situated in the proprietary context, helps to alter our understanding of Locke and colonialism.

The Journey

In the summer of 1669, Lord Ashley and his seven associate Lords Proprietors launched three ships bound for the Carolina province.[12] The venture was their largest attempt yet to settle the American territory, transferred to their care by Charles II in 1663, and the task posed considerable challenges. By securing Charles II's proprietary charter (1665), the eight designated Lords Proprietors—Albemarle, Ashley (who would become Earl of Shaftesbury in 1672), Berkeley, Clarendon, Craven, and the three commoners Sir William Berkeley, Sir George Carteret, and Sir John Colleton—committed to an enterprise that had eluded English designs in the area for more than thirty years.[13] Twice before, letters of patent had been granted for the territory—once in 1663 to some of the proprietors and earlier, in 1629, to Sir Robert Heath. Both of these earlier charters were similar to the 1665 authorization: They referenced the powers of the "bishop of Durham" and allowed proprietors to create laws subject to the "assent & approbation of the Freeholders."[14] In all three charters, as well, the laws were subject to some ambiguous qualifications—for example, political representation of the freeman could be direct or indirect, and there was no clear designation of when and how often such ratification would take place.

The most indefinite issue was the content of the law itself. The Carolina charter, like the Maryland charter, permitted multiple forms of law, as long as they were "conveniently, agreeable to the laws and customs of this our kingdom of England."[15] The Carolina charter reproduced many sections—particularly the passages on the palatinate of Durham and the "advise assent and approbation" of the colonists—of the Maryland charter verbatim.[16] And like Maryland's charter, the Carolina charter's open-ended legal terms were as much a sign of privilege as an indication of the challenge of settlement. While Carolina was granted virtually full access to the range of English law, the charter's condition of "repugnance" signaled that the colony might not be able to re-create conditions in England and might have to assemble unusual, even offensive, combinations of law. For example, ordinances were conditioned with the caution that they be "reasonable" and "not repugnant or contrary, but as near as may be, agreeable to the laws and statutes of this our kingdom of England; and so as the same ordinances do not extend to the binding, charging, or taking away the right or interest of any person or persons, in their freehold, goods, or chattels, whatsoever."[17] In many ways, the similarities between Carolina's charter and Maryland's charter should not be surprising. Calvert was a prominent figure in elite English political and diplomatic circles, and he was acquainted with several of the Carolina proprietors.[18] It would be reasonable to assume that the Carolina investors would seek to enhance their claim with a charter that possessed Maryland's distinctive quasi-sovereign palatinate powers.

Nonetheless, while the basic template of the charter was the same in both colonies, notable differences cropped up in Carolina's founding. Conspicuously, the political climate in which Charles II granted the Carolina charter was quite different. Just three years after restoration, Charles II's grant of charter to a proprietary association headed by the "Cabal" member Lord Ashley was no simple bequest. Recently appointed by Charles II as chancellor of the Exchequer, Lord Ashley personified the fragility of the king's mystique of restored hereditary privilege. Eager to secure a broad base of power and finances, Charles II sought to strengthen connections with the city, dissenters, and former commonwealthsmen and thus found Ashley's associations with merchants in London and his skills at financial administration desirable.[19]

Viewed within this context, Charles II's grant of charter to the Carolina proprietary association served as a gift of privileges to solicit a mixed body of merchants and gentry. The Carolina proprietors took full advantage of their chartered liberties by constructing formal establishing orders for their fledging colony. Along with provisions of "brass wire," "penny nailes," "cork," "white salt," and "dried peas," the Lords Proprietors encouraged the prospect of a populated "county" with the *Fundamental Constitutions of Carolina*.[20] A highly intricate document, the *Fundamental Constitutions* proclaimed the province of Carolina as equipped with the lavish privileges of a "county palatine."[21] The first thirty articles in the *Fundamental Constitutions* dealt with the roles and functions of the proprietors, nobility, offices of state, and division of land.[22] The next forty articles focused on the courts, grand council, and administration of justice.[23] Finally, the concluding passages of the *Fundamental Constitutions* delineated the requirements of towns and corporations in the colony, in particular tackling the issue of religious practice and the taking of oaths.[24]

Numerous historians view the *Fundamental Constitutions* as a distinctive but ultimately ineffective tool of governance. It relied on what Anthony McFarlane characterizes as "a hierarchical social order of nobles and freeholders ruled by a political oligarchy."[25] Similarly, as H. F. Russell Smith comments, the *Fundamental Constitutions* may have been well known at the time, but "it never enjoyed anything but a partial existence."[26] Theorists, by contrast, have had a quite different perspective, treating the document as evidence of Locke's colonial investments and of the colonial subtext of the *Two Treatises*.[27] Both of these approaches have limitations. Historians who dismiss the *Fundamental Constitutions* as overly elaborate tend to underplay the rhetorical and dynamic effects of the document, treating the text's adaptation and revision into a temporary form as a failure. Meanwhile, theorists who claim the *Fundamental Constitutions* as Locke's creation overlook not only the document's ambiguous authorship but also Locke's more clerical role as secretary for the Carolina proprietary association.

There is another interpretation of the document that conceptualizes Carolina's constitution in a more dynamic way and better delineates Locke's role in colonial administration. When situated within the atmosphere of Restoration politics, the numerous articles of the *Fundamental Constitutions* appear as an elaboration of civic humanist and republican features prominent in the period, most obviously in James Harrington's *The Commonwealth of Oceana* (1656). This adaptation can be read as part of the Lords Proprietors' interest in the territory and their attempt to respond to the numerous challenges that plagued viable settlement.[28]

After all, the addition of a formal constitution was not entirely without basis, given the practical realities of settlement. Several of the proprietors had already been or were concurrently engaged in colonial ventures in the West Indies and the contiguous Americas. As a whole, the proprietary association requested a variety of surveys, reports, and travelogues from scouts journeying through the Carolina area.[29] These variegated sources of information would have equipped the proprietors with essential knowledge of the Carolina region, such as its recent history, topography, and climate. The materials likewise would have alerted the proprietors to possible concerns and obstacles that might arise in their attempt to bring greater productivity and calm to the colony—namely, calamities of mutiny, instability, starvation, and factional conflict.[30] In addition, while a number of the proprietors had been involved in planning settlements in parts of the Carolina territory at various times in the early seventeenth century, few of the settlements survived. As a result of these failures, the 1663 patent was declared void, since the purposes for which it was granted were not fulfilled.

The creation of the *Fundamental Constitutions* helped to signal this current attempt at colonization as a new and different endeavor, as the opening lines of the *Fundamental Constitutions* firmly announce:

> Our sovereign lord the king having, out of his royal grace and bounty, granted unto us the province of Carolina, with all the royalties, propri-

eties, jurisdictions, and privileges of a county palatine, as large and ample as the county palatine of Durham, with other great privileges; for the better settlement of the government of the said place, and establishing the interest of the lords proprietors with equality, and without confusion; and that the government of this province may be made most agreeable unto the monarchy under which we live, and of which this province is a part; and that we may avoid erecting a numerous democracy: we, the true and absolute lords and proprietors of the province aforesaid, have agreed to this following form of government, to be perpetually established amongst us, unto which we do oblige ourselves, our heirs and successors, in the most binding ways that can be devised.[31]

Yet while the Lords Proprietors fully accept the authority granted to them by the king, secure settlement still awaited them. Thus, the challenges overcome by the Lords Proprietors in this preamble paragraph can be seen as twofold. It assured prospective settlers of the stability of the colony, and it reassured the king that their interest in the area was already justified and worthy of the authority delegated to them, "and that the government of this province may be made most agreeable unto the monarchy under which we live, and of which this province is a part."[32]

This was a familiar refrain in charters of the period, and the document still needed to firm up what prior charters had left unclear: the structure of the law and the terms for the execution of governance. This gap was a standard feature of proprietary charters; it was also underscored by the palatinate privileges of the Carolina charter more specifically, which emphasized the quasi-sovereign and frontier powers of the proprietor. What the *Fundamental Constitutions* did was to better bolster the sense of forthcoming polity, clarifying the structure of the government by crafting a specifically civic humanist and republican framework that put forth an image of Carolina as a commonwealth not only governed by an organized leadership, but also populated by situated colonists.

A Colonial Republic

As idiosyncratic as the *Fundamental Constitutions* might appear to modern audiences, it actually shared a remarkable similarity to a popular work of the period: Harrington's *The Commonwealth of Oceana*. Both the

Fundamental Constitutions and *Oceana* stressed several issues: careful and proportionate allotment of land for agrarian settlement; specific directions to create and maintain tiers of political activity; and explicit rules aimed at reducing laws and eliminating lawyers. While the first text was an official issuance drawn up by a proprietary association and the second a quasi-fictional historical account set forth by a political pamphleteer, both evoked a corresponding temporality in their revivals of the Machiavellian "republican ideal" as a response to exigency.[33] Strikingly, as Mark Goldie explains, both the *Fundamental Constitutions* and Harrington's *Oceana* possessed fanciful titles and warnings against the proliferation of lawyers. The two texts also affirmed toleration in matters of religion and made marriage a civil matter. Finally, they both mandated training in military skills and use of ballots in elections.[34]

Of all of these shared features, the strongest concurrence was their agreement on the basic practicalities of landholding. In both *Oceana* and the *Fundamental Constitutions*, land was carved up into elaborate divisions, which served as the basis for political status and civic membership. In the *Fundamental Constitutions*, the territory was first divided into fifths, with one-fifth of the land held in equal shares by the eight Lords Proprietors, another fifth given to the hereditary nobility, and the rest of the territory granted to the people. The fifth article of the *Fundamental Constitutions* stated, "Leaving the colonies, *being three-fifths, amongst the people; that so, in the setting out and planting the lands, the balance of government may be preserved.*"[35] While Harrington described this requirement using different terminology, his rendition followed similar proportions: Every office possessed a property qualification, and the land was divided into fifty tribes, with twenty hundreds in each tribe and ten parishes in each of the hundreds.[36]

Harrington's account has given us some clues to understand more clearly the political rationale at work in using independent freehold as a revision of agrarian law. In *Oceana*, proportionate holdings of land were an innovation to solidify and secularize Machiavelli's republic. Machiavelli famously sought to balance fortune and virtue in the republic, and he turned to the agrarian law as a possible solution that might offset decline.[37] But in the *Discourses*, the law was still not a firm guarantee of stability. "It was evident that the agrarian law was in some respects defective," commented Machiavelli. "It was either in the beginning so made that it required constant modification; or the changes in it had been so long deferred that it became most obnoxious because it was retrospective in its action; or perhaps it had been good in the beginning and had afterwards become corrupted in its application."[38]

Harrington responded to Machiavelli's dilemma with reform of the agrarian law. Independent freehold was a mechanical contrivance to prevent the variability of power in the different groups of populace, elite, and monarch by solidifying social and political identity in property. Through Harrington's proposal, Machiavelli's republican virtues were territorialized and thus better stabilized to withstand the vicissitudes of *fortuna*. As Harrington explained, "This kind of law fixing the balance in lands is called *agrarian* . . . wherever it hath held, that government hath not altered, except by *consent. But without an agrarian, government, whether monarchical, aristocratical or popular, hath no long lease.*"[39] The agrarian provided more than just a technical remedy to confusions in property. It also offered a regulatory principle that maintained the proportion of various political, economic, and social identities over time, stabilizing the dynamic flux and swell of political power.[40] In adopting a similar tripartite polity occupied by lords, freeholders (titled in Carolina as landgraves and caciques), and even servants (referred to as leet-men), the *Fundamental Constitutions* provided a tactical response to the potential conflict, instability, and dissolution that colonial settlement faced. First, the *Fundamental Constitutions* established the primary executive offices (chief justice, chancellor, constable high steward, treasurer, chamberlain, admiral, and palatine) at the very start of the document. The Lords Proprietors were to fill these executive positions, and by signing on to the *Fundamental Constitutions* they became—at least, in principle—the executive officers they sought to create (although, to be sure, in practice, Lords Proprietors were to rule via deputies in the early years of the colony). Their constitutional agreement to "this following form of government" not only indicated their proper position in the territory. It also demonstrated the colony as a political place with a present *and* a future, of "which we do oblige ourselves, our heirs and successors, in the most binding ways that can be devised."[41] Above all, however, it was the *Fundamental Constitutions'* adaptation of the elaborate civic republican features, akin to Harrington's *Oceana*, that most clearly signaled that the "county" was a populated place where rules and orders could be exercised.[42]

What can one make of this choice? Certainly, many of the Lords Proprietors were or had been heavily involved in colonial ventures, and they were well aware of the failures that had attended similar colonial settlements.[43] They were also likely familiar with the ways in which civic humanist and republican forms were being used in the period to respond to the challenges of faction and instability. As Andrew Fitzmaurice has suggested, colonial proprietors were typically elites who had been educated in the civic humanist tradition, and they viewed the ideals of the republic as strategies for motivating action. Colonial pamphlets, instructions, and other legal documents drew on these languages and put forth civic humanist and republican images of the legislator, aristocrat, and active citizen to motivate and energize investors and colonists to the activity of colonization.[44] "Humanist culture," as Fitzmaurice has written, "sometimes referred to as rhetorical culture, placed great emphasis upon the contingency of knowledge. In such an environment, in which knowledge was a matter of plausibility rather than certainty, the ability to persuade was crucial to social and political action. . . . Speech, in particular, was believed in its various forms, including writing and printing, to be one of the most important means through which to pursue action."[45]

The *Fundamental Constitutions* can be read as similar in spirit. A number of the Lords Proprietors, such as Lord Clarendon and Lord Berkeley, had been associated with the Virginia Company, and given their involvement in Virginia and their elite status it was likely that they were familiar with the civic humanist tropes of the period.[46] At the same time, the vision of polity offered by the *Fundamental Constitutions* differed in notable ways from the classical commonwealth that was depicted in the Virginia Company's pamphlet literature.[47] Like the Virginia Company's promotional literature, the *Fundamental Constitutions* addressed corruption and decay as part of the languages of civic humanism. In addition, however, the *Fundamental Constitutions* allowed for other political and legal structures, including feudal law and common law.[48]

The *Fundamental Constitutions* was not just a product of civic humanism and republicanism; it was more promiscuously a *hybridized* creation that grafted strange and even ungainly features of feudalism and paternalism onto familiar supports. We can see this in the way the constitution mixed an image of county palatine with an *Oceana*-type republic in which virtue and glory subsided as lesser dilemmas. This republicanism, structured by a revised agrarian law, expressed a more vigilant and defensive ideology than that of the early Virginia Company. As Quentin Skinner argues, the version of republicanism that appeared by the middle of the seventeenth century was closely associated with the state and its interests. No longer city-state republics, the early modern republics possessed standing armies and war powers. These features were exemplified by Harrington's *Oceana* and its leanings toward expedience and security.[49]

From this vantage point, the *Fundamental Constitutions* illustrates a telling model of how the ambitions of colonization drew together republican, feudal, and authoritative rule. Even as an ideal, reference to civic humanist and republican ideals could, in the guise of political participation and virtue, maintain both elite privilege and social and economic hierarchy while also encouraging colonists to engage in active practice on the ground. However, while the *Fundamental Constitutions* may have crafted an image of polity as an initial organizing idea that helped make founding intelligible as a project calling for support, this model often proved impossible to achieve fully in practice.[50]

Imaginaries and Grounded Practices

Despite its elaborate construction, the *Fundamental Constitutions* was never fully implemented. There were not enough settlers to fill all the positions ordered by the *Fundamental Constitutions*, and in the first few months of the Carolina settlement the proprietors supplemented the original model with temporary laws and directives. As the proprietors themselves admitted in 1669, "In regard the number of people which will at first be set down . . . will be so small . . . it will not be possible to put our Grand Model of Government in practice at first, and that notwithstanding we may come as nigh [the] aforesaid Model as is practicable."[51] Still, the adaptation of the *Fundamental Constitutions* did not necessarily mark the failure of the republican ethos.

The *Fundamental Constitutions* was akin to what Cornelius Castoriadis describes, in more modern parlance, as an "imaginary." The "imaginary," he explains, "ultimately stems from the originary faculty of positing or presenting oneself with things and relations that do not exist, in the form of representation."[52] The distinction is a subtle but essential one. The

Fundamental Constitutions brings together discourses "in the broadest and most radical sense: norms, values, language, tools, procedures and methods," and it does so to craft a well-rendered starting point for the colony's founding.[53] The constitution, through its careful detail, provides a way to make a prospective colony apprehensible. This was part of the process by which a collective came to "exist," in Castoriadis's conception, "to pass from the virtual to anything more than this."[54] Indeed, the imaginary conjured by the *Fundamental Constitutions* was not vague or amorphous. Even before any colonists glimpsed sight of the Carolina shore, the civic republican features of the *Fundamental Constitutions* conjured up an imaginary of a society with laws and rules already populated with three social tiers of colonists, whose different virtues and abilities were cast in the land and managed with regularity.[55]

Yet, as it turned out, the *Fundamental Constitutions* was not executed literally. From the start, founding both went beyond and fell short of the terms outlined in the document. In the years between 1669 and 1680, the Lords Proprietors drew up at least four sets of temporary laws and instructions for the colony, noting among their various reasons "the paucity of Nobility" and "[the] better ordering of affairs."[56] There have been different explanations for this situation. The adaptation of the original constitutions was perhaps a sign that the Lords Proprietors had relinquished their interest in the Carolina colony, as some historians maintain.[57] Alternatively, the creation of temporary laws could have been evidence of the outright failure and inadequacy of the first constitutions—another oft-repeated explanation among historians.[58]

There is some validity to all these accounts, for the *Constitutions* was highly elaborate, and there were too few settlers to fill the enumerated political positions. At the same time, as the initial Carolina proprietary correspondence illustrates, many still saw the new laws as capable of maintaining an ethos that was similar to the original *Fundamental Constitutions*. Even Russell Smith, who claims that the *Fundamental Constitutions* had little practical effect, agrees that the Lords Proprietors felt that the Temporary Laws were able to retain the balance of the original. "In the *Fundamental Constitutions*," Russell Smith clarifies, "they had made references to the theory; in their 'Temporary Agrarian Laws' of June 1674, they still asserted that 'the whole foundation of the government is settled on a right and equal distribution of laws.'"[59] Ashley's earlier letter to Joseph West and the council, dated June 20, 1672, likewise expressed this sentiment:

> In the mean time *I recommend it to your care (whose prudence and integrity we already have had experience of) to keep unbiased to those rules you will find in our Fundamental Constitutions Temporary Laws and Instructions* and particularly our Deputies are to remember that they represent our Persons & therefore they ought not to diminish our right by making themselves but ciphers and submitting too much to the will of any Governor whatsoever nay of Sir Peter Colleton himself or any of the Lords Proprietors should come upon the place our Deputies ought to maintain our authority and share in the Government according to the Fundamental Constitutions which we have to that purpose put into their hands. Having been so careful to balance one another[']s power to prevent the ingrossing it into any one hand that the Palatine himself and so his Deputy the Governor hath but his limited proportion of it suited to the dispatch of affairs beyond which we never intended nor are our Deputies to suffer it to extend.[60]

Ashley thus affirms the proprietors' attention to proportion and balance of power in the Temporary Laws. He similarly cautions against diminishing "our right" or unbalancing the careful construction of power.

Just as crucial, independence and self-sufficiency were key elements of the original *Fundamental Constitutions'* agrarian revision of the republican imaginary, and with the Temporary Laws, the proprietors still seemed highly attuned to the difficulties of balancing prosperity against sloth.[61] Most notably, the proprietors were desperate to enlist colonists to the territory, and the issue of the colony's "speedy" settlement was double-edged. These concerns were reflected in the early Carolina correspondence between the settlers and the proprietary association. Locke, for instance, summarized letters from the Carolina Council, Governor Sayle, and settlers such as Joseph West and Thomas Colleton in the Carolina "memoranda" of 1670. Locke noted variously that the colony "wants more men clothes powder" and that "the people there depend lazily on the Proprietors supplies."[62] By 1671, Lord Ashley put the issue even more plainly to Joseph West (who was later appointed temporary governor):

We intend from time to time so to furnish our Stores that Industrious People who will pay ready truck may be supplied with things they want at reasonable and moderate Rates, but do not intend that the Lazy or debauched who will never be good for themselves or the Plantation shall run further in our Debts to the increase of our charges and disparagement of our Settlement.[63]

In its preoccupation with "stores," "rates," and "debts," Ashley's directions freighted economic concerns with degrees of political and moral weight. If laziness and indolence could lead to the unattractive prospect of limitless proprietary subsidy and potential bankruptcy, the emergence of these problems also indicated the Lords Proprietors' lack of knowledge: Were the colonists truly unable to subsist on their own? Were they hoarding or bartering the proprietary supplies? Were they manipulating the settlement's resources for their own interests?

The instructions of the Lords Proprietors thus reflected a striking combination of paternalism and republicanism. In particular, Ashley's instructions frequently exemplified this combination, as when he told the colonist Maurice Matthews to follow the temporary constitutions of the colony as the "compass you are to steer by" but also added more forcefully that "you are therefore obstinately to stick to those Rules and oppose all deviation from it since by our Frame no bodies power nor not of any of the Proprietors themselves were they there is so great as to be able to hurt the meanest man in the Country if our Deputys have but honesty and resolution enough to keep things tight to those rules wherein their own welfare and security with that of the whole plantation is so carefully provided for."[64] In a way, Ashley's directive seems to imitate the *Fundamental Constitutions'* hybrid mix of palatine privilege and civic humanist republican structure. To wit, the *Fundamental Constitutions* stated openly from the outset that these "large and ample" privileges were not simply for "the better settlement of the government of the said place" and to "avoid erecting a numerous democracy," but also for "establishing the interest of the lords proprietors with equality, and without confusion."[65] As Mark Goldie explains, this combination was not unusual: There was no necessary contradiction between a republican form and paternalistic interests in early modern English political theory. The *Fundamental Constitutions* and other, similar republics and utopias were, in Goldie's apt phrase, "unacknowledged republics." They held no promise of egalitarianism; they co-existed with significant political hierarchy and social and economic inequality, where great distinctions of wealth and status flourished within a civic humanist structure of governance.[66]

The example of Carolina, in this way, deepens the picture of hybrid constitutionalism. As in Maryland, the constitution of Carolina heavily stresses discretion and flexibility. In addition, perhaps because of the elaborateness of the *Fundamental Constitutions*, we can more distinctly see how constitutionalism is shaped by privilege as well as by the prospect of failure and conflict. This can be seen in the frequent modifications of the *Fundamental Constitutions* and in the tempered paternalism practiced by the proprietors, who sought to dominate their settlers but were often forced to confront the limits to their powers and allow colonists to act according to their own judgment. The authoritative power of the Lords Proprietors did not always coincide with the interests of the colonists, and colonists often could and did refuse to follow proprietary command.

Native Knowledge and Adaptation

The Lords Proprietors knew that limited supplies, unseasoned settlers, and neighboring settlements all posed serious threats to founding. To mitigate the risks of debt and the difficulties of conflict, the proprietors encouraged colonists to develop relationships with local tribes and to learn indigenous farming and navigation practices. Both the colonial correspondence and Locke's memoranda for the colony documented these interactions, and these colonial materials have a complex resonance for a modern audience. First, and most important, they intimate the broad range of colonial activities and anxieties: the different, often combative perspectives of administrators and colonists on the ground, and the messy complexities of founding practices. Second, these texts portray colonization not in terms of philosophical treatises or arguments but, rather, in a more piecemeal fashion. The memoranda were compilations of notes on colonial concerns, not a straightforward narrative about colonial ideology, and these texts allow us to resituate and reconsider Locke's relationship to colonization, for Locke has now become an iconic figure in the knotted history of English colonialism and constitutionalism.[67] As informal secretary to the proprietors of the Carolina colony, secretary of the Council of Trade and Plantations, and member of the Board of Trade and Plantations, Locke certainly participated in early modern colonialism in practice and addressed it in theory. Yet his relation to colonial implantation, especially in the Carolinas, was far from authorial: Carolina was not his colony; nor was he the sole architect of the *Fundamental Constitutions*. As Maurice Cranston explains, Locke became heavily involved in colonial affairs as a consequence of meeting Anthony Ashley Cooper, then Lord Ashley, the king's chancellor of the Exchequer, in 1666.[68] Locke's colonial activities as the secretary to the Lords Proprietors of Carolina involved compiling advertisements for the fledgling colony, keeping minutes of meetings, negotiating grievances and requests from colonists and proprietors, drafting temporary laws and executive instructions, and drawing up the notes and memoranda of the colony's correspondence. Locke also, as Roger Woolhouse notes, reviewed the flow of trade and supplies between Carolina, its neighboring colonial settlements (especially Virginia and Barbados), and England. Especially noteworthy, Locke endorsed and summarized the many letters, directives, and orders that circulated between colonists, proprietors, and administrators in Carolina, the Caribbean, and England. The brief summaries were then compiled into loosely organized "memoranda" and divided according to various topical headings, ranging from "Country" to "Westos," and then further detailed with a notation of the source. In these tasks, Locke was not a political philosopher or a theorist of colonialism involved in creating or defending new political ideas. Rather, he was an administrative functionary, and the records, correspondence, and instructions he reviewed as secretary help to illuminate the complex flow of colonial information across the Atlantic between England, the Caribbean, and the British southern colonies.

More specifically, Locke's memoranda indicated that colonists turned to local indigenes for provisions and aid. For example, his excerpts of colonists' letters in the memoranda of December 1670 noted:

The Emperor hath 1000 bowmen in his town Woodward says tis a 2nd Paradise.

Mr. T. Colleton.

Indians. Assisting with provisions intelligence and arms.

Council.

Stout and when the Spaniards came ready to fight.

West.

Honest, Just Two Cassiques [sons] clothed and civilly treated by him in Barbadoes. The Indians supply provisions and help to plant.

Mr. T. Colleton.

Faithful friendly and in league perpetual.

Sir. Jo. Yeamans.[69]

As illustrated in these memoranda, the "Indians" helped to supply "provisions intelligence and arms" as well as aid in planting.[70] These were colonial–indigenous relations evident in the letters of settlers and endorsed in the Lords Proprietors' instructions. For example, Ashley complimented the actions of the settler Henry Woodward in a letter to Stephen Bull dated August 13, 1673: "However it may be discountenanced by some there, looks on as very wisely done and very agreeable to our design which is to get and continue the friendship and assistance of the Indians and make them useful without force or injury. Should be very glad that all the tribes of Indians round about had each an English man for their Cassique."[71]

Equally significant, as demonstrated in the memoranda and Carolina colonial materials, the Lords Proprietors encouraged the colonists to be self-sufficient to better support the colony and to relieve the proprietors of debts. Associations with the local Edistos and Kywaha provided early Carolina colonists with opportunities to develop navigational information and agricultural skills.[72] For instance, the promotional "Barbados Proclamation," which was endorsed by Locke and signed by Governor Sayle, noted that "the Indians that boarder on them being so friendly for an inconsiderable value they supply [the colonists] with deer fish and fowl in a great abundance as likewise in assisting them to clear and plant their land."[73] Local tribes provided this resource because they possessed and operated settled crops and fields, as described in the Carolina journeyman Robert Sandford's pre-settlement account in 1667: "All round the Towne for a great space are several fields of Maize of a very large growth . . . amongst it a great variety of choice pasturage I saw here besides the great number of peaches which the more Northerly places do also abound in some store of fig trees very large and fair both fruit and plants and diverse grape vines."[74] Indigenous knowledge of planting and cultivation proved to be highly useful for the new colonists, particularly since the Lords

Proprietors were reluctant to provide seed, tools, and other provisions to new Carolina settlers unless deemed absolutely necessary. Moreover, by encouraging colonists to develop relationships with local tribes and learn indigenous farming and navigation practices, the Lords Proprietors sought to mitigate the risks of proprietary debt and the difficulties of intra-colonial conflict. Local Indians were viewed as capable of certain forms of agricultural production (to "clear and plant their land" in fields) and as possessing skills of foraging, hunting, and gathering (supplying "deer fish and fowl"). Meanwhile the subjects of concern for the Lords Proprietors were the colonists, who may have been "Lazy or debauched" and "run further in our Debts."

Perhaps not surprisingly, then, the Lords Proprietors' ambitions for colonial self-sufficiency were not always agreeable to colonists on the ground, who repeatedly asked for greater assistance, funds, and supplies. First, the precise particulars of colonial self-sufficiency could not be predetermined or fully prescribed; they could only be gathered and acquired in situ. Second, colonists were quite aware that proprietors were loath to lay out funds for provisions and resources, which were difficult to keep track of. For example, Captain West wrote to Locke in 1673:

> I could not omit this opportunity to present you with this my humble service, and to entreat your assistance by importuning the Earl of Shaftesbury to hasten a ship from England with more People and supplies of Clothing, and Tool &c for the people are not able to subsist long without they are supplied by the Lords Proprietors. . . . If we were but once stocked with cattle, that we might fall upon English Husbandry it would quickly be a very plentiful place, *I suppose before this you have heard of our extreme wants of provisions this year, which now God be praise we have almost overcome,* for about a month hence we shall have corn enough of our own [growth]; and hope we shall never fear wanting Indian corn again, *for this want will do much good in the country, by teaching people to be better Husbands, and more industrious for the future, and not depend any more upon supplies.*[75]

West's entreaty illustrated the Carolina settlers' need for provisions and the insufficiency of colonial adaptations to local, indigenous practice. More precisely, West's letter reflected the mixed status of Indian practices, since "Indian corn" was viewed by settlers as serviceable, but only for the time being. It was clearly just a stop-gap measure. The self-proclaimed goal of settlement, "English Husbandry," was a more difficult endeavor that could not be satisfied simply by learning indigenous skills and knowledge. Thus, settlers made the claim that farming and "husbandry" required the proprietors to provide additional supplies and funding.

How might we conceptualize this state of affairs? One way contemporary theorists have characterized the impact of indigenous knowledge on the colonies is to argue that indigenous forms of governance, such as the Iroquois Chain, shaped American constitutionalism.[76] Yet in the Carolinas, it was not indigenous governance per se that molded Carolina's constitution. Rather, the relationship between colonists and indigenes seemed to be more ambiguous and more fluid, particularly with respect to theory and practice. To an extent, indigenous culture, custom, and information proved important to making the colonists the kind of durable and independent actors articulated by the *Fundamental Constitutions*. For instance, in posing a civic republican form, the *Fundamental Constitutions* established a type of political imaginary in which the pursuit of stability and adaptation were central features. As illustrated in the early correspondence and memoranda, the colonists were encouraged by the proprietary association to adopt and adapt indigenous surveying, planting, and trading to pursue these goals. At the same time, these indigenous knowledges, although certainly useful, were also not treated with esteem by either proprietors or colonists. Local practices of tilling, farming, and navigation were practices of subsistence—necessary but nonetheless menial.

This was, therefore, in many ways an understanding of cultural knowledge that was not identity-oriented but, rather, a conception primarily driven by a concern for locale. Michel Foucault describes these particular, immediate, and non-totalizable types of understanding as "subjugated knowledges."[77] In *Two Lectures*, he explains that there are "a whole set of knowledges which have been disqualified as inadequate to their task or insufficiently elaborated: naive knowledges, located low down on the hierarchy, beneath the required level of cognition or scientificity . . . a particular, local, regional knowledge, a differential knowledge."[78] In colonial founding, these indigenous knowledges are *needed* knowledges, prudential and effective in that they are locally and immediately relevant. But they are still not quite legitimate. They are rarely described in full; nor do they often garner official praise. Yet we should still note that, while there are clearly strong hierarchical dimensions in the *Fundamental Constitutions*, they also do not correspond directly to a stadial map of culture. Following the civic humanist and republican sentiments of the *Fundamental Constitutions*, proprietors and colonists employed these knowledges *tacitly*—through observation and engagement in context—and without any more complete commitment to group rights or interests.

This instrumental approach was also evident in the *Fundamental Constitutions*, which, most notably, encouraged the conversion of "natives of that place . . . whose idolatry, ignorance, or mistake gives us no right to expel or use them ill." It also gave the chancellor's court "all state matters, dispatches, and treaties, with the neighbour Indians or any other, so far forth as is permitted by our charter."[79] Similarly, Article 8 of the Temporary Laws of 1671 stated, "No Indian upon any occasion or pretense whatsoever is to be made a slave or without his own consent to be carried out of our Country."[80] These articles, like the colonial memoranda, illustrated the mixed approach of the proprietors who acknowledged some rudimentary elements of indigenous agency—that is, the power of indigenes to make treaties and to offer consent—but also encouraged proselytizing indigenes and patronizing them for their "idolatry" and "ignorance."

In the view of the proprietors, the "Indians were indigenous, free, and in possession of existing rights to the land," Alan Gallay explains. Proprietors "did not dismiss Indian ownership of land within their domain, but they believed that their patent gave them ownership of non-Indian land and the exclusive right to negotiate with the Indians for land."[81] In fact, the Lords Proprietors often felt that the colonists' various economic activities threatened the security of the colony and their own interests; the proprietors thus sought to restrict, as enumerated in the *Fundamental Constitutions*, diplomatic and treaty relations largely to the proprietary association, and they were particularly wary of unregulated explorations by colonists in indigenous territory. As stated in Article 102/112, "No person whatsoever shall hold or claim any land in Carolina by purchase or gift or otherwise, from the natives or any other person whatsoever, but merely from and under the lords proprietors, upon pain of forfeiture of all his estate, moveable or unmoveable, and perpetual banishment."[82]

Yet even though the *Fundamental Constitutions* expressly stated that no one other than the proprietors were to trade with the Indians, at times trades by colonists were viewed by the proprietors as expedient and useful for specific "furs and other commodities" and for creating more general diplomatic advantage. As the *Instructions* drafted by the Lords Proprietors for the surveyor Henry Woodward in May 1674 demonstrated, proprietors viewed relations of trade, exchange, and diplomacy with local tribes as supports for the colony's growth and stability:

1. You are to treat with the Indians of Edisto for the Island and buy it of them and make a Friendship with them.
2. You are to settle a Trade with the Indians for Furs and other Commodities that are either for the Supply of the Plantation or advantageous for Trade.
3. You are to consider whether it be best to make a peace with the Westoes or Cussitaws which are a more powerful Nation said to have pearl and silver and by whose Assistance the Westoes may be rooted out, but no peace is to be made with either of them without Including our Neighbour Indians who are at amity with us.
4. You are in management of the trade and treaty of the Indians always to have the consent and Direction of Mr Percivall my principal Agent.
5. You are to consider what other Commodities besides these we already know are to be had from any of the Indians which may be profitable unto us.[83]

More practically, Gallay notes, "Not all the local Indians welcomed the colonists. . . . The Kussoe, for instance, had refused to ally with the English."[84] The proprietors thus had a vested interest in negotiating with indigenes that would be amenable to diplomatic and trade relations. Proprietors sought to bolster trade and to strengthen local alliances, and they worried, in particular, that the "enslavement of Indians would initiate wars, which might not only prove expensive but bring unwanted attention from forces within England that might wish to take away their patent." As Gallay concludes, "The proprietors thus repeatedly urged their officials and colonists to treat Indians fairly."[85]

Perhaps not surprisingly, the Lords Proprietors' ambition to protect and cultivate indigenous relationships also prompted challenges from colonists and even appointed officials in the colony, revealing a split in colonial ambitions with respect to indigenous power.[86] For example, as Gallay explains: "With the governor and council typically placing their interests above those of the proprietors, there was little respect for the law. The colony's elite split into factions and jockeyed for power."[87] One of the biggest sources of competition was the Indian trade. "The colony's economy for its first fifty years," Gallay notes, "revolved around the Indian trade: colonists wanted Indians to hunt to bring in the animal skins and furs they could exchange for European goods."[88] As Gallay comments, "The contest for power among elites effected a struggle over who would control the Indian trade. *Within the colony, colonists could trade with local Indians, which they did for foodstuffs, pelts, and slaves.* But the proprietors reserved for their agents the potentially profitable trade with the large tribes outside the colony, which local elites eyed greedily."[89]

In a prime example of the contrasting interests of proprietors and colonists, Henry Woodward, an interpreter for the Carolina settlement, allegedly located mines in the Tatikequias country of the lower Carolinas in April 1671. In response, Lord Ashley explained to Woodward:

> If those inland countries have given you any knowledge or conjecture of mines there *I earnestly desire you not to give hint of it to anybody whatsoever for fear our people being tempted by the hopes of present gain should forsake their plantation and so run themselves into certain ruin* which has followed all those who formerly though in greater numbers than we have there now marched into this country in search of gold and silver.[90]

Ashley also informed interim Governor William Sayle in a different letter that the "mines" that Woodward had found could lead to the loosening of colonial discipline and self-reliance within the colony. But most prominently in his correspondence, Ashley was concerned that the discovery might incite extra-colony conflicts and tensions with the multiple groups in and around the Carolina territories—the various Spanish and Kywaha settlers: "This may be apt to tempt some of our people covetous of present booty to some attempt that way. . . . *We do absolutely prohibit you and you are to take care not only that you suffer not the people out of greediness to molest either the Spaniards on that side or any of our neighbour Indians in their quiet possessions.* . . . Neither do we think it advantageous for our people to live by rapine and plunder which we do not nor will not allow Planting and Trade is both our design and your interest."[91]

Ashley's two letters mixed a number of different quandaries. He viewed "Planting and Trade"—a familiar staple in the *Two Treatises*—as the primary colonial task. Yet he also intimated that the temptation of "present gain" or "booty" could easily distract colonists from "Planting and Trade." Moreover, Carolina agriculture did not negate the "quiet possessions" of neighbor Indians; nor did it definitively upend the claim of the "Spaniards." Ashley's primary concern was to make sure that the tentative settlement established in Carolina would not be undone by the excesses of "rapine," "plunder," and "greediness." The riches of the mines could allow settlers to establish interests and trade relationships independent of proprietorial oversight, potentially leading to the abandonment of the colony.[92] In addition, it was reasonable that the Lords Proprietors sought to avert the possibility of war over the mines with either the indigenes or the Spanish, especially since war would have required even more outlay of aid and supplies. Thus, as a potential threat to the stability of the colony and to the prospects of agriculture and trade, the mines were to be suppressed and put out of the colonists' heads.

Ashley's queries reflected that proprietary founding in many ways was a process of managing *insertion*. The colonists' reliance on indigenous aid and the proprietors' interest in accommodating local tribes were attempts to gain a steadier foothold in a territory already occupied by numerous parties. Adaptation, more prosaically, was just a modus operandi for colonists prone to conflict and lacking resources and local knowledge. Moreover, even if proprietors and Carolina colonists attempted to weave themselves into the grid of local practices and understandings to ground the colony, adaptive skills alone neither prevented hostilities nor fully stabilized settlement. In fact, proprietors and colonists frequently antagonized one another and instrumentalized relationships with various groups of indigenes and African slaves.

For example, at numerous times colonial administrators ordered and sanctioned violence. Notably, the Council Journal of August 30, 1673, recorded, "It is ordered & c that a party of men be raised under command of Lieutenant Colonel. John Godfrey & Captain Maurice Matthews jointly & be expedited to march against the said Indians to kill & destroy them or otherwise subject them in peace."[93] Just as significant, the proprietors' interest in negotiating indigenous relationships did not extend more broadly into intercultural respect. The indigenous accommodation proposed by the *Fundamental Constitutions*, as I discuss earlier, stressed conversion and toleration, not equitable political and cultural recognition.[94] Even treaty relationships, although they required mutual participation by indigenes and colonists, were not exactly impartial because the treaties' participants often had very different conceptions of *what* was being negotiated and, as the terms of the *Fundamental Constitutions* made clear, the treaty was seen as an instrument of proprietary power.

Meanwhile, African slavery was a prominent feature from the start of the settlement of Carolina, and the *Fundamental Constitutions* made strong differentiation between "negro slaves" and Indians and other non-colonists. Most notably, as Article 101 proclaimed, "Every freeman of Carolina shall have absolute power and authority over his negro slaves, of what opinion of religion soever."[95] In contrast to the "Indians," African slaves were not granted treaty rights; nor were they accorded the lesser accommodations of toleration and conversion. In a similar vein, the "Barbados Proclamation," the promotional report that sought to recruit Caribbean settlers to Carolina, encouraged the transport of African slaves: "Now for the better Expedition in settling of the said province and encouragement of all manner of people that have a desire to transport themselves servants negroes or utensils the Lords proprietors of the province of Carolina hath provided the Carolina friggot aforesaid for the transportation of the said people who will be ready to depart this island."[96] Slaves were thus treated by the *Fundamental Constitutions* and other supporting texts, such as the "Barbados Proclamation," as barely capable of agency; they were primarily described, as seen here, as if they were property, akin to "utensils." Only at certain rare points was their agency and humanity asserted. "Since charity obliges us to wish well to the souls of all men, and religion ought to alter nothing in man's civil estate or right, it shall be lawful for slaves, as all others, to enter themselves and be of what church any of them shall think best, and thereof be as fully members of any freeman," Article 98/107 of the *Fundamental Constitutions* stated.[97] What the *Fundamental Constitutions* thus established was a standard of the most *minimal recognition*. Slaves were legally property—"no slave shall hereby be exempted from that civil dominion his master has over him, but be in all other things in the same state and condition he was in before"—but they were also moral and religious actors whose religious beliefs could be shaped.

Especially egregious, this conveyance of minimal recognition was part of a broader context in which African slaves were crucial actors in the early part of Carolina's history.[98] As Peter Wood discusses in his seminal study *Black Majority*, Carolina colonists relied heavily on the agricultural and territorial knowledge of the Caribbean and African slaves who came to dominate the population in the Carolinas by the 1700s. Caribbean slaves, especially, who were familiar with the heat and humid conditions typical of the Caribbean and southern American territories, were extremely knowledgeable about farming practices for rice and other staple crops.[99]

The complex tensions among colonists and between colonists and indigenes, slaves, and other non-English settlers help to recast the character of the struggles over power in the territory. There was certainly colonial reliance on indigenous culture, and there was also strong evidence of the exploitation and manipulation of indigenous polities. Yet the relationship was not strictly hierarchical. Rather, what emerged were various struggles of power that occurred both within and beyond the colony, where indigenous agents and groups were differentially and diversely engaged.[100]

Differential Relations and the Politics of Post Hoc Interpretation

By turning to the founding of Carolina, I have sought to examine the feature of *adaptation* in proprietary constitutionalism. As I have argued, adaptation did not create harmonious relationships between colonists and indigenes. It was certainly a strategy to facilitate colonial interests and ambitions, but it took form in ways that can be hard to assess, neither ordering total violence and coercion nor erecting a hard and fast opposition between colonists and indigenes. Instead, it was more ambiguous and elastic in its openness to useful knowledge and local practices. In that way, adaptation helped to facilitate what we might describe as a constitutionalism not simply of *insertion* but also of *opportunism*. This constitutionalism did not require or enforce stable categories of identity. Instead, local conditions and events determined the salience of particular choices, and thus contingency and ambition often worked hand in hand. At moments, accord could certainly be produced between various actors, but that accommodation could be just as easily withdrawn if events and interests changed.

Although the Carolina founding represents just one element in a complex era, it can help reorient our contemporary sensibilities to an equivocal past in which colonial ambition and the pursuit of profit resided alongside insecurity and ignorance. First, in the absence of a formal structure of colonial imposition, the early years of the Carolina colony involved a process of relinquishing direct authority to those on the ground—initially from the Crown and then from the Lords Proprietors—to respond better to the contours of the local. The wide assemblage of rights, laws, and statutes available for proprietary governance appeared as a theoretical range from which specific legal instruments might be recombined to better provide for *relative* stability within *norms* of instability. Second, this responsiveness was a critical part of the colonizing process, and yet it relied on adaptive skills—learning, exchange, and incorporation—that often are not associated with colonial powers. Finally, these practices of adaptation command attention because they recast the character of the struggles over power between colonists and indigenous peoples not as impositional and assimilative but, instead, as elastic and instrumental.

This is a recasting that can be extended even further to contemporary assessments of liberalism. Commentators have long focused on Locke's *Two Treatises* and emphasized the colonialist ambitions of his account of appropriation, making particular note of his assessment that "there cannot be a clearer demonstration of any thing, than several nations of the Americans are of this, who are rich in land, and poor in all the comforts of life. . . . A king of a large and fruitful territory there, feeds, lodges, and is clad worse than a day-labourer in England."[101] However, in his position as secretary Locke reviewed letters and documents that illustrated a wide range of colonial concerns and anxieties. While Locke's compilation of memoranda does not confirm his support of the activities of either the colonists or the Lords Proprietors, it does indicate his familiarity with local conditions, and it suggests a new perspective from which to assess the *Two Treatises*.[102]

From the vantage point of Carolina, the *Two Treatises* appears less a confident defense of English appropriation and assimilation than a strategic rendering of colonial practices that were relatively new (and perhaps not even fully acquired): Carolina colonists under Locke's clerical review learned types of stationary planting, cultivation, and gathering from various local indigenous tribes—in essence, adapting the skills and knowledges of local tribes to develop some measure of the productivity and stability attributed to the presumptively progressive, "civilized" actors articulated by the *Two Treatises*. Equally relevant from the perspective of Carolina were the colonial dependences, insecurities, and contingencies that may have been rewritten or written away in the *Two Treatises*. Are, for example, indigenous, African, and other knowledges the exiled underpinning of the "progressive" modern constitution?

What is at stake are questions of constitutional and colonial interpretation today. Locke's association with the founding of Carolina serves as a useful example for pluralizing and deepening longstanding conceptions of English colonialism and constitutionalism. For example, the association between Locke and the republican *Fundamental Constitutions* was perhaps not so aberrant. He had strong ties with Ashley, who had been aligned with the republican project, and Locke's library contained copies of Harrington's *Oceana* and other utopian and republican literature of the period, such as Sir Thomas More's *Utopia* and Henry Neville's *Isle of Pine*. There is evidence that, even if he did not directly write the original *Fundamental Constitutions*, Locke did assist in revising later portions of the document. The proprietor Sir Peter Colleton complimented Locke on "that excellent form of government in the composure of which you had so great a hand."[103] Other friends and colleagues also discussed the *Fundamental Constitutions* and the Carolina colony frequently with Locke.[104]

Based on the account offered here, I do not wish to make the case that Locke should be viewed as a civic republican rather than a liberal. Much critical work has already been done that effectively complicates Locke's status as a liberal.[105] My point instead is more open-ended. Locke is a ripe example for reconsidering the fluidity and fecundity of political languages and forms in circulation in the period, where English colonialism and constitutionalism were not only polyvocal but also highly unsettled—and even contradictory—in their mix of feudal, humanist, republican, and authoritarian elements. Likewise, Locke's role as scribe helps to illustrate the tensions between *claims* of colonial authority and territorial possession and *practices* of founding that were more tentative, adaptive, and negotiated on the ground. Such re-castings can help us move to construct different genealogies of colonialism and constitutionalism. As Foucault explains, genealogy functions as an "effective history" in that it undercuts presumed foundations: "[It] disturbs what was previously considered immobile; it fragments what was thought unified; it shows the heterogeneity of what was imagined consistent with itself."[106] Genealogy permits us to "liberate" divergent and marginal elements, allowing previously unseen perspectives, ideas, and voices to gain greater regard. To adopt such a view allows us to cast some skepticism on the claims of progress, while simultaneously mobilizing energies to attend to the many colonial debts and dependences that the triumphal narrative has sought to erase.[107]

In turning next to the colony of Pennsylvania, I examine a founding that was shaped in part by the developments of prior proprietary settlements. Penn had sought a charter similar to those of Maryland and Carolina, and he constructed a formal, written constitution, the *Frame of Government*. Yet although Pennsylvania was strongly influenced by earlier examples, it did not imitate them wholesale; nor was it dependent on their form. Proprietary powers gave Penn enough latitude to use proprietary legal and political powers in new ways, but the distinctiveness of Pennsylvania's governance was also a sign of significant shifts in British rule. For with the growing centralization of colonial administration and increased restrictions on chartered privileges by the Privy Council, Penn was to use the assemblage of "customs, statutes, and rights" still remaining to him as proprietor to more fully stretch the possibilities of negotiation from a practice of the colony's populus to a practice of an elite few. These changes did not signal the elimination of hybridity but, instead, revealed its flexibility.

UNDER NEGOTIATION

Treaty Power and Hybrid Constitutionalism in Pennsylvania

4

A treaty is more than just a transient agreement to exchange a few furs
for European trade goods. . . . Through dialogic interaction, the sharing
of sufferings, the clearing of barriers to communication, the reciprocal
exchanges of gifts and goodwill, and the mutualization of interests and resources, different peoples could attain one mind, and link arms together.
—ROBERT WILLIAMS, *LINKING ARMS TOGETHER*

Negotiation is impure.
—JACQUES DERRIDA, *NEGOTIATIONS*

The treaties negotiated between William Penn, the seventeenth-century proprietor of the colony of Pennsylvania,
and various Lenape and Susquehannock tribes have long stood
as iconic images of cultural accommodation. In particular, this
view was memorialized in Benjamin West's famous nineteenth-
century portrait of the treaties at Shackamaxon, where Penn
was depicted in mythic historical terms as amicable "Onas
(Brother)" to indigenous peoples, "shaking hands with some Indian or, seated beneath a tree on a sunny day, passing the native
a peace pipe across a cheerful fire."[1] "Penn's 'Holy Experiment,'"
Thomas Sugrue notes, "has been continually depicted as a representation of the possibility, however fleeting, of harmony between the European colonists and the North American Indians."[2]
More recent accounts, however, have substantially challenged
the romantic image of William Penn as selfless partner to the

Delaware tribes. Once treated as noble exceptions in the history of English conquest and acquisition, Penn's treaties now appear, in the assessments of Mary Geiter, James Merrell, Steven Craig Harper, Daniel Richter, and others, as much more complex practices with at times contradictory moral, religious, economic, and political motivations.[3] Penn did indeed negotiate treaties and agreements with local tribes, but he also did so in part to secure proprietary power, to fend off counter-claims by neighboring English colonies, and to quiet challenges from his own settlers.

Drawing on primary and secondary materials on the founding of Pennsylvania, I approach the treaties negotiated between Penn and various Lenni Lenape and Susquehannock tribes in and around the Delaware territories during the 1680s and 1690s as one of the key tactics used by the proprietary settlements in the pre-Revolutionary period. As we have seen, the colonies of Maryland and Carolina were given powers to use treaties, if needed, to better secure settlement and negotiate grievances and conflicts. In fact, as Anthony Pagden has made clear, the English were far from the only colonists to negotiate purchase. French, Dutch, and Swedish settlers made wide use of various formal and informal treaties for land, and their motivations for purchase varied widely, as well. At times, treaties were pursued to ease religious scruples about land possession, but they also enabled colonists to sidestep Crown or proprietary oversight.[4] In addition, free sale or concession allowed colonists not simply to claim that they had acquired lands legitimately from indigenous holders; they also might evade "the monarch's right to limit the movement of his subjects—the right of *ne exeat regno*—which the monarch held under common law (and, many would argue, under natural law)."[5]

As we will see in this chapter, treaties, from the vantage point of hybrid constitutionalism, were far from neutral to colonial interests. As long as relations with indigenes were useful to proprietors, traders, farmers, and other English settlers, treaties shaped by Indian practice were part of English constitutionalism and influenced English legal conduct. In Pennsylvania and elsewhere, proprietors used treaties to amass colonial power and control, but treaty relations also revealed the fragility of the proprietor's power in territory variously inhabited, trafficked, and claimed. Penn's situation was particularly telling, for while he received a charter that set him up as a proprietor with quasi-sovereign powers, he was also restricted from using the wider array of palatine liberties—among them, the power to make war, pardon major crimes, and create churches—that had been granted to earlier proprietors, such as Calvert and Ashley.

The Pennsylvania treaties also provide suggestive historical material for a conceptual expansion of the third feature of hybrid constitutionalism, *negotiation*. This is especially pertinent given contemporary political theory's interest in the history of treaty making between English colonies and indigenous tribes. Among the most notable of recent interventions are the works of James Tully, Robert Williams, and Iris Marion Young.[6] Tully, for example, looks to the treaties established between agents of the Crown and aboriginal nations from the 1630s until 1832, drawing out three conventions of constitutionalism—mutual recognition, continuity, and consent—that arose out of treaty practices of "dialogue and mediation."[7] Williams similarly emphasizes the spirit of reciprocity, sharing, and connection set in motion by Iroquois treaty rituals of condolence and gift giving.[8] In one of the most expansive conceptions, Young takes inspiration from the treaty relations between Mid-Atlantic indigenous tribes and English settlers in the seventeenth century and eighteenth century, where "each regarded the other as distinct political formations." In turn, she proposes a de-centered, diverse, democratic federalism guided by principles of relationality and dialogue.[9]

These works bring attention to long-overlooked dimensions of colonialism and constitutionalism, and each focuses on slightly different moments in the seventeenth-century and eighteenth-century history of colonial–indigenous treaties. For example, both Williams and Tully focus on the treaties established by the Iroquois confederacy, or Haudenosaunee, during and after the Encounter era. Young primarily concentrates on late-seventeenth-century and early-eighteenth-century treaties established in the Mid-Atlantic region, citing Pennsylvania as a key case for reconsidering the ways negotiation and dialogue shaped multicultural relations. Tully, Young, and Williams all nonetheless emphasize that treaties are conducted through distinctive cross-cultural forms of dialogue, accommodation, and consent.

All three also share the view that the making of treaties represents a compelling alternative to modern constitutionalism's presumptions of imperial conquest and colonial implantation. As opposed to charters that grandiosely claim territory or constitutions that are established in the displacement or assimilation of previous inhabitants, treaties allowed different parties to *negotiate* settlement. No particular resolution is anticipated, as Young suggests. And as a result, treaties present an interactive and multicultural model of adjudication—one that sidesteps and may even relieve the chronic oppression between colonizer and colonized.[10] As Williams indicates in the opening epigraph, "A continuing bond of trust and solidarity" is established by the agreement "to link arms" in a multicultural treaty relationship.[11]

However, while Tully, Williams, and Young are highly attuned to the ways treaties negotiate political diversity and cultural difference, each theorist also tends to insulate hybrid constitutionalism from certain elements of power. The most prominent are inequality on the ground and aspects of aggression and conflict. To a degree, these omissions happen for heuristic reasons. For example, Tully sets aside the "vast inequalities of wealth and power" between colonists and native peoples to better isolate the conceptual features of what he describes as "treaty constitutionalism." "Treaty constitutionalism" provides the setting for an "intercultural common ground," where "negotiators" "recognize their differences and similarities, so that they can reach agreement on a form of association that accommodates their differences in appropriate institutions and their similarities in shared institutions."[12] Similarly, Young depicts treaty negotiations as a process of "widespread cooperation" that is set in contrast to the eruptions of "conflict between Indians and colonists."[13] Indeed, as she aptly cautions, "I do not wish to romanticise the relations among native peoples of this period, or between the native peoples and the European-descended settlers. . . . The point is only to find in the past grounds for bracketing ossified assumptions about jurisdiction, governance and the relation of self-determining people."[14]

My focus in this chapter is in part intended as a historical addition to contemporary accounts. By focusing on the Lenape and Susquehannocks, I add historical examples that address and go beyond the covenant chain. But I also aim to retrench power more explicitly as an integral and dynamic dimension of treaties and proprietary constitutionalism.

Framing Proprietary Power

One of the most popular advertisements for the colony, *Some Account of the Province of Pennsylvania* (1681), described Pennsylvania as the "seed of a nation" blessed by both God and Charles II, a nation "begun and nourished by the care of wise and populous countries, as conceiving them best for the increase of human stock and beneficial for commerce."[15] At founding, however, this "increase of human stock" was far from harmonious. Even before the colony's charter was officially granted in 1681, Penn promised thousands of acres to prospective colonists and "First Purchasers." Furthermore, Penn advertised in *Some Account of the Province* that such parcels were to be "free from any Indian encumbrance."[16] Many of the members of Penn's private business association, the Free Society of Traders, received the desirable lots near Philadelphia. Others who paid Penn for lots on the Schuylkill River or near Philadelphia found themselves saddled with smaller plots far off the river or in the dense woods of the Delaware Valley with Swedes, Dutch, and Finnish settlers.[17] Unsurprisingly, many of the first settlers were upset about their land. As Thomas Holme, surveyor, wrote to Penn in November 1683, "I find it may be requisite for your affair in the concerns of this City (where many people may (probably) come, more then formerly expected) to reduce the breadth of the high street lots . . . & yet leave sufficient room, to make way for new purchasers amongst them to some content, to prevent being {all} placed backward, of which many are unwilling."[18]

The size of the burgeoning settlement further exacerbated the challenge of providing land. Between the years 1681 and 1682, more than twenty-three ships sailed to Pennsylvania, and even in the first year of the colony's founding, nearly two thousand people of English, Welsh, Scottish, Irish, German, and French Huguenot origin settled in the territory, and more than four times that many moved to the colony within the first five years. Penn needed not only to harmonize relations among the new colonists but also to *insert* these diverse newcomers within a territory already inhabited by various local tribes, such as the Lenape and Susquehannocks, and by the Swedish and Finnish settlers who remained in the territory following the decline of the New Sweden settlement.[19] This was not so different from the other proprietary territories, which also grappled with the common issue of insertion. But the scale differed dramatically. Penn had to harmonize and transplant thousands, not hundreds, of settlers, while he encountered increasing Crown restriction.

More precisely, Charles II and the Committee of Trade and Plantations severely curtailed the proprietary privileges granted to Penn. Rather than a grant that referenced the expansive privileges of the "Palatin of

Durham," as Penn initially favored, he ultimately was granted the status of a proprietor "as of our Castle of Windsor, in our County of Berks, in free and common socage, by fealty only, for all services, and not *in capite*, or by knights service."[20] According to the terms of the *Charter of Pennsylvania* (March 4, 1681), Penn was granted the privilege to settle and sell lands in the area between Maryland and New York and the power to draft a constitution for the colony. This was no small grant. As Mary Geiter explains, "Only Maryland had a single proprietor like Pennsylvania, the proprietorship being held by the Calvert family headed by Lord Baltimore." Still, despite Penn's position as sole proprietor, he did not possess many of the liberties that had been granted to Calvert—namely, the authority to issue hereditary titles, pardon treason or murder, establish churches, or engage in unrestricted war or trade.[21] Moreover, Penn's powers were curtailed in a number of ways. He was required to enforce the Navigation Acts; he was to admit customs inspectors to the province; and he was not able "to make, or cause to be set or made, any imposition, custom, or other taxation, rate, or contribution whatsoever, in and upon the dwellers and inhabitants of the aforesaid province."[22] Most important, the Privy Council had the legislative oversight to "adjudge" and "void" the colony's laws.[23] Although the colony could still create laws, the council possessed final review.

In a refrain of Maryland's charter, the *Charter of Pennsylvania* thus began in a familiar tone and stated:

> We . . . do grant free, full, and absolute power (by virtue of these presents) to him and his heirs, to his and their deputies and lieutenants, for the good and happy government of the said country, to ordain, make, and enact, and under his and their seals, to publish any laws whatsoever . . . appertaining either unto the public state, peace, or safety of the said country, or unto the private utility of particular persons, according unto their best discretions, by and with the advice, assent, and approbation of the freemen of the said province.[24]

The charter gave the proprietor and freemen the ability to create laws, and it provided special mention of the "discretion" and "advice, assent, and approbation" of the Pennsylvania Assembly. Moreover, the charter recalled Maryland's mixed privileges to make laws, incorporating the exact language of the earlier 1632 charter: "Provided nevertheless, that the same laws be consonant to reason, and be not repugnant or contrary, but (as near as conveniently may be) agreeable to the laws and statutes, and rights of this our kingdom of England." However, according to the new restrictions, "a transcript" or "duplicate" of the laws would be sent "within five years" for the Privy Council's review, with a turnaround time for the council's evaluation set as a "space of six months."[25]

These constraints on Penn's proprietary privileges marked a critical turning point in English colonialism and in the forms of governance used by English settlements. For much of the early and mid-seventeenth century, the proprietary model was especially useful, as Christopher Tomlins notes, in allowing the Crown to expand colonial reaches with relatively limited outlay of funds and military support.[26] The most influential examples of proprietary settlement were styled as palatinates and characterized as frontier marchlands that faced unforeseen challenges and were equipped in kind with a wide range of political, military, economic, and religious privileges. Colonies such as Maryland and Carolina, as we have seen, often lacked arms and funds. Partly commercial and partly private, proprietors settled territories by using a hybrid assemblage of legal and governmental forms and by employing strategies of negotiation with neighboring European settlements and indigenous tribes and nations to gain a foothold in trade and settlement within occupied ground.

By the end of the century, the "proprietorial design for English colonization was fast being eclipsed by the expanding English state," as Tomlins and others have argued.[27] Penn's restricted powers as proprietor represented the Crown's greater interest in consolidating and nationalizing colonial enterprise. Particularly during the years 1675–80, English authorities attempted to tighten control over the colonies, increasing supervision and gaining greater information about colonial activities toward the last third of the seventeenth century. They did so by focusing on a number of areas, according to Richard J. Ross: increased enforcement of the Navigation Acts; increased scope of general supervisory capacities with expanded customs powers; the creation of vice-admiralty courts; and general reduction of colonial autonomy as proprietary and chartered colonies were transformed into royal colonies.

More specifically, the Crown sought to regulate judicial and legislative process through governors' instructions. Parliament used the Navigation Acts to wrest control of colonial trade from Charles II. The Committee of Trade and Plantations, a body of the Privy Council staffed by members of the Lords of Trade, attempted to centralize administration over independent proprietary and covenant English settlements in the Americas. It aimed to revoke independent powers, regulate colonial assemblies, and appoint royal governors to strengthen defense against hostile French and Indian neighbors.

Still, burgeoning English administrative power over the colonies was not necessarily an omnipotent force of governance and unification. The Crown may have planned from the mid-1670s onward to rein in the English mainland and island colonies in the Americas (two-thirds of which were run by private consortiums and individuals). "Yet," as Ross notes, "as it proceeded, the colonies' legal systems remained significantly diverse and subject to local (more than imperial) direction."[28] Even through the middle of the eighteenth century, Ross explains, quoting Stephen Botein, "the legal apparatus of empire still amounted to little more than an overlay on localized habits of colonial governance."[29]

In addition, vehement protests by the colonists, combined with disputes over policy within the Privy Council, compromised and halted comprehensive colonial management.[30] As Jack Greene notes, the English empire was not created by fiat but "negotiated."[31] In many ways, the characterization that administrative rule was *centralizing* was relative only to the previous autonomy experienced by the colonies. More to the point, Penn and the Pennsylvania colony still grappled with hybridity, albeit under changing conditions and new restrictions.

With his charter, Penn thus faced the challenge of managing a diverse religious, ethnic, and economic population without expansive resources to settle arguments relating to trade, war, faith, or crime. In part, Penn attempted to soften the risks of transporting a wide range of Quakers and others into a terrain already populated by Marylanders, Dutch, Swedes, and Delawarean indigenes by creating a constitution entitled *The Frame of the Government of the Province of Pennsylvania in America: Together with Certain Laws Agreed upon in England by the Governor and Divers Freemen of the aforesaid Province* (1682).

The *Frame* intimated from the start that the polity would be an admixture of peoples. To accommodate this populace, the *Frame* offered up a public representation of the colony as unifying thousands of peoples diverse in religion and ethnic affiliation—Quakers from Europe, Protestants from England, and previous European settlers near the Delaware

River—through "representation" in a bicameral assembly and a "carefully propagated" and "virtuous Education of Youth." It guided both "men of virtue" and "loose and depraved people" in "just administration" of manners, behavior, and customs.[32] Although the Privy Council possessed the ability to review the colony's laws, Penn still held the right to produce what laws he saw fit for the "public state, peace, or safety" of the colony.[33]

By drafting the *Frame*, Penn was employing part of the proprietary privileges that still remained to him by the charter, and the details of the *Frame* reflected Penn's familiarity with the ideas of former and current colonial proprietors. As Mary Geiter argues, Penn often associated with English elites, grandees, and merchants with clout. He was educated at Oxford as a gentlemen commoner, where he met John Locke. As the son of an English admiral, Penn also was familiar with many of the men involved in overseas settlement and trade in the Americas, such as George Monck, Duke of Albemarle, who had been one of the Carolina proprietors. Indeed, to acquire the charter Penn received support, as Geiter notes, in the "period between November 1679 and June 1680 from 'The Chits,' as they were known"—Sunderland, Sidney, Godolphin, and Laurence Hyde—who "formed the new inner circle of the king's cabinet. Between the three, Penn's support was assured."[34] Indeed, even those who often challenged Charles, such as the Earl of Shaftesbury, offered their support to Penn. As one of twenty members on the Privy Council, Shaftesbury had been one of the proprietors of the Carolina colony, as Geiter comments, and Penn sought to appeal to Shaftebury's mercantile interests and to enlist "his efforts to promote the cause of toleration and the acquisition of a new colony."[35]

In addition to his relations with power brokers, Penn's gambit for a proprietary charter was enabled by internal tensions in the king's court. "The granting of Penn's charter," Geiter comments, "became part of a larger plan on the part of the 'Chits' to counter the threat to the monarchy by appeasing those elements in the City which were sympathetic to the Crown's opponents. . . . The decision to grant [a new colony] to Penn as a proprietor stemmed from the political situation. The alternatives, to create a Crown colony or to grant one to a trading company like the Virginia or Massachusetts Bay companies, were apparently never seriously considered."[36] To create a Crown colony would have been problematic because it could be passed on to the king's brother James. Yet to establish a purely merchant colony might have also been troublesome because it would be difficult for the Crown to oversee. Proprietary rule, which was oriented toward profit and yet also accountable to the Crown, offered a still reasonable model. As Geiter explains, "Charles required a proprietor who had experience as well as integrity, but who was not fully aligned with the City Whigs. Penn was an ideal choice for the king. He was connected with the City merchants, and yet his own religious philosophy appeared to be more tolerant than some of the more radical sects in the country. However, a proprietorship, to make economic sense, had to be kept under control," and thus Penn's charter was restricted relative to earlier patents.[37]

With the *Frame*, Penn signaled his ambition to take on the challenge of control. The *Frame* proposed the establishment of a popular legislature in a bicameral house, joined with a quite vigilant code of moral behavior to manage the new settlement. First, Penn incorporated elements similar to James Harrington's *Oceana* and its institutions of voting and represen-tation. The salience of a neo-Harrington republican frame was manifold for Penn, who sought to establish a working order offering the possibility that all settlers, present and future, could be incorporated into the polity. While the republican order was unpopular in the aftermath of the Restora-tion, Penn and many of his contemporaries, such as Algernon Sidney and Thomas Rudyard, still drew on it to evoke an ideal of a balance of power that could withstand an ensuing disruption: in particular, the republican order gave a promise of inclusion in a commonwealth—a vision of an or-der in which diversity could be unified within a single polity.[38]

Second, according to the *Frame*, an organization of freemen in a bi-cameral legislature made up of a Provincial Council and General Assem-bly should compose the government. Through a two-thirds quorum, laws were to be proposed by the Council—a body of seventy-two representa-tives chosen by a yearly meeting of freemen and ratified by the General As-sembly and governor.[39] In addition, terms were limited and balanced: "No one Person shall continue therein longer than Three Years: And in case any Member shall decease . . . another shall be chosen to supply his place for the remaining time . . . and no longer."[40] Like Calvert in the Maryland colony, Penn sought to have the freemen of the polity in the Provincial Council and General Assembly serve to offer "assent and approbation" to the laws of the polity.[41] But in sharp contrast, Penn also included in the sixth and ninth articles a specific provision to prevent the Provincial Council from making laws that would be in "subversion of this *Frame of*

Government"—namely, "that in this Provincial Council the Governor or his deputy shall or may always preside and have a treble voice."[42]

This system of rotating election and service helped portray Pennsylvania's political balance in space and time, as it attempted to convey flexibility. Likewise, while Penn professed no specific preference for either "Monarchy, Aristocracy, or Democracy" in the preface to the *Frame*, his attention to the primacy of the legislative "in the Form of a Provincial Council and General Assembly" was a notable neo-republican combination of all of these features.[43] For instance, the *Frame* described government as a form in which "the laws rule" as long as the "people are a party to those laws."[44] Thus, the "laws" decided by an assembly represented the people. But that legislature was also protected from "confusion" by the triple voice of a "Governor or deputy" presiding.[45] The laws that governed held a degree of external force to the individual and diverse interests of the colonists.

However, even with these features, Penn did not seem fully satisfied that the processes of election, representation, and legislation could guarantee the province's "wisdom, virtue, and ability."[46] As he argued in the introduction to the *Frame*:

> Good Men will never want for good Laws nor suffer Ill ones. . . . But a loose and depraved People (which is the Question) love Laws and an Administration like themselves. That therefore which make a good Constitution must keep it; (viz.) Men of *Wisdom and Virtue*; qualities, that because they descend not with Worldly Inheritances, *must be carefully propagated by a virtuous Education of Youth*; for which After-Ages will owe more to the care and prudence of Founders and the successive Magistracy, then to their Parents for their private Patrimonies.[47]

Therefore, for Penn the question that arose prior to the creation of a balanced legislature was one of the polity's "wisdom and virtue" and "virtuous education." This was an issue of some controversy. For Penn explicitly situated the cultivation and propagation of "virtue" as a matter for "civil government" and the "founders and successive magistracy," not the familial body or "their parents." As such, the power to "propagate"—if not life, then virtue—was covered by the dictates of the *Frame*. As the Quaker Benjamin Furly complained to Penn, the *Frame* had "Parents deprived . . . of a power of countenancing & rewarding Virtue, obedience & sweetness, & discountenancing Vice & refractoriness in their children."[48]

More specifically, the *Frame* established four supervisory committees for managing the customs and manners of the colonists.[49] In the thirteenth article of the *Frame*, Penn gave orders "for the better Management of the Powers and Trust aforesaid" that the Provincial Council should divide itself into four committees "for the more easy Administration of the Affairs of the Province." The first committee attended to the physical and financial order of the colony "to situate and settle Cities, Ports, Market-Towns, and High-ways, and to hear and decide all Suits and Controversies relating to Plantations." Following in kind, the Committee of Trade and Treasury was next instituted to regulate "Trade and Commerce" and to "encourage Manufacture and Country-growth." The third was the Committee of Justice to secure peace and "punish the Maladministration of those who subvert Justice to the Prejudice of the public or private Interest." Last, Penn established a Committee of Manners, Education, and Arts to oversee civil education and manners of the people, "that all Wicked and Scandalous Living may be prevented, and that Youth may be successively trained up in Virtue and useful Knowledge and Arts."[50]

The *Frame*'s four committees, like the colony's Provincial Council, were composed of elected representatives. In that respect, the administration of manners, education, trade, and plantation was not regulation from the proprietor alone. Nevertheless, the committees supervised matters that traditionally were the prerogative of parents and families. Initially, the risk of having Penn the proprietor coerce and compel one's own virtues and manners might have been outweighed by the equal regulation that would be imposed on others "of differing Humors and engagements" or "loose and deprav'd People."[51] Yet by the end of the *Frame*, readers of the constitution may have worried about a quite different problematic: Although Penn most likely held the core Quaker presupposition that the righteous would govern, the heterogeneity of the newly arriving colonists and of those already on the ground disturbed that familiar sentiment. Who would serve on the Committees, and whose sense of "manners" and "education" would dominate in "civil government"?[52]

In this way, the *Frame* had some similarities to other proprietary constitutions, such as the *Fundamental Constitutions* of Carolina. For example, an early draft of the *Frame*, entitled the *Fundamental Constitutions*, had similar reference to "tribes" electing those of "virtue, wisdom, and integrity."[53] And like the Carolina document, the *Frame* had a revised republican form. Yet Penn's *Frame*, with its self-consciously administrative civil government, also differed in a number of ways, and Penn's contemporaries were not always supportive of the results. For instance, Penn's Quaker friend Benjamin Furly critiqued the earlier *Fundamental Constitutions* and the *Frame*, arguing that the constitution lacked adequate legal protection for foreigners; possessed untenable inheritance laws and social services; and needed better guarantees for freedom of conscience.[54] In addition, while Locke and Penn did have friends in common, Locke also criticized the *Frame*, querying the document's harsh treatment of adulterers and its conditions of religious toleration.[55]

Indeed, to an extent Penn's language of "civil government" and "just administration" aligns in many ways to the "empire of uniformity" that Tully argues was initiated by the tradition of "rights, manners, and virtues" theorized by John Locke, James Harrington, and Adam Smith.[56] As Tully explains, "When theorists of what John Pocock calls the competing traditions of rights, virtues, and manners debated the nature of modern constitutional societies in terms of Locke's rights-bearing and industrious labourers, James Harrington's virtuous republicans, and Adam Smith's polished commercialists, they gave the implantation of European institutions and traditions of interpretation the impression of historical inevitability. All three conceptions of modern constitutionalism are defined in contrast to the Aboriginal peoples they displaced in practice—the propertyless and wasteful hunter gatherer, the vicious savage, and the rude native respectively."[57] In fact, Penn was quite familiar with the writings of Harrington, Hobbes, and Sidney, and Penn had attended Oxford when Locke was there.[58] The *Frame*, in this mode, does seem to manage behavior and virtues in a "modern" way, especially since it does so with civil processes—arts, education, trade, commerce, and adjudication. But Penn's *Frame* combined these "civilizing" elements with more irregular and unpolished features—elements that strongly mimicked the hybridity of previous constitutions, such as Carolina's *Fundamental Constitutions*.

First, the *Frame* did not definitively secure settlement. Instead, when viewed in context Penn's explicit attention to moral training and supervision was a pragmatic attempt to secure a foundation of stability within the *Frame*'s call for toleration. The population of Pennsylvania was heterogeneous in both religious and cultural terms, a pragmatic result of the colony's recruitment. However, according to the charter, no churches could be created in Pennsylvania. As a result, in the rhetoric of the *Frame*, an administrative structure of "manners, education, and art" supported toleration of religious diversity and it helped to promote unification against factions or disturbances.[59] Toleration here was as much a commitment to preserving peace between those of differing faiths as it was an asset for creating colonial support and stability.[60]

Equally telling, these "civilizing" and "socializing" provisions did not mitigate contestations on the ground. Pennsylvania colonists, such as Jasper Batts, complained about Penn's proprietary powers and the restrictions of the *Frame*.[61] Other settlers quarreled with each other and with their leadership over land allotments.

Penn ended up revising the constitution more than twenty times between the years 1681 and 1682, and the repeated changes to the *Frame* suggest something of the unstable and ever-changing nature of constitutionalism in the period. Penn had been influenced in many ways by the examples set by earlier proprietary colonies and by the civic humanist and republican ideals circulating in the period. At the same time, Penn's version of these values, as they were outlined in the *Frame*, were clearly not in sync with the sentiments of his contemporaries. These incongruities suggest as much about Penn's particular predilections as of the wide variation possible in the period's constitutionalisms.

Moreover, despite the heavy labor Penn had taken to revise the *Frame*, it was not the only element in the colony's founding. Rather, it was one of a number of legal and political instruments used to establish governance and sovereignty in the new settlement. In particular and in addition, treaties offered Penn a pivotal way to pursue an informal, monopolistic power that could service both expansionary and defensive interests. Contrary to conventional understanding, Penn's practice of treaty making was not unique or particularly enlightened but, rather, a policy long practiced by other British and European settlements seeking to extinguish Indian land claims by purchase.

Treaty Negotiation as Monopolistic Power

Penn's turn to treaty practices were as much attempts to circumvent the restrictions of the Crown as they were attempts to consolidate power and influence in contested indigenous ground. Set within rivalries over land and borders, the negotiations with the Lenni Lenape and Iroquois-speaking

Susquehannocks served as a means, unrestricted by the charter, to establish better control of land that remained ambiguous in the terms of the charter, particularly to the south on the Maryland border and to the north and west along the Delaware.[62]

For example, in the south Penn sought to secure his claim to land threatened by Maryland agents, who alternately intimidated and bribed Pennsylvania settlers to abandon their loyalty to Penn.[63] Meanwhile, to the north and west Penn challenged previous alliances and agreements made by the Lenape and Susquehannocks with European settlers. In the 1620s, Swedish and Finnish settlers established extensive trade and exchange relationships with Susquehannocks and Lenape, according to the ethnographers Terry Jordan and Matti Kaups, "and produced a mixed backwoods culture that later pioneers carried to large areas of America."[64] Lenape tribes, such as the Siconese (who were also known as the Sickoneysinks or Ciconicins), made agreements with representatives of the New Netherlands for territories on Delaware Bay and Swanendale in 1629 and 1630.[65] From the 1640s until the collapse of New Sweden, Swedish and Finnish settlers purchased land and formed trade relationships with Susquehannocks and Lenape tribes. "New Sweden's masterstroke," Karen Kupperman explains, "was to take up an intermediary role in the vital trade between Europeans and Indians."[66] By learning indigenous languages, practices, and customs, Swedish setters facilitated trade between Indians and other Europeans, such as the Dutch and English to the north. Kupperman reflects that "sharing one major advantage—location—the Swedes and Indians made up for their drawbacks: lack of support from Sweden and the Susquehannocks' fear of interference by the powerful Iroquois League to the north."[67] Even after the official seizure of New Sweden by the Dutch, Swedish and Finnish settlers continued to reside in settlements on the Delaware River and Delaware Bay, maintaining their fur and crop trade with various Delaware tribes.[68]

These challenges prompted Penn to use treaties to claim, against the counter-claims of Maryland and the previous Delawarean settlers, his legitimate authority over ambiguous borders.[69] In the early years of the colony's settlement, he was detained in England negotiating territorial claims with the Duke of York. He sent his agents and administrators to negotiate treaties with a variety of local tribes—first, with the Lenni Lenape, located near the Delaware valley, and subsequently with the Iroquois-speaking Susquehannocks, who lived farther north. As the words of the deeds and memorandum indicated, Penn did not speak directly with tribal chiefs and kings, although he often intimated that he had in his promotional materials, such as the popular *Letter to the Society of Traders*.[70] Rather, Penn's agents conducted most of the treaties. They brokered exclusive, proprietary, and final transfers of lands in Penn's name, as expressed in his *Memorandum of Additional Instructions to William Markham & William Crispin & John Bezer* on October 28, 1681:

> First, To Act all in my Name *as* Proprietary & Governor
> Secondly, To buy Land of the true Owners which I think is the Susque
> hanna People
> Thirdly, To treat Speedily with the Indians for Land before they are Fur
> nished by others with things that Please them take advice in this.[71]

The treaties were conducted explicitly for Penn as proprietor; they were not directly representative of Crown interests, nor did they necessarily benefit Pennsylvania colonists, who at times expressly opposed them.[72] Furthermore, the *Memorandum* indicated several of the instrumental features of treaty making for Penn: While identifying the "true Owners" of the land was important, it seemed essential largely because Penn sought to challenge competing claims "by others." Most of all, as Penn's third instruction indicated, the "Indians" needed to be treated "speedily" because their preferences were perceived as fluid and changeable.

Penn's representatives acted in kind, offering provisions and gifts to solicit tribes. The account book for the *Deed at Passyunk*, August 1682, recorded the provisions and gifts that the Indian interpreter Captain Lasse Cocke supplied to the members of the Lenape tribe. Specifically, he laid out funds for "Maintaining the Indians in Meat & Drink when Governor Markham & others that came with him to make first Purchase of Land" and for "Presents [such as shot and alcohol] given to the Indians": " 8ib Powder at 2/8 per & 20ib of Lead at 5d per & 6 Gallons Rum 5 per."[73] These agreements, despite their cost and effort, helped consolidate Penn's proprietary power in three critical ways. First, they allowed Penn to enforce greater control over the conduct of trade, especially with the cultural and linguistic knowledge of translators and representatives. Second, treaty negotiations enabled him to manage guns, alcohol, and other provisions—key resources used to establish peace. And third, the treaties granted Penn possession of exclusive title with native tribes.

Nevertheless, this process required a careful balancing act, as is evident in Penn's public proclamations and letters. Notably, Penn suggested that his treaties were more moral and less corrupting than the agreements that local tribes had made previously with Swedish and Finnish settlers. Penn, for instance, decried gifts of alcohol, suggesting in his *Letter to the Free Society of Traders* (1683), one of the most popular accounts of the new colony, that "since the Europeans came into these parts, [the indigenes] are grown great lovers of strong liquors, rum especially, and for it exchange the richest of their skins and furs . . . but when Drunk, [they are] one of the most wretched spectacles in the world."[74] However, in practice his representatives and interpreters relied on similar kinds of gifts and solicitations: "Lead," "rum," and "shot" were all frequent and customary presents given to the Lenni Lenape and Susquehannocks, according to deed records.[75] Penn also made sure the representatives regularly offered rum and ammunition to the Lenape and Susquehannocks as incentives—signs of good faith unavailable to most Pennsylvania colonists. Notably, Penn passed a law in the First Legislative Assembly of Pennsylvania on December 5, 1682, that explicitly prevented any "person within this Province to from hence forth presume to Sell or exchange any Rum or brandy or any Strong Liquors at any time to any Indian within this Province & if any one shall offend therein the persons convicted Shall for every Such offence pay five pounds." Penn further decreed that "diverse Persons as English Dutch Swedes &c: have been wont to sell to the Indians Rum & brandy and Such like distill'd Spirits." Alcohol, Penn concluded, had a deleterious effect on both the "Indians" and the "colonists"; the "Indians are not able to govern themselves in the use thereof but do commonly drink of it to such excess as makes them sometimes to destroy one another & grievously annoy and disquiet the People of this Province & Peradventures those of Neighbouring Governments."[76]

In the guise of providing a resource—unencumbered title to land—to the colonists, Penn thus strengthened both his *internal* and *external* power in the colony. Internally, Penn's restrictions dissuaded Pennsylvania colonists from engaging in their own negotiations with local indigenes. Externally, Penn used his ability to conduct treaties to service a variety of ends. Most of all, treaties allowed him to circumvent the new restrictions placed on his proprietary authority by the Crown. The Privy Council did not need to review the treaties, for they did not have the status of colonial law. In addition, Penn styled the treaties to pose both a moral and commercial challenge to other colonial settlements, English and European, described by him in print as corrupting and greedy. Finally, the peace Penn offered to the Lenape and Susquehannocks was also in many ways peace in the form of *protectionism*; Lenape and Susquehannock alliances with Penn served as a buffer against Iroquois tribes and other European settlers. From the perspective of Penn and his representatives, treaty negotiation both intersected and attempted to change a number of contested relations: the authority of the British metropole over the colonial peripheries; the regulation of commercial entities by Crown institutions; the competitive relations between English settlements and other European empires, such as the French, Dutch, and Spanish settlements; and the interactions between colonists and indigenes.[77]

In this way, Penn's interests in treaties recall some elements of Charles Tilly's assessment of state making as "organized crime," in which "the makers of state" look to "monopolize the means of violence within a delimited territory."[78] My point, to be clear, is not to characterize Penn as a criminal. Instead, I call on Tilly's account to better delineate the ways in which proprietary power could amass monopolistic control and could work in and around the constraints of formal regulations. By offering pacification to local tribes, Penn was able to open up various trading and diplomatic opportunities without excessive arms or financial investment. To an extent, Penn's power can be seen as conventionally realist in its preoccupation with territorial control and relative diplomatic power; however, his pacific outlook added dimensions of moral and ethical complexity to familiar realist interests. Entrepreneurial and diplomatic aims intermingled with—indeed, even amplified—moralizing messages, allowing a proprietor with limited political and economic resources to forestall conflict, create alliances, and pursue territorial ambitions.

At the same time, Penn's treaties far from ensured colonial dominance. Treaties were fairly rough instruments; they did create some opportunities for the proprietors to acquire and manage land and resources, but they were nonetheless a crude, if unrestricted, instrument of governance. Penn did attempt to use formal agreements between indigenous and colonial elites to better manage uncertainty, but continuing tension on the ground demonstrated that any easement obtained by treaty was often relative and limited, especially since there was an enduring practical difficulty of including all parties affected by negotiation—directly or indirectly.

As a matter of fact, the treaties sometimes worked against certain types of colonial unity. In a notable example, as the *Remonstrance for the Inhabitants of Philadelphia* (1684) showed, Pennsylvania colonists were still unhappy about the lands they held, despite Penn's treaties. Pennsylvania settlers claimed that Penn had "wronged" them, fueling their "fears & apprehensions" that their loss would not be remedied, and they threatened to turn their loyalties to Maryland and to use representatives in England to protest their wrongs to the Committee of Trade and Plantations.[79] While he may have sought to "pacify" relations and claim privilege in contestations over disputed sections of land, treaties did not fully resolve the thicket of conflicts (on the ground.) If treaties sometimes sparked intra-colonial conflict, they also added to burgeoning inter-colonial tensions. Proprietary colonies such as Maryland, Carolina, Pennsylvania, New York, and New Jersey, among others, were often in heavy competition with each other, vying for territory and trade, and, as we will see, the ability to develop agreement with Lenape and Susquehannocks was critical to establishing comparative colonial security.

Treaty Negotiation as De-centered Power

Although Penn was able to service a number of proprietary interests in treaty negotiation, the treaties were far from unidirectional. They were, as Robert Williams reminds us, agreements made with the dialogue and engagement of *multiple* groups, and the various indigenous groups in the territories associated with Pennsylvania were actively enmeshed in treaty arrangements. For the Lenape and Susquehannocks in the period, treaty negotiation with Penn offered a way to respond both to changes in Iroquois power and to waves of European colonialism. Three tribes dominated in the Pennsylvania region during the seventeenth century: the Lenni Lenape, who occupied the lower Delaware Valley and were close allies of the Minisinks; the Susquehannocks, who lived in the Susquehanna Valley above Chesapeake Bay; and the Iroquois Confederacy of the Oneidas, Onondagas, Cayugas, and Senecas to the north.[80] Within the "artificial bounds" of the territory claimed by Penn, indigenous interests never revolved exclusively around the English, as Daniel Richter and James Merrell contend.[81] Instead, in the period between 1650 and 1700, tribes grappled with a variety of inter-indigene conflicts. Equally factoring into diplomatic concerns were incursions from English, Dutch, Swedish, Finnish, and French settlers in and around the territories associated with Pennsylvania, New York, and Maryland.

Much of my account in this section relies on contemporary ethno-historical studies. These works largely rely on extant English and Swedish sources to assess the concerns of Lenapes and Susquehannocks; thus, they are not without gaps and inaccuracies, because the colonial sources come from individuals with economic, military, and religious agendas. Moreover, the contemporary ethno-historical materials tend to focus more on group dynamics than on individual actions. These studies, in consequence, sometimes run the risk of generalizing indigenous interests and intent. My intent here is not to definitively reconstruct the indigenous perspective but, rather, to clarify the ways in which colonial power related to and intersected with indigenous actors and polities. Thus, I emphasize the ways in which these contemporary studies help trace tendencies and patterns in indigenous governance while also indicating variations in and among various native tribes. There is, to be sure, some risk of generalizing. Yet particularly since treaties were multicultural instruments, it would also be highly problematic to omit discussion of indigenous participation and agendas.

In particular, the growing centralization of Iroquois governance over the course of the seventeenth century deeply affected Lenapes and Susquehannocks. Over the past twenty years, scholars have contested and redefined the precise nature of the "empire" attributed to the Iroquois, but a rough consensus remains that the Iroquois—though more divided among themselves and less dominant than previously portrayed—heavily influenced indigenous nations in the East and in the Mid-Atlantic region.[82] Significantly, the Five Nations struggled with a series of substantive internal and external challenges after the 1660s. Major population losses had resulted from European disease and settlements. Moreover, with the escalation of English and French imperial rivalry in the middle of the seventeenth century, the Iroquois faced increasing pressure to overcome factionalism at home and to consolidate military and diplomatic ties with treaties.

In response, the "people of the Five Nations," explains Daniel Richter, "drew upon their traditional patterns of warfare to shore up both their economy and their population. When warfare itself threatened Iroquois existence, headmen modified old rituals of peacemaking to evolve a system of intercultural diplomacy."[83] Prior to 1660, Iroquois treaties emphasized *reciprocity and exchange*. Robert Williams explains that the Iroquois used words of peace and rituals of condolence and offered gifts to conduct the treaty negotiations in 1645 at Trois-Rivières between Mohawk headmen and Frenchmen, Hurons, and Algonquians. But by the mid-1660s, the Five Nations struggled to maintain internal stability as they faced new conflicts with the Mahicans, New England Algonquians, and Susquehannocks, all of whom had developed military and diplomatic strength in alliances and on their own. Most of all, the Iroquois adapted old traditions. As Richter maintains, it was these skills of adaptation—"the capacity to innovate within a framework of tradition"—that "provides a key to Iroquois survival."[84] Iroquois treaty negotiations subsequently placed greater emphasis on establishing a hierarchy of power and status, reinforced by geographic centers of authority and payment of tribute.

To the Iroquois, this outcome represented a step toward an ideal of peace and cooperation among multiple peoples. However, to those either excluded from or subordinated by the processes of treaty negotiation, such as the Susquehannocks and Algonquians, changes in the Iroquois covenant chain after the 1660s resulted in a significant loss of political autonomy. In markedly different ways the Lenapes and Susquehannocks responded to these shifts in Iroquois power.

The Lenape used treaty negotiations to pursue their interests as members of small bands and communities not linked by an overarching political structure of representation. Prior to European settlement in the Americas, the Lenapes defined themselves by kinship and organized in small communities where neither men nor women held positions of exclusive authority.[85] The decentralized, scattered Lenape bands, according to Sugrue, based their contact on reciprocal exchanges with "little evidence of political structures that transcended kin groups."[86] At various points they were semi-agricultural and horticultural, but in the mid-seventeenth century the Lenape increasingly relied on fishing, hunting, and gathering, along with growing participation in the fur trade. The shift in activities came as a consequence of massive population losses due to epidemics in the wake of the settlement by the Dutch, Swedes, and Finns in the 1620s. By the end of the century, the Lenape were located in and around the Delaware River and near European trading posts, and they relied even more heavily on European goods. Due to their limited involvement in the harvesting of beaver, these Lenape tended to serve as mediators between markets and farther-flung tribes.[87] Historically, the Lenape sought to avoid conflict, and they turned to treaties as a way to create limited, local regions of protection and isolation from Iroquois authority. Francis Jennings describes the impact of Lenape agreements: "The Iroquois found considerable difficulty speaking even for themselves in Pennsylvania because of inter-colonial jealousies: New Yorkers wanted to keep the Iroquois from falling under Pennsylvania's sway, and Pennsylvania wanted to preserve 'their' Indians from outside influence, as New York's via the Iroquois. During William Penn's lifetime, Pennsylvania stayed out of the Covenant Chain confederation."[88]

In contrast, the Susquehannocks were organized along distinctly different political, social, and economic lines. Susquehannocks, along with the Five Nations of the Iroquois League and the five Huron nations, were descendents of the Late Woodland Owasco culture. They formed political structures around large horticultural communities, ranging in size from several hundred to one thousand members. "Owasco communities," Richter notes, "seem to have been extremely independent, isolated, and hostile toward outsiders. Warfare was prevalent, and reciprocal retaliation produced an ongoing cycle of feuding not easily stopped."[89] While the Lenape took on a mediating role in the seventeenth century, the more aggressive Susquehannocks were frequently embroiled in a number of European and native conflicts. For a time, Richter comments, the Susquehannocks prospered materially and "turned their village into a fortress bristling with European firearms."[90] They had access to Maryland traders on the Chesapeake and to the Swedish, Dutch, and English on the Delaware. They also had firm control of hunting territories throughout the Susquehanna watershed and points west. But the Susquehannocks also came into intense conflict with the Dutch in New York and English settlers in Maryland and Virginia.[91] Over the course of the century, peoples of both the Delaware and the Susquehanna watersheds became increasingly dependent on European trade for clothing, tools, and weapons.[92] By the 1680s, substantial waves of new English settlers had arrived; trading conditions had worsened for local tribes, while the pressure to sell native land had increased substantially. Because of the increasing competition, the Susquehannocks sought to exclude the Lenape from the fur trade. In addition, Susquehannock conflicts with the Iroquois splintered and weakened the nation; some Susquehannocks returned north to the protection of the Iroquois, and others fled to the New York and Virginia settlements.

Thus, the Lenape and Susquehannock tribes appeared to negotiate treaties with Penn's administrators for a number of reasons: to draw defenses against the Iroquois Confederacy to the north, to secure more local support in regional conflicts, and to avoid taking sides in the wars against France or in neighboring conflicts. Treaties thus enabled Lenape and Susquehannocks to pursue various forms of *decentralized* power that differed in structural terms from Penn's. Penn reserved a monopolistic power to himself as proprietor and head of the Society of Traders while restricting Pennsylvania colonists, Finns and Swedes, and nearby Marylanders from developing their own relations with the Lenape and Susquehannocks. But for the Lenape, treaties helped to establish realms of mediation and pacification. The decisions made by Lenape bands were not connected to a wider indigenous infrastructure or political hierarchy. Rather, power in intimate Lenape bands was fluid and diffuse. Agreements reflected communal decisions based on discussion and persuasion. In contrast, the larger bands of Susquehannocks used treaty negotiations more defensively to construct a diplomatic and economic alternative to the covenant chain.

This period of treaty negotiation between Penn and the Lenape and Susquehannocks is theoretically pertinent because it illustrates the *variable* forms of power that shape and can be shaped by hybrid constitutionalism. For Penn, proprietorial insecurities motivated interest in treaties as an instrument to supplement and consolidate monopolistic power. By contrast, the more hierarchical Susquehannocks viewed treaties as defensive measures that could create and fortify an alternative system of alliances; the agreements served as a zone of protection in the face of increasing threats by the Iroquois and other regional neighbors, such as the Dutch in New York. In yet another way, treaties facilitated Lenape communal life, providing limited protection and mediation.

Like Young's work on inclusion and democracy, the treaty negotiations under examination here remind us that it is not simply that groups can possess different conceptions of power in the processes of treaty negotiation but also that those conceptions of power are often further affected by differences within groups. Unequal positioning on the ground, where access to resources, opportunity, and information can vary widely, also heavily affects the dynamics of treaty negotiation. Treaties thus facilitated power in multiple and subjective ways. And if these agreements did not impose wholesale domination or exploitation, neither did they eliminate personal and group interest and influence. Here instead as in Michel Foucault's characterization, power was "employed and exercised through a net-like organization," where "individuals circulate between its threads" and are "always in the position of simultaneously undergoing and exercising this power. They are not only its inert or consenting target; they are always also the elements of its articulation."[93] This is a tempering reminder, for Foucault's description acknowledges that power does not remain stable, but is more sinuously shaped and changed over time.

Especially in light of contemporary concerns and the deep desire to reform accommodation and adjudication, it is worth considering what a historicized account of treaty negotiation might imply for us today. Does it spur us to renew our processes of intercultural engagement? Or does it serve more as a cautionary tale for avoiding treaties altogether? As we will see next, there can be a shape shifting quality to treaty practices of negotiation and dialogue, a quality that is open to the possibilities of multicultural engagement but also is powerfully vulnerable to miscommunication and deception.

Treaty Negotiation as Relational Power

Many claim that treaties between English and indigenous nations were fatally flawed from the start because treaty participants possessed such different—and, arguably, mutually exclusive—conceptions of land possession and use.[94] The English tended to view land as a commodity to be bought and sold: Deeds conveyed absolute right to land, and gifts of rum, wampum, and goods were seen as payment for land title. By contrast, indigenous conceptions of territory emphasized land usufruct: Deeds were largely viewed as provisional agreements that needed to be revisited and renewed over time, and any gifts were seen as part of ongoing protocols and customs of greeting and negotiation. "The Lenape notion of the transfer of partial or usufruct rights in a land transaction," Sugrue writes, "had no impact on the wording of deeds, all of which stipulated the permanent and absolute renunciation of Indian rights to the land conveyed."[95] Similarly, James Spady affirms, "Penn actively sought to 'extinguish' the 'Indian encumbrance' on the land through English property law, but the Lenapes apparently expected to receive regular payments for the colonists' continued residence upon the land."[96] Thus, on first appraisal the treatied deeds between Penn and the Lenape and Susquehannocks seem to illustrate a clash of cultural and political understanding, where indigenous conceptions of land and culture were possibly misunderstood or, more likely, manipulated to serve Penn's interests. If Penn and his interpreters and "go-betweens" did possess knowledge of Lenape and Susquehannock protocols and values, these understandings did not appear to compel any necessary commitment or sense of responsibility to treaty participants over the long term.

For example, Penn made frequent and public indication of his knowledge and validation of Lenape and Susquehannock cultures in promotional materials, such as *The Letter to the Free Society of Traders*. In addition, Penn and his administrators recognized that Lenape and Susquehannocks perceived the pacts as open-ended and subject to ongoing review and renewal. Even though the deed agreements referred to the permanent transfer of land to the English, Penn and his representatives nonetheless revisited and renewed "confirmatory" treaties with Lenape and Susquehannocks from the 1680s until as late as 1718. Penn was willing to make multiple payments to tribes until 1700 when financial difficulties beset the colony.[97] These "confirmatory" treaties suggest that the open-ended nature of treaty negotiations could be turned to multiple ends. Penn and his administrators knew of Lenape protocols and practices, and they used Lenape customs when it was useful for diplomatic reasons. However, these decisions were often changed and revisited, at times causing conflict with and even betrayal of earlier agreements.

This element of indeterminacy appears in greater detail in the *dialogic* aspects of treaty negotiation. In general, elites arbitrated treaty negotiations, relying on interpreters whose interests, knowledge, and capabilities revealed a core ambiguity in intercultural dialogue and accommodation. For example, the Swedish colonist Lars Parsson (Lasse) Cocke, fur trader and magistrate, negotiated many of the early treaties (1682–99) with the Lenape, Susquehannocks, and members of the Iroquois Confederacy. Similarly, James Logan, an early secretary to Penn, negotiated treaties with the

Lenape for land and trade access.[98] Negotiation practices extended beyond simply translating speeches and trading wampum. In arranging meetings, interpreting manners and gestures, and providing incentives, representatives of the proprietor required a cross-cultural understanding of language, custom, and culture.

James Merrell points out that such practices of translation, reciprocity, and diplomacy were deeply imbued with power *and* contingency. Although fluent in cross-cultural practices, negotiators were often partisan. For instance, Penn's secretary, James Logan, was conversant in Iroquois protocols of condolence and Algonquian practices of orientation. He owned a copy of the Bible in Algonquian, and he housed Lenape representatives during treaty negotiations. However, he also referred to local tribes and nations as "children" and famously showed little commitment to intercultural understanding beyond matters relating to trade and land. Lasse Cocke expressed a different kind of cultural fluidity. He had been raised in the Delaware lower counties prior to the Pennsylvania settlement, and yet he eagerly naturalized to Penn's colony to expand his fur trade.[99]

Cocke and Logan were not unique. As Merrell comments, "The very preoccupation that gave the trader valuable negotiating tools—the traffic in peltry—might also hinder him when called to serve. Intent on satisfying the demands of his Indian and Philadelphia customer, with an eye always on 'the sweet profits' to be made in trade, the fur peddler 'can with eagerness go thro the greatest hardships and Difficaltyes for sake of Gaine.' "[100] Despite—or perhaps because of—their cross-cultural facility, negotiators used their skills to serve instrumental, even coercive, interests. "However skilled he was, chicanery was also part of the go-between's repertoire," Merrell notes. "Moreover, for all the talk about these figures standing squarely between native and newcomer, mediators themselves saw, and set, limits to their acquaintance with another world. *A good ear and a glib tongue could achieve a meeting of the minds. . . . A meeting of the hearts proved another matter.*"[101]

Of course, Cocke and Logan, strictly speaking, did not address cultural identity in our more modern sense, where practices, customs, and sensibilities delineate specific group, ethnic, or even civilizational membership. Rather, in seventeenth-century Pennsylvania, cross-cultural knowledge was a *relational* type of power, allowing individuals to gain access to modalities of living and survival. This form of power was rooted in a conception of locale in which knowledge meant developing the skills and relationships needed to survive in a specific time and place. Treaty parties depended on one another to some degree, and each sought to rely on others—whether through discussion, exchange, or alliance—to forward various respective interests. Engagement with other cultures was thus a practical acknowledgment of dependence. What was at stake was not recognition of culture or even the assimilation to a dominant culture. Instead, culture for interpreters and go-betweens appeared more prosaically to be a skill set to be mastered for prudential ends.

How might this conception of culture reconfigure our political understanding? The treaties are a feature of hybrid constitutionalism in which certain forms of cross-cultural understanding did seem to take place, but they were often variable and indeterminate as guarantees of enduring respect or harmony. This is a situation that calls to mind the epigraph by Jacques Derrida that opened this chapter.[102] For Derrida, the "shuttle" of negotiation is not "noble."[103] He submits that "there is always something about negotiation that is a little dirty, that gets one's hands dirty . . . something is being trafficked, something in the order of a traffic, or the relations of force."[104] Treaties may have allowed for the inclusion and the expression of overlapping jurisdictions and multiple authorities, but they were also haunted by a history of instrumentality and indeterminacy.

Such work prompts serious reconsideration of the ways in which hybrid constitutionalism worked with and for colonial ambitions. I have sought to argue that, in its hybridity, proprietary constitutionalism was plural, local, and elastic. These attributes, however, were not geared toward honoring or protecting cultural, ethnic, or political difference. They were instead motivated by a more abiding colonial desire to establish and insert a working polity into already occupied ground. What do these aspects suggest about how we might think about the colonial past today? And what instruments of governance and adjudication are best suited to responding to that history?

From a historical perspective, the treaties negotiated between Penn and the Lenape and Susquehannocks help to challenge broad-brush accounts of English empire as a monolith erected only by territorial conquest and cultural assimilation. Such accounts can overlook the degree to which cross-cultural agreements, understandings, and knowledges supported and supplemented English colonial order. Notably, the treaties revealed Penn's reliance on Lenape and Susquehannocks to provide land and alliances. Equally pertinent, historical examples of treaty negotiations illuminate the wide variety of indigenous diplomatic, territorial, and social interests and agendas in the past and allow insight into the many agreements and conflicts that historically altered indigenous communities.

On a conceptual level, the example of Pennsylvania's founding prompts renewed consideration of the possibilities for potent cross-cultural connection and the risks of inequality, exclusion, and indeterminacy. Treaty negotiations, after all, did include cross-cultural adjudication, but they did so in ways that created moments of exclusion and fostered opportunism. In fact, as Peter Charles Hoffer clarifies, while the English viewed treaties as useful, once their settlements became more prosperous, much of the provisional "middle ground" between indigenous and colonial elites disappeared.[105]

We might consider, in that respect, whether hybrid constitutionalism may be particularly prone to a type of indeterminacy of outcome, not only because groups are fluid and their conditions on the ground are subject to change, but also because the institution of treaty negotiation is itself open-ended. To an extent, the treaties negotiated between the Lenape, Susquehannocks, and Penn were ill-fated because Penn manipulated the open-endness of the treaties to service his own interests. But it is also the case that the more general structure of the treaty allowed for the expression of miscommunication and even deception. Treaties operated in spaces when multiple understandings of power and influence overlapped in animated and mobile ways. At times, consensus may have occurred, but given differences among groups and the changeability of conditions on the ground, participant understandings shifted easily.

We might then wonder whether modern treaties might not also possess similar vulnerabilities. By admitting multiple actors and allowing agreements to be subject to ongoing review, treaties seem to possess an agonism that renders participants vulnerable—some, arguably, more than others. This is an agonism that Tully poignantly raises in his discussions of democracy, where he notes, "No agreement will be closed at a frontier; it will always be open to question, to an element of non-consensus, and so to reciprocal question and answer, demand and response, and negotiation."[106] Such agonism pushes us to develop more pointed questions. Are there tactics we can take to ameliorate miscommunication and deception? And if not, will we be able to persist in pursuing change, even in the face of the risks of co-optation? Perhaps, for example, better distribution of resources (political, social, and economic) may enable us to better guard against the exclusions and instrumentalities present in hybrid constitutionalism. As we have seen in the historical examples discussed earlier, elements of exclusion, elitism, and opportunism emerged because of inequalities in resource and opportunity. At the same time, some of the deception also occurred due to divergent ideas about power among culturally and socially distinct groups. And perhaps these elements of diversity may not be eliminable. In that case, rehabilitating negotiation may also have to involve cultivating the energies and sensibilities needed to sustain action even in light of such risks. This process might be aided by a critical reframing of the practices of negotiation that de-couples the intention of negotiation and the more ambiguous effects of its practice.

A deeper understanding of hybrid constitutionalism's relationship to power is an opportunity to acknowledge the vulnerabilities as well as the strengths in speaking, engaging, and negotiating across cultural difference. As we will see next, hybrid constitutionalism also suggests a way to differently view the legacy of colonialism itself.

NEGOTIATING CULTURE

Plurality and Power in Hybrid Constitutionalism

5

Thus has our whole country been granted by the crown while in the occupation of the Indians. These grants purport to convey the soil as well
as the right of dominion to the grantees. . . . These various patents cannot
be considered as nullities; nor can they be limited to a mere grant of the
powers of government.

—*JOHNSON V. M'INTOSH*

Beyond the causal role they play in influencing people's dispositions, the
narratives preserved by collective memory sometimes play a normative
role—that is, they may in various ways provide criteria, implicit or explicit, by which contemporary models of action can be shaped or cor-
rected, or even by which particular ethical or political proposals can be
authorized or criticized.

—STEVEN KNAPP, *LITERARY INTEREST*

With this work, I have sought to push beyond a framework
of conquest and assimilation to address the hybrid features of proprietary constitutionalism. Sometimes, as I argued,
these elements were rough and awkward, as in the political and
legal assemblages of ordinances, statutes, and temporary instructions in Maryland. At other moments, the hybridity seemed
quite subtle, whether in the elaborate claims of the *Fundamental Constitutions* or in the diplomatic and cultural negotiations
of the treaties between the Lenni Lenape, Susquehannocks, and
William Penn. Taken collectively, these proprietary examples

illustrated forms of constitutionalism that were mixed not only in their political, cultural, and temporal features, but also in their combination of insecurity and ambition. Hybridity in this way was not a form of alternative privilege—a resolution to the dilemmas of the present. Instead, it calls to be treated more critically and even circumspectly for its involvement in what Bonnie Honig evocatively describes as the "irrevocably, structurally arbitrary and prelegitimate" conditions of founding.[1]

Yet while the focus in this book was largely directed to the seventeenth-century English American proprietary context, and particularly to the conditions of founding, the project as a whole was prompted by a question pursued by contemporary political theory: In what way did English colonialism shape (and, indeed, does it still affect) modern constitutionalism? In this concluding chapter, I consider the issue of impact and address it more fully. Can the features of hybridity identified in this study be extended beyond the constitutional and political framework of the proprietary settlements? Do the hybrid constitutionalisms discussed thus far speak to current conceptions of adjudication and governance?

The task of extending this account of proprietary constitutionalism is a bit tricky and, in a way, runs contrary to the basic premise of this study. The book, after all, began with the desire to look at the colonial emergence of modern constitutionalism from a particular, not general, viewpoint. The approach adopted in this work followed much of the spirit of Wittgenstein's comments in *The Blue and Brown Books*—namely that the "craving for generality" can produce "a contemptuous attitude towards the particular case."[2] A focus on particularity, as I have argued, allows us to apprehend not simply dynamic relationships between language and action in the processes of colonial founding but also features of discretion, adaptation, and negotiation that often fail to register in more wide-ranging accounts. Therefore, it is not my intention to suggest that the examples of the proprietary colonies should be used to re-characterize the entire swath of English colonialism and constitutionalism in the past three hundred years. Such a projection would problematically overstate the influence of the English proprietary settlements, as it would also overlook essential issues of institutional and juridical change over time and relevant changes in colonial and indigenous policy. Nor should the proprietary examples considered thus far be seen as normative illustrations of either hybridity or constitutionalism more broadly.

At the same time, it is possible to use the specificity and particularity of the proprietary example as a theoretical and historical *provocation*. A provocation, as the *Oxford English Dictionary* explains, is an "action of provoking or inciting," but it also refers to the "senses relating to incitement"— the faculties of hearing, seeing, and feeling that prompt "incitement, impulse; instigation."[3] When an example tries to provoke, in other words, it attempts to draw on the senses and emotions to produce actions that signal not just irritation, but also a stance of retaliation and even challenge.

The ambiguous colonial beginnings of the proprietary colonies can be positioned as examples that provoke *both* the modernity and the uniformity of constitutionalism in its so-called emergence, where *emergence* can be thought of not just as a new start to a long familiar story, but also as a contested period in which we can unearth marginalized and submerged understandings. James Tully, notably, depicts modern constitutionalism as a language of cultural uniformity and unity that has come to dominate as impartial and universal in the past three hundred years. This picture of the "modern constitution," he explains, is underpinned by a stadial map of mankind; modern Western culture stands as superior to the traditions of ancient constitutionalism and the "long contests of Aboriginal and non-Aboriginal peoples . . . unnoticed and forgotten."[4] This is a self-conscious contrast that arises with and through the period of European colonial and imperial expansion that emerged from the seventeenth century to the twentieth century.

Yet some important ambiguities are built into Tully's influential account. First, the early modern period was a period in which neat designations of ancient and modern were hard to sustain. As we have seen, charters and constitutions relied on the example of the English constitution, which was irregular with respect to temporal distinctions. Second, stadial histories, which were commonly associated with the conjectural histories of the late eighteenth century and nineteenth century, do not map neatly onto the seventeenth-century and eighteenth-century contexts of the classic theorists such as Hobbes, Locke, Harrington, and Smith, whom Tully commonly cites. Third, the variegated aspects of proprietary colonialism and constitutionalism are not adequately represented by the image of the "empire of uniformity."

What the examples of the proprietary settlements help to do is to reconceptualize the colonial roots of modern constitutionalism as hybrid.

This hybridity does not signal the elimination of colonial ambition and desire. Instead, it proposes different dynamics and different structures of power. As we have seen, entangled commercial and political interests drove proprietary colonization, producing settlements that sought to insert themselves into occupied and contested ground. In response, these polities created and drew on hybrid constitutions that encouraged discretion, adaptation, and negotiation. These constitutions did not wholly reject the modern or take recourse only in tradition. More confusing, what emerged were assemblages that shifted shape, where modernity and ancient tradition were crucially intermixed, adapted, and reconfigured.

This is not to suggest that the development of proprietary constitutions was simply haphazard. To draw on a different vernacular, proprietary constitutionalism demonstrated some of the central qualities of path dependence, although, of course, it is not an archtypical case. Path dependence, as James Mahoney explains, offers a way to assess and understand the development of regime structure over long periods of time. It means more than "history matters" or that "past events influence future events."[5] Most typically, path development is broken down into five key steps: antecedent conditions (historical factors that define available options and shape selection processes); critical juncture (selection of a particular option, such as a policy option, from among multiple alternatives); structural persistence (production and reproduction of institution or structure pattern); reactive sequence (reaction and counter-reactions to institution or structural pattern); and outcome (resolution of conflict generated by reactions and counter-reactions). Path dependence thus tends to focus on the crucial role of *structures and institutions* in long-term development, and while it is not wholly structuralist, individuals are granted a less active role.

In the proprietary colonies, there was certainly strong evidence of many of the major elements of path development—most notably, in the antecedent conditions for founding. The repeated use of charters and written and unwritten orders; delegation of authority; and even discretion, adaptation, and negotiation all served as common historical factors in the proprietary settlements. Yet in a number of ways, the proprietary colonies did not fit the standard model of path development. The charter itself was extremely open-ended and hybrid, as we have seen, in terms of the political and legal institutional structures made available to proprietors and colonists. Indeed, even if proprietors and settlers did repeatedly use certain legal and institutional structures, such as treaties and ordinances, each of the proprietary settlements was independent and not necessarily inclined to align with neighboring colonies. In fact, the very flexibility and openness that colonies individually sought often became the source of contention between colonies, at times undermining imperial cohesion. Finally, there were frequently "failures" of proprietary institutions and structures on the ground, as in the many revisions made to the *Fundamental Constitutions* and the *Frame of Government*. Proprietary constitutionalism, to that end, was an odd combination of structure and contingency, ambition and insecurity.

To re-characterize colonization in this way shifts the terms of debate. There may have been unabated English colonial desire for settlement during the seventeenth century and eighteenth century, but those ambitions were nonetheless shaped by practices that stressed flexibility and change over time. These practices were certainly instrumental and served as tactics to promote colonial interests. Yet they were also contingent in an important way: They were not bolstered by sizeable administration, arms, or wealth, and they did not provide any guarantee of domination. This study, as a consequence, reveals elements of English insecurity and instability that are often overlooked, and it brings to light how indigenous knowledges and skills were central to English colonial settlement, a point that is typically hidden in both triumphalist and anti-triumphalist narratives. Moreover, founding did not create unanimity among proprietors, investors, colonists, traders, farmers, and settlers. Proprietors and colonists often distrusted each other and turned to native and other settlers for assistance and instruction. Similar tensions abounded between proprietors and Crown authorities. Such conditions thus complicate and unsettle the more grandiose claims of proprietors by highlighting the insecurities and anxieties of settlement.

Cast in this way, hybridity can serve as a critical concept that draws attention to operations of power, privilege, and interest. It is especially attuned to the *contextual* and *operational* effects of constitutionalism over time and place. Reframing the concept in this way makes it possible to move beyond the confines of modern constitutionalism and its features of uniformity and to conceptualize political and legal hybridity in much more expansive geographical terms. For example, by turning to James Muldoon's account of early modern empire, we can see hybridity, as Muldoon notes, in the "composite monarchies" of early modern Europe, which were a complex assemblage of political territories governed according to a variety of laws, customs, and principles.[6] The central role of medieval legal theory in the governance of these "composites" illustrated that, although governed by universal dominion in theory, the Holy Roman Empire lacked comparable governmental or administrative infrastructure in practice. A similar site of resonance is in C. H. Alexandrowicz's classic study of European treaty making in the East Indies in the sixteenth century. As Alexandrowicz explains, although the Europeans in principle had a "unilateral" legal title, "they had in practice to fall back on negotiation and treaty making in preference to resorting to war." Moreover, as Alexandrowicz aptly illustrates, Europeans discovered that Asian diplomatic and interstate relations "were more ancient than their own and in no way inferior to notions of European civilization."[7]

Even in the English colonies, hybridity was not limited to the proprietary settlements. Consider, for instance, the examples of Rhode Island and New York in the seventeenth century. Elements of hybridity, as Bilder clarifies, were evident in the legal practices of the colony of Rhode Island, which drew on the various, irregular legal traditions in England. This, she argues, resulted in a "transatlantic constitution" that lawyers actively modified and debated.[8] Comparable in manner, New York had constitutional orders that were an irregular admixture of common law and assembly law. Empire, as Hulsebosch explains, was marked by legal pluralism and polyvalent authority and was more akin to a collection of competing power centers than to a pyramid of authority.[9] In the exemplary studies of Hulsebosch, Bilder, Hoffer, and Tomlins, among others, hybridity emerges as a central feature in early modern English colonization and colonialism that illuminates the negotiated, pragmatic quality of colonial power.

Forms of hybridity, moreover, persisted well beyond the seventeenth century. Numerous historians, such as Konig, Ross, Greene, and others, have amply documented that the English colonies long supported legal and political processes of "regional differentiation" that were "shaped not only by the contingencies of the historical moments that had launched them but also by succeeding self-definitions—as settler societies developing in a hostile environment, as colonists joining together in collective separation from England, and finally as members of political and culturally distinct entities in a federal republic attempting to balance the sovereignties of state and union."[10] The colonies, as Konig and others make clear, differently used the open-endedness of colonial charters, and their legal systems reflect the many ways in which the irregular English constitution could be altered and re-formed in colonial contexts. This is also a point that Jacob Levy made in his account of the ancient constitution and non-contractarian tradition in colonial law until the end of the eighteenth century.[11]

This persistence, in fact, continued even with the substantial growth of British imperial administration after the late seventeenth century. As Richard Ross comments, despite their ambitions, imperial powers were often much less effectual than they aspired to be. For example, by 1696, the Crown and Parliament attempted to construct a more unified system of imperial administration that they hoped would "produce, among other positive results, a more efficient and uniform administration of law in the colonies." But, as Ross notes, this unified system largely failed because of "bureaucratic inefficiency, special interest lobbying by colonists and British traders, and resistance from colonial courts and legislatures. These locally entrenched legal departures defied any and all imperial attempts at uniformity, and in 1730 an exasperated imperial official could complain 'that throughout the whole continent of North America, there are not two colonies, where the courts of justice or the methods of proceedings are alike.' "[12] Such constitutional irregularity was not a secret during the Revolutionary era; instead, it was frequently observed and commented on. In a notable example, as Konig explains, Edmund Burke, in representing New York's interests, recognized "how different conditions create different social and political forms, and he understood how the successful governing of British North America must not demand conformity to 'abstract ideas of right' or 'mere general theories of government.' " Burke thus rejected a plan for establishing a single state and instead, as Konig explains, proposed a plan of reconciliation that "rested on 'a wise and salutary neglect' that conceded 'the legal competency' of each colony to choose its own way." After all, the colonies, in Burke's estimation, had developed according to their particular and different circumstances, and "only on that basis could the empire continue their loyalty."[13]

Tracking hybridity rather than modernity or even civility allows us to focus on different features of power and privilege—as they appear, for example, in moments of negotiation, aspects of imitation, and periods of confusion. Of course, these hybridities were not static over time; nor were they necessarily causally related to one another. In that respect, the instances that I discuss here are not linked in a teleological account of progress and development in which hybridity leads to a determinative order. Instead, I treat these cases in a more genealogical and speculative fashion—as an opportunity to collect diverse examples and to excavate obscured features and assumptions that, as in Nancy Fraser's and Linda Gordon's proposal for a genealogical approach, would "defamiliarize taken-for-granted beliefs in order to render them susceptible to critique and to illuminate present-day conflicts."[14] To be sure, the examples that I survey here offer only preliminary points of consideration. To do justice to a genealogical account would require another study altogether. Yet these elements still can serve to heighten awareness to the possibilities and pitfalls of hybridity.

As such, the illustrations that I include here are not meant to be comprehensive or definitive. They are, instead, occasions for reevaluating the past in different terms. Genealogy, Foucault explains, "does not pretend to go back in time to restore an unbroken continuity . . . to demonstrate that the past actively exists in the present, that it continues secretly to animate the present, having imposed a predetermined form to all its vicissitudes."[15] Instead, genealogy is more aware of possible interruptions, thwarted ambitions, and submerged meanings. Although not primarily concerned with tracking a key linguistic term, as in Fraser's and Gordon's study, my account is similarly attentive to broad historical shifts in the usage of terms such as "treaty," "charter," and "constitution." This genealogy is equally interested in bringing together ranges of meanings that are open to, if not dependent on, "normative political reflection."[16]

Rewriting Modernity

If hybridity—and its associated features of particularity and multiplicity—were obvious in the seventeenth century and eighteenth century, why have they fallen away from view now? In part, English American colonists and theorists of the eighteenth century, such as John Bulkley and Samuel Wharton, reinterpreted the hybrid character of colonial charters and constitutions. They solidified tenuous territorial claims as facts of legitimate right, casting Locke's arguments for appropriation and cultivation as incontrovertible defense.[17] In addition, as Konig comments, Jefferson and others constructed a narrative about early American law that stressed its distance from the English constitution. Namely, Jefferson and others sought to reject the imposition of the eighteenth-century British century "imperial constitution" by constructing a simplified narrative of American legal development that, as Konig comments, "imposed a misleading[ly] unsophisticated uniformity on the regionally varied legal landscape of early America."[18] "According to this story—which has been embellished through time—the colonists devised a simpler, purer law better suited to the common needs of British North America. Theirs was a generic system of law lacking the complicated forms and actions of English secular and ecclesiastical law."[19] As effective as this story may have been in establishing a sharp contrast between the English constitution and the American legal tradition, according to Konig, "it intentionally neglected the English antecedents of a continuing American legal tradition of instrumentally crafted regional variation. Legal regionalism among the colonies had existed as a reality long before it became a consciously articulated ideal when Americans reexamined their colonial past in search of a workable foundation for a new legal order in the 1780s."[20]

Even more definitively, the U.S. judicial decisions of the nineteenth century, such as *Johnson and Graham's Lessee v. William M'Intosh* and *Cherokee Nation v. Georgia*, firmed up as manifest what was initially far from settled. Such cases strongly asserted the certainty of English possession, giving full assent to the legal title of U.S. possession of native land. "It has never been doubted," Chief Justice John Marshall wrote in *Johnson and Graham's Lessee v. William M'Intosh* (1823) that "either the United States, or the several States, had a clear title to all the lands within the boundary lines described in the treaty, subject only to the Indian right of occupancy, and that the exclusive power to extinguish that right, was vested in that government which might constitutionally exercise it."[21] Marshall also bolstered the U.S. claim to territory with a supporting account of the sociocultural contrast between colonists and indigenes. In Marshall's rendering, "The tribes of Indians inhabiting this country were fierce savages, whose occupation was war, and whose subsistence was drawn chiefly from the forest. To leave them in possession of their country, was to leave the country a wilderness; to govern them as a distinct people, was impossible, because they were as brave and high spirited as they were fierce." Marshall thus characterized the "frequent" wars and conflicts between colonists and indigenes as unavoidable until "European policy, numbers, and skill, prevailed."[22] Thus, as he submits, "As the white population advanced, that of the Indians necessarily receded."[23]

These constitutional decisions were highly influential, and they offered complex accounts that recast—whether deliberately or not—the initially hybrid conditions of founding in the terms of an oppositional dichotomy between "hunting and gathering" Indian nations and "agricultural" settlers.[24] As P. J. McHugh indicates, the "progressive" modern constitution banished such dependences from its claims, as did some of the stadial histories of eighteenth-century theorists who amended and eliminated the negotiated intercultural knowledges of colonists. "By the early mid-nineteenth century," McHugh explains, "British officials and practice regard the nature of Crown sovereignty in its (remaining) American possessions as thorough-going and exclusive. A more doctrinaire and absolutist approach superseded the essentially improvisatory ways of the old jurisdictionalism."[25] More to the point, as we have already seen, the constitutional dichotomy between the primitive "hunting and gathering" Indians and the modern "agricultural" colonists occludes the cross-cultural history of events on the ground. Nineteenth-century decisions imposed a regulated formality on overlapping and messy jurisdictions, as they also recast charters, constitutions, and treaties to be more uniform and orderly than they initially were. For instance, even *Worcester* v. *Georgia* (1832), which famously set the stage for Native American treaty rights, nonetheless relied on an imagined history in which treaty participants were perceived as coeval and representative.[26] Citing the examples of Maryland, Pennsylvania, and Georgia, among others, the court noted:

> Certain it is, that our history furnishes no example, from the first settlement of our country, of any attempt on the part of the crown to interfere with the internal affairs of the Indians, farther than to keep out the agents of foreign powers, who, as traders or otherwise, might seduce them into foreign alliances. The king purchased their lands when they were willing to sell, at a price they were willing to take; but never coerced a surrender of them. He also purchased their alliance and dependence by subsidies; but never intruded into the interior of their affairs, or interfered with their self government, so far as respected themselves only. . . . Such was the policy of Great Britain towards the Indian nations

inhabiting the territory from which she excluded all other Europeans; such her claims, and such her practical exposition of the charters she had granted: she considered them as nations capable of maintaining the relations of peace and war; of governing themselves, under her protection; and she made treaties with them, the obligation of which she acknowledged.[27]

What might it mean, then, to reconceptualize the colonial and pre-Revolutionary period as an era marked less by a triumphal march to modernity than by a persistent hybridity that emphasized regional particularity and variously mixed the ancient and the modern? This is a question pursued in Levy's account. For Levy, the contractarian tradition customarily associated with the modern constitution did not really take hold until the nineteenth century. Until that point, Levy explains, colonial forms of constitutionalism expressed much more continuity with the English tradition, particularly in its emphasis on the ancient constitution and common-law practice. As such, Levy argues that "it cannot be said that modern constitutionalism has no intellectual or in-practice room for the kinds of institutional complexity and protection of customary liberties that was evident in the old order, and that may again be called for to protect multiculturalism today."[28] The persistence of ancient, gothic, and other non-modern constitutional forms through the nineteenth century supports, for Levy, a normative point about the value of non-contractarian legal and political instruments, where more traditional forms of adjudication hold quite a bit of promise in dealing with group rights. Both Madison and Jefferson, according to Levy, hoped for Indians to adapt to agriculture, Christianity, and republican forms of government. However, Madison's account in the constitution of 1787 did not emphasize uniformity but, instead, according to Levy, "recognized the need for jurisdictional pluralism and institutional accommodation of cultural difference; it made no claim to dissolve whites and Indians into a common atomistic contract; it sought to protect Indians' prescriptive rights. The empire of uniformity, the systematic attempt to coercively assimilate Indians into the American social, economic, and political order and to deny the legal standing of tribes altogether was a late nineteenth-century development, not a late eighteenth-century one."[29]

I do agree with Levy that it is necessary to challenge the dominant narrative of modern constitutionalism, which unduly emphasizes uniformity and centralization of power. I am also sympathetic to the move he makes in resituating the emergence of modern constitutionalism in the nineteenth century. In this way, I also agree with Tully that modern constitutionalism does wield tremendous power in asserting conceptions of culture and custom that delegate indigenous peoples to a lower status. But I am more wary of according privilege to ancient constitutionalism and other non-contractarian forms.

What the example of the proprietary constitutions suggests is that there was a significant period of time in which hybrids of ancient and modern constitutionalism worked in the service of colonial interests. After all, non-contractarian elements, such as the ancient constitution and feudal law, which focused on diversity, complexity, and particularity, were often closely associated with forwarding colonial ambitions. While some accommodation between colonists and indigenes was possible because of features such as discretion, adaptation, and negotiation, it was also the case that accommodation did not prevent exploitation and coercion. For this reason, these features were not cures for the inequalities and violence produced by colonialism; nor is it clear that they necessarily hold promise as better tools to adjudicate group rights and cultural difference. In light of this past, the perspective that I endorse is one that looks to enlarge our focus to contend with forms of hybridity that are not normative ideals but indications of myriad and changing flows of power and privilege.

An excellent example of this is illustrated in Lauren Benton's comprehensive account of legal regimes.[30] Benton demonstrates that "legal regimes" emerged in the fifteenth century and sixteenth century across a diverse span that encompassed Africa, Europe, Asia, the Indies, and the Americas. These local regimes were neither uniform nor consistent with each other, but each did have a common basis in the mutual recognition of distinct spheres of jurisdictional authority and a shared interest in negotiating on-the-ground processes for exchange and interaction. As she argues, "Jurisdictional complexity, in fact, has been viewed by some scholars as the defining characteristic of Western law after the twelfth century. State sponsors of European overseas expansion were far more accustomed to ruling over subjects with multiple political or corporate group loyalties than to asserting unqualified claims to sovereignty."[31]

Distinctive in Benton's account is her illustration of the way hybridity can serve as a *critical concept* linking a wide range of temporal and geographical colonial orders throughout more than three centuries of European overseas expansion. These hybridities developed in the interplay between open-ended conflicts for jurisdiction and sovereignty; the contingency of power and influence on the ground; and ethnic, religious, and political complexity. As Benton notes, "The construction of the colonial state proceeded haltingly and in response to myriad conflicts over the definitions of difference, property, and moral authority."[32] Colonizing powers sought to limit the costs of judicial administration, and the jurisdictions established were "precise but inherently unstable and, therefore, subject to frequent revision."[33] In Benton's survey, these hybrid states were less the *precondition* for or necessary consequence of colonial rule than they were an object created and disputed by colonial cultures and legal structures:

> In India, the tensions between Company and Parliament influenced debates about the shape of the legal order. In South Africa, European authority was split between frontier colonists (largely Dutch descendents) and colonial administrators (both Afrikaner and British) who fought openly over the rights to control and discipline Africans. In French West Africa, local administrators interpreted the pragmatic imperatives of rule far differently from French-trained magistrates and Parisian colonial officials. And in Latin America, early jurisdictional conflicts centered around Church-state tensions built into imposed law. Later, the diverging interests of local magistrates and royal administrators, and the metropolitan focus on reform, shaped a divided judicial bureaucracy. Imperial-local divides were salient in each case and were sometimes compounded by other sources of factionalism among colonial elites, particularly diverging economic interests.[34]

Colonizers both relied on jurisdictional ambiguity and introduced it into colonial legal order. Moreover, the hybridity available in colonial contexts, in Benton's account, often were new opportunities for special classes of colonists and indigenes, such as litigants, governors, and other elites, to amass local power and to use plurality on the ground to their benefit. What comes to be prominent in her assessment is an alternative narrative of state development. Benton argues, through exhaustive case study, that "strong" colonial states in the nineteenth century did not develop because of colonial power and law systematically imposed on subordinate territories or because the "weak" legal regimes were subsequently taken over.

Colonial states were created "through a series of conflicts over the nature and relation of its subjects," not by imposition or planned design.[35] Hybridity in this way can exemplify both the overt and the subtle dimensions of the colonial period, and, as I will argue, it continues to linger at the heart of contemporary politics.

Negotiation and Adjudication

The "grip" of what has become our "hegemonal account"—to invoke the terms of Quentin Skinner—makes disruptions to triumphal narratives more than mere oddities in our collective history.[36] As Skinner points out, the hegemonal account can all too easily set the terms of interpretation for the events being evaluated. This is particularly troubling for critics who seek to challenge the triumphal narrative but get caught up in its narrative grip. What is at stake in challenging the "hegemonal account" is not simply an adjustment to chronology, but a shift in our understanding of how tradition and modernity are constituted, and such work can play a critical role in reorienting our awareness of the complexity of intercultural relations on the ground.

Still, while the task of recuperating hybridity allows us to elucidate the complicated political and cultural terrain of the past, it does not necessarily resolve into a project of rehabilitation, where, for example, reconstructing past hybrid conditions can remedy past grievances or claims. The account that I have offered can help to spur new thinking about the nature of colonial power and the ways indigenous and other knowledges were adapted and appropriated by colonists. But it also makes evident that these hybrid political and cultural structures were messy and difficult not only to characterize but also to respond to. Can current legal and political frameworks be revised to eliminate the more partisan, instrumental elements of hybridity? What would this entail? changes to the distribution of power on the ground, or alterations to the institutions, processes, and components of negotiation and adjudication?

An examination of some of the current examples of treaty negotiations and other alternative constitutional forms can help to clarify these questions, and relevant examples can be seen in virtually all of the British colonial, decolonized, and postcolonial territories. One of the most notable is the landmark Australian case *Mabo v. Queensland* (1992), in which, as Jeremy Webber explains, "the High Court broke with Australia's long his-

tory of denying indigenous title and recognised indigenous title's continued existence with Australian law."[37] More specifically, as Andrew Fitzmaurice has clarified, "It is often stated that the *Mabo* judgment rejected
the doctrine of terra nullius. In fact, the judgment was consistent with
a five-hundred-year tradition of employing natural law—and in this instance, the idea of *terra nullius*—to consider the justice of colonization."[38]

In this way, *Mabo* is an exceedingly tricky case. When the *Mabo* decision rejected terra nullius and supported the common-law conception of
native title, it did so by relying on an ahistorical conception of terra nullius. As Fitzmaurice and others, such as David Ritter and Bain Attwood,
have noted, terra nullius was not used originally in the eighteenth century and nineteenth century to justify the dispossession of Australian
Aborigines. Instead, as Attwood clarifies, "While the Australian colonies
were indeed judicially classified as 'desert and uncultivated' and Aboriginal people were apparently treated as having no common law right to
their traditional lands, there was no judicial decision that created a nexus
between the former legal proposition and the latter historical fact. That
is, no early Australian or English case ever stated that because Australia was '*terra nullius*' or 'desert and uncultivated,' Aboriginal people possessed no common law right to their tribal lands."[39] But what *Mabo* did, as
Fitzmaurice explains, was offer an argument that was "consistent with the
negative use of the natural law tradition and its instruments *ferae bestiae*,
res nullius and, to a lesser degree, *territorium nullius* and terra nullius, to
defend the rights of indigenous peoples." More simply, "The judges were
not rejecting terra nullius so much as reviving it for a longstanding critique of colonization."[40]

The *Mabo* decision, in which the court sought to affirm indigenous
sovereignty in the eighteenth century by rejecting the legal concept terra
nullius, which itself was created not in the eighteenth century but from
various nineteenth-century contexts, reflects the complex strains of hybridity and constitutionalism. While terra nullius can be used powerfully
as a legal tool that demonstrates the ideological and juridical colonial
mindset that looked to dispossess Aborigines, its ahistorical application in
Mabo does raise a number of pressing issues. What complex interplay of
events constituted the original English occupation of the Australian territories in the eighteenth century? Is the judicial framework that now looks
to provide a remedy to past colonial crimes sufficient? As Attwood has

noted, the legal, political, economic, and social operations of colonization in Australia were much more varied and full of "complex messiness" than the argument of terra nullius would suggest.[41] Although many aspects of "the myth of *terra nullius*" have "a ring of truth about [them]," as Attwood notes, the *Mabo* decision, particularly as it was narrated by popular historians such as Henry Reynolds, hides another highly pertinent truth: "Indigenous people's rights to land in Australia were denied because this is the nature of colonialism. It dispossesses indigenous people of their land and uses its own law to try to disguise the violence of this. This is the law of the land in colonial societies. In the case of Australia this was all the more so because there was little by way of countervailing forces to prevent the colonizers seizing what was not theirs."[42]

Moreover, relying on the concept of terra nullius, which retrospectively quiets messiness and hybridity, has had some significant blowback for aboriginal groups and individuals in Australia. In particular, as Michael Brown has noted, *Mabo* created a problematic conception of aboriginal occupation that relied on a rigid account of identity that required the "traditional" (that is, indigenous) owners to demonstrate their ongoing connection to the land. As Brown explains, while the *Mabo* decision validated elements of indigenous title and sovereignty in overturning Queensland's extinguishing of all native land titles, it did not resolve but merely highlighted the more open-ended question of how "traditional" indigenous and culture would be determined.[43] The standard for identity used by *Mabo* tended to rely on traditional practice and clan and community affiliations for aboriginal status, potentially putting urban and "non-traditional" Aborigines at a loss. Just as problematically, as a consequence of *Mabo*, issues of identity and authenticity increasingly became matters to be determined by the law and legal institutions—leading the way, as Brown comments, to "unexplored legal paths, some of which hint at troubling possibilities."[44]

The legacy of hybridity serves as a reminder that treaties, constitutions, charters, and other constitutional arrangements mediate economic, social, and institutional forces in complex—and not easily resolvable—ways. This situation is further highlighted by the fact that, as Jeremy Webber notes, in "indigenous societies, there tends not to be the same sharp differentiation between law and other forms of social normativity; there may not be the same emphasis on the posited quality of law, there may be less emphasis on rules, and of course there may be no specialized agencies for the enforcement of law."[45] Thus, as Webber further contends, "The simple enforcement by the courts of interests held under indigenous law would produce detrimental results: it would displace indigenous methods of social ordering, freeze the development of indigenous law, and place the administration of that law in the hands of non-indigenous tribunals."[46]

The limits of cross-cultural mediation are not limited to colonial constitutional structures. Even in treaty agreements, such dilemmas arise, as can be seen in one of the most striking modern examples of treaty debate: the Waitangi Tribunal in New Zealand. Māori tribes and the British Crown signed the Treaty of Waitangi in 1840, but Māori and English versions of the treaty gave the parties different expectations about the extent of British sovereignty and land possession. In 1975, after bitter conflicts in the nineteenth century between the Crown and the Māori and a long period in which the dual nature of the treaty was ignored, the Waitangi Tribunal was established by statute to research Māori claims and to make recommendations to the government for adjudication.

The creation of the tribunal, as Giselle Byrnes deftly explains, helped to galvanize Māori *rangatiratanga* (autonomy) movements in the twentieth century. It also pushed the Crown to accommodate Māori political, cultural, and territorial claims.[47] At the same time, Byrnes finds that the tribunal and its operations of historical inquiry exposed the tensions of adjudicating treaty relations. The tribunal encountered numerous difficulties in determining the historicity of the treaty document and in portraying the timelessness of Māori and Crown treaty principles. More important, the tribunal struggled to adequately characterize Māori and Crown interests. In Byrnes's account, the tribunal depicted Māori agents as "active victims" in an attempt to signal both past colonial wrongs and Māori agency. According to Byrnes, descriptions of Māori, Crown, and settlers were often rough and undifferentiated, and these characterizations were further complicated by the tribunal's status as a statutory body beholden to the Crown. The tribunal, initially created to head off confrontations over Māori claims, had only an advisory role; the Crown had the ultimate power of settlement.[48] The tribunal debates, Byrnes ultimately found, represent the possibilities *and* the limitations of historical inquiry in redressing past grievance and creating new possibilities for just treaty partnerships. Just as significant, the institutions that were charged with facilitating and negotiating new treaty relations often were also implicated in the colonial structures of power that were being addressed.[49]

These dilemmas of power and privilege, of course, are not exclusive to constitutional or treaty relations. Many cross-cultural projects (such as environmental agreements, industrial ventures, and land claims) that involve the state/Crown, indigenous peoples, and other bodies such as nongovernmental organizations face similar predicaments, and the remedies to such situations are far from clear. Brown, for instance, is wary of the recent turn to protect indigenous culture with formal legal measures, such as intellectual-property law, copyright law, and United Nations Total Heritage Protection statutes. Although these legal instruments offer the promise of defined enforcement, they also risk imposing more rigid, procedural norms on the complex, animated, and elusive qualities of a lived culture.[50] "Such approaches," Brown writes, "have a disturbing tendency to reshape the world in unforeseen and harmful ways . . . to foster bureaucratized and lifeless cultures that operate by a proprietary logic perilously close to that of the corporations they seek to resist."[51]

In the United States, these dilemmas can be seen in the complex negotiations between state, tribe, federal, and business interests—examples that strongly resonate with the economic and political ambitions of the proprietary colonies. Consider, for example, the current disputes over the restoration of more than 100,000 acres of Oneida land. The U.S. Supreme Court decided in 1974 to sustain the Oneidas' position that their lands had been transferred by illegitimate treaties that lacked approval by federal "Non-Intercourse Acts."[52] While this decision facilitated a surge of territorial and economic development for the New York Oneidas, it also spurred a set of complicated controversies about Oneidas' use and governance of lands. Most notably, the New York Oneida created Turning Stone Casino outside Syracuse, New York, which became the fifth most popular tourist attraction in the state. According to Bruce Johansen, the casino has created 1,900 jobs and spurred a number of secondary businesses, such as a 285 room luxury hotel and a textile-printing facility. "By 1997," according to Johansen, "the casino and other Oneida businesses were employing 2,600 people, making the Oneida Nation the second largest employer in central New York."[53] Profits from the casino and related industries also had a considerable effect on social conditions among the New York Oneida.

Profits helped fund a council house, a health-services center, a cultural and recreation center, scholarship programs, job training, and educational and elder-care services. Thus, many within New York and Oneida territory saw the return of Oneida lands as a boon, not only because it boosted the local economy, but also because it ostensibly restored and affirmed the validity of past agreements between states and tribes. Yet more than a few indigenous parties saw the decision as a coercive reinforcement of state, national, and business interests.

In particular, by the late 1990s the New York Oneida were involved in a variety of entangled conflicts. A number of vocal dissidents within the New York Oneida Nation, including Maisie Shenandoah, a Wolf Clan mother, and Rick Hill Sr., a Tuscarora leader, challenged the nation's new emphasis on a gaming economy and focused their criticism on the behavior of Ray Halbritter, who had taken on leadership roles in the nation and in the Turning Stone casino. Halbritter in particular was accused of using his power in the Men's Council to force dissident members from their homes, withhold federal stipends, and organize with state and federal police to disenfranchise oppositional voices.

In addition to the internal conflict, the New York Oneida were being challenged by Oneida in Wisconsin and Ontario for access and rights to land.[54] In the 1990s, about 270,000 acres in and around Madison and Oneida counties in New York still needed to be returned, according to the Supreme Court decision. By 2000, Governor George Pataki, Halbritter, and a number of local officials had announced a proposed settlement of the long-stalled land claim. Notable by their absence at the announcement were representatives of roughly twenty thousand Oneidas living in Wisconsin and Canada.[55] As Johansen explains, "The proposed agreement [which allowed New York Oneida to reacquire 35,000 acres of reservation land] contained a major political problem: It excluded from land claims the Oneidas now residing in Wisconsin and Canada, groups much larger in number than the New York Oneidas. The Oneidas represented by Halbritter represented less than 5 percent of those who asserted rights in the land claim. While the New York Oneidas asserted a membership of about 1,000 (not counting expelled dissidents), the Oneidas of the Thames, in Ontario, have roughly 5,000 enrolled members, and the Wisconsin Oneidas have 15,000 members. Governor Pataki, in other words, was attempting to settle a 200-year old claim with the consent of roughly

5 percent of the aggrieved parties."[56] Similar to *Mabo* in Australia and the Waitangi Tribunal in New Zealand, the Oneida conflict illustrates the power of state and national institutions, such as the judiciary, to make determinations about proper title. In different ways, these decisions illustrate the possibilities of new forms of negotiation and adjudication as they also reveal the attendant risks of excluding and marginalizing various indigenous and non-indigenous actors. These processes are further complicated by the ways in which economic incentive and political influence combine to lend strength and putative legitimacy to some voices over others.

My review of examples in Australia, New Zealand, and the United States are not meant as criticism of treaties, court decisions, or alternative mediation processes. They are instead intended as a call to cultivate critical attention to both past and current forms of hybrid complexity. Often the ambitions and agendas that structured past treaties and hybrid arrangements find themselves recovered and reconfigured in altogether different political, economic, and cultural contexts. Hybridity—when conceived critically—encourages consideration of colonial and postcolonial relations that are not structured only in terms of hierarchical constructions of ethnic/cultural difference or hegemonic conceptions of colonial rule. Hybridity refocuses attention on elements of constitutionalism, law, and governance that are *in process* as it heightens the attention that we give to ideological aspiration and practical affect.

Particularly in light of the vexed historicity of hybrid constitutionalism, increased scrutiny of proposals and remedies such as treaties, power-sharing agreements, and new covenants and charters seems warranted. Just as pertinent, attention to hybridity can help explain why many have taken stances of contention to reformed constitutional arrangements. As Taiaiake Alfred argues, when the Crown or the nation-state and indigenous nations are situated in positions of radical inequity, what may superficially appear as a "balanced" treaty or constitutional arrangement can be belied by the institutional, economic, and political forces of the Crown or nation-state. As a result, indigenous interests can be easily co-opted by the mechanisms of treaty making, where even tribal leaders find their interests and ambitions acquiescent "to the state's agenda."[57] For instance, in a 2002 case in British Columbia, native leaders sought to bar native treaties from being brought to a public referendum that would have permitted more than four million residents of the province to mail in their votes on native issues. The concerns ranged from whether hunting and fishing on Crown land should be maintained for all residents to whether aboriginal self-government should have the characteristics of municipal government. Local chiefs of bands such as the Hupacasath in Port Alberni protested that the referendum would diminish aboriginal rights, because while in principle public input was desirable, the practical effect of the public's sizeable influence made it impossible for native leaders to fully discuss and deliberate highly contentious issues.[58]

Moreover, it is important to recognize that threats to treaty negotiation do not just come from non-native participants. In addition to external challenges, struggles *within* indigenous tribes can undermine leadership and representation, as in the Oneida case. Thus, at times, as Alfred maintains, a stance of "contention" may be more appropriate for indigenous nations, a "non-cooperative, non-participatory position vis-à-vis the state, its actors, and its policies."[59]

Ultimately, my focus on hybridity has been intended as a way to mark the shifting and at times contradictory states of proprietary colonial governance and discourse. While such work can complement and help revise wider-ranging accounts of colonization and constitutionalism, there is also an essential limitation to the situated, contextual approach that I have pursued, a point equally demonstrated in the specific subject of this work. Along these lines, I do not argue that situated knowledge is a panacea for the deep conflicts of power and privilege between peoples on deeply contested land. The challenges for us today are multiple. Strengthening contemporary treaty and alternative constitutional arrangements will likely require the cultivation of *both* skepticism and responsiveness to modalities of power and privilege. This in many ways is a call for a form of agonism in which struggle is persistent, and energy and attentiveness are needed to remain responsive. But this agonism is also specifically shaped by the legacy of colonialism, where any active engagement is shadowed by self-conscious acknowledgment that action can be spurred by and can engender ambition, instrumentality, and even co-optation. The cultivation of inclusive and sustainable forms of hybrid adjudication thus will need not simply further redefinition and expansion of the terms of interaction, but also a vigilant attention to current and future relations of exclusion, conflict, and opportunism.

Abbreviations

Archives Md	*Archives of Maryland*, ed. William Hand Browne et al (Baltimore: Maryland Historical Society, 1883–).
Assembly Proceedings	*Proceedings and Acts of the General Assembly, 1637–1747*, vol. 1 (Baltimore: Maryland Historical Society, 1883–).
BPRO	British Public Records Office, London.
CSCHS	*Collections of the South Carolina Historical Society*, ed. Langdon Cheves, vol. 5, rev. ed. (2000 [1897–]).
Narratives Ca	*Narratives of Early Carolina, 1650–1708*, ed. Alexander S. Salley Jr. (New York: Charles Scribner's Sons, 1911).
Narratives Md	*Narratives of Early Maryland, 1633–1684*, ed. Clayton Colman Hall (New York: Charles Scribner's Sons, 1910).

1. Hybrid Constitutionalisms

Epigraphs: Foucault, *Language, Counter-Memory, Practice*, 215; Burke and Burke, *An Account of the European Settlement in America*, 2: 288–89.

1. Bilder, "English Settlement and Local Governance," 78–79.
2. Tomlins, "The Legal Cartography of Colonization, the Legal Polyphony of Settlement," 338. See also Tomlins's argument about the polyphony of English charters in idem, *In a Wilderness of Tigers*; idem, *The Legal Cartography of Colonization*.
3. For edited collections of colonial charters, patents, and constitutions, see Thorpe, *The Federal and State Constitutions*; Lucas, *Charters of the Old English Colonies in America*. See also the seminal work of Andrews, *The Colonial Period of American History*, and, more recently, Thornton, "The Palatinate of Durham and the Maryland Charter," and Palumbo, "The Boundaries of Empire," on the development of palatine jurisdiction in the seventeenth-century English Atlantic empire.
4. Bilder, "English Settlement and Local Governance," 64–65; emphasis added.
5. Bagehot, *The English Constitution*, 9.
6. Konig, "Regionalism in Early American Law," 149.

7. Ibid., 150.

8. Arendt, *The Human Condition*, 63–64.

9. See, for example, Ivison, *Postcolonial Liberalism*; Young, *Inclusion and Democracy*, esp. 236–75; Armitage, *The Ideological Origins of the British Empire*; Parekh, *Rethinking Multiculturalism*, 185–90; Ivison et al., *Political Theory and the Rights of Indigenous Peoples*; Tully, *Strange Multiplicity*; Arneil, *John Locke and America*.

10. Parekh, "Liberalism and Colonialism," 84.

11. Young, "Hybrid Democracy," 240, 246–47.

12. The influence of Tully's argument is difficult to overestimate. Cited not only in contemporary work concerned with colonialism in both its specific and general nature, Tully's work has become a touchstone for a wide variety of scholarship dealing with multiculturalism, constitutionalism, and liberal and democratic deliberation. In addition to the works cited earlier, see, for pertinent examples, Hendrix, "Moral Error, Power, and Insult"; McHugh, *Aboriginal Societies and the Common Law*; Barry, *Culture and Equality*, 26; Honig, *Democracy and the Foreigner*, 123–24; Deveaux, *Cultural Pluralism and the Dilemmas of Justice*, 13–14, 34; Alfred, *Peace, Power, Righteousness*, 63; Walzer, *On Toleration*, 116; Hindess, "Divide and Rule"; Mills, *The Racial Contract*, 149; Gutmann, *Multiculturalism and "The Politics of Recognition,"* 26–28. My point is not that Tully's argument is adopted uniformly but that it serves as one of the essential elements of the theoretical framework in which current arguments about modern constitutionalism are established.

13. Tully, *Strange Multiplicity*, esp. 1–29, 58–98.

14. Ibid., 58.

15. Ibid., 62–70.

16. Ibid., 79–80.

17. Ibid., 64.

18. Ibid., 78.

19. The Maryland charter, for example, states, "Laws aforesaid be consonant to Reason, and be not repugnant or contrary, but (so far as conveniently may be) agreeable to the Laws, Statutes, Customs, and Rights of this Our Kingdom of England": *Charters*, 1679–80, sec. VII.

20. Pocock, *The Ancient Constitution and the Feudal Law*, 21–29, 255–305. See also Peltonen, *Classical Humanism and Republicanism in English Political Thought*.

21. In a sense, then, the charter revived a version of what Charles McIlwain described as the medieval tension between *gubernaculum* and *jurisdictio*, a tension left unresolved by the charter's lack of specification. In addition, given distance and new settlement, the charter's relation of "agreeableness" to the kingdom of England was no simple thing to measure. Variation in judges and proprietors might render both judgment and statute unstable and open to question: McIlwain, *Constitutionalism*, 1–40, 123–46; Cross and Hall, *The English Legal System*, 5–10; Tubbs, *The Common Law Mind*, 179–90; Klein, "The Ancient

Constitution Revisited"; Sommerville, "The Ancient Constitution Reassessed"; Baldwin, *Bouvier's Law Dictionary*, 196–97, 1129–30.

22. Bilder, *The Transatlantic Constitution*, a study of colonial Rhode Island, is especially adept at illustrating how "repugnancy" formed a limit for how far colonial law could diverge from English tradition, allowing colonial legislators to adapt to local circumstances while drawing on English tradition.

23. Hulsebosch, *Constituting Empire*, 8.

24. Hont, *Jealousy of Trade*, 155.

25. Greene, *Negotiated Authorities*, 25–26.

26. Rousseau, *The Social Contract*, 16.

27. Locke, *Two Treatises of Government*, 330–33. After all, as Locke notes, "It is not every compact that puts an end to the state of nature between men, but only this one of agreeing together mutually to enter into one community, and make one body politic; other promises and compacts men may make one with another, and yet still be in the state of nature."

28. Pocock, *The Machiavellian Moment*. See also Appleby, *Liberalism and Republicanism in the Historical Imagination*. Houston, *Algernon Sidney and the Republican Heritage in England and America*, largely focuses on the Revolutionary period in America but contains a nuanced account of the period's various republicanisms.

29. On elements of republican thought, see also Peltonen, *Classical Humanism and Republicanism in English Political Thought*, 2–18; Collinson, "De Republica Anglorum"; idem, "Afterword"; Goldie, "The Unacknowledged Republic"; Skinner, *Visions of Politics*.

30. Fitzmaurice, *Humanism and America*, 27.

31. Hall, "The Chesapeake in the Seventeenth Century," 58–59. Patricia Seed makes a similar point in *Ceremonies of Possession in Europe's Conquest of the New World*.

32. Anderson, *Imagined Communities*, 21. But, as Anderson notes, "In Protestant North America printing scarcely existed at all in that century. In the course of the eighteenth, however, a virtual revolution took place. Between 1691 and 1820, no less than 2,120 'newspapers' were published, of which 461 lasted more than ten years": ibid., 61.

33. Ibid., 24.

34. Ibid., 35.

35. Axtell, *The European and the Indian*, 250. See also Nash, *Red, White, and Black*; Breen, "Creative Adaptations," 195–232; Jennings, *The Invasion of America*, 32–104.

36. *Oxford English Dictionary*, online ed., Oxford University Press, 2000, available at http://www.oed.com (accessed May 20, 2009). The online edition contains the text of the second edition (1989), along with the additions and entries from the third edition (1993–97).

37. Notably, Hobbes, *Leviathan*, book II, chap. 31, 183: "In the first sense the labour

bestowed on the earth is called *Culture*, and the education of children, a *Culture* of their mindes. In the second sense, where mens wills are to be wrought to our purpose, not by Force, but by Compleasance, it signifieth as much as Courting." Multiple in its period meanings, the term suggested a concatenation of growth, training, and inducement.

38. Ibid. See also, Thucydides, *The History of the Peloponnesian War*, 5.

39. Derrida, *Negotiations*, 12. Derrida's reflections on negotiation are directed largely at deconstructive theory's relationship to morality. In an adapted form, his invocation of the "impurity" of negotiation reverberates with considerations of cultural negotiation's colonial historicity.

40. Letter from Capt. Croghan to Col. Henry Bouquet, 1763, in Stevens et al., *The Papers of Col. Henry Bouquet*, series 21649, 80–82.

41. For more contemporary studies, see Merritt, *At the Crossroads*; Kupperman, *Indians and English*; Calloway, *New Worlds for All*; White, *The Middle Ground*.

42. For a wider view of the work relating to the recovery of native experience, see Axtell, "The Ethnohistory of Early America," 110–14. See also idem, *The Invasion Within*; Gray, *New World Babel*; Murray, *Forked Tongues*; Merritt, *At the Crossroads*; Kupperman, *Indians and English*; Calloway, *New Worlds for All*; White, *The Middle Ground*; Chaplin, *Subject Matter*, 24–26.

43. On this issue of authenticity, see also Clifford, *The Predicament of Culture*; Spivak, *A Critique of Postcolonial Reason*.

44. See esp. Bhabha, "Signs Taken for Wonder," 114; idem, "Of Mimicry and Man," 125–33.

45. Skinner, *Liberty before Liberalism*, 116.

46. Ibid.

47. See Pocock, "The Concept of a Language and the *Métier d'Historien*," 21–25. See also idem, "Virtues, Rights, and Manners," 37–50.

48. Skinner, "Meaning and Understanding in the History of Ideas."

49. Foucault, *Language, Counter-Memory, Practice*, 208.

50. Fitzmaurice, "American Corruption," 217–32. See also idem, *Humanism and America*; idem, "The Civic Solution to the Crisis of English Colonization"; idem, "Classical Rhetoric and the Promotion of the New World"; Peltonen, *Classical Humanism and Republicanism in English Political Thought*; Armitage, *The Ideological Origins of the British Empire*; idem, "The Cromwellian Protectorate and the Languages of Empire"; Brett, "The Development of the Idea of Citizens' Rights"; Skinner, *Reason and Rhetoric in the Philosophy of Hobbes*; idem, *The Foundations of Modern Political Thought*.

51. Young, "Hybrid Democracy," 239–40.

52. Connolly, "The Liberal Image of the Nation," 183–98.

53. Tully, *Strange Multiplicity*, 37.

54. Ibid., 211.

2. Colonial Founding in Maryland

Epigraphs: Hobbes, *Leviathan*, 146; de Tocqueville, *Democracy in America*, pt. I, 54–55.

1. In this chapter and in pertinent sections of the book, I refer to the edition of the charter printed in Thorpe, *The Federal and State Constitutions*, 3:1677–1686, as *Charter*, with references to page numbers and sections. The charter was also printed in 1635 in the promotional tract *A Relation of Maryland*, A2-D.
2. *Charter*, 1677–78, sec. II.
3. Ibid.
4. For background, see Rountree and Davidson, *Eastern Shore Indians of Virginia and Maryland*; Quinn, *Early Maryland in a Wider World*, esp. Jennings, "Indians and Frontiers in Seventeenth-Century Maryland"; Ferguson, *Moyaone and the Piscataway Indians*.
5. On the wide networks of settlers prior to Maryland's settlement, see Jennings, "Indians and Frontiers in Seventeenth-Century Maryland."
6. David B. Quinn, "Introduction," in idem, *Early Maryland in a Wider World*, 22–27; Scharf, *History of Maryland from Earliest Times to the Present Day*, 39–40. See also Bergmann, "Being the Other."
7. See *Oxford English Dictionary*, online ed., http://www.oed.com (accessed May 20, 2009).
8. Hobbes, *Leviathan*, 146. On definitions of the charter, see also Baldwin, *Bouvier's Law Dictionary*, 165.
9. *Charter*, 1677–78, sec. II.
10. Ibid., secs. II–III.
11. On the senior Lord Calvert and his colonial experiences, including the Avalon settlement, see esp. Jordan, *Foundations of Representative Government in Maryland*, 1–7; Menard and Carr, "The Lords Baltimore and the Colonization of Maryland"; Krugler, "Our Trusty and Well Beloved Councillor." On the Avalon colony particularly, see Coakley, "George Calvert and Newfoundland."
12. Quinn, "Introduction," in idem, *Early Maryland in a Wider World*, 22–27; Scharf, *History of Maryland from Earliest Times to the Present Day*, 39–40.
13. Hoffer, *Law and People in Colonial America*, 9–15.
14. *Charter*, sec. III. On the charter's chorographic elements, see Tomlins, "The Legal Cartography of Colonization, the Legal Polyphony of Settlement," 322; Hadfield, *Amazons, Savages, and Machiavels*; Helgerson, "The Land Speaks."
15. *A Relation of Maryland*, F2.
16. Quinn, "Introduction," in idem, *Early Maryland in a Wider World*, 22–27.
17. Jordan, *Foundations of Representative Government in Maryland*, 2.
18. Ibid., 1.
19. Quoted ibid., 2. For the original source, see Pocock, *The Machiavellian Moment*, 419–21.
20. Jordan, *Foundations of Representative Government in Maryland*, 2.

21. *Charter*, 1678–79, sec. IV; emphasis added.

22. The term "palatinate" arises from the Latin *palatinus*, associated with the imperial palace or designating the specially privileged; the *palatine* is the ruler of a palatinate. "Palatine" can also serve as an adjective. The term, borrowed from Germany, came into use in England in the fourteenth century. In the English context, a palatinate—or county palatine—was an area whose lord, although a subject and feudal tenant-in-chief of the king, possessed quasi-regal jurisdiction. Four English palatinates were created after the Norman Conquest, mainly for military reasons: Cheshire and Shropshire on the Welsh border; Durham to the north; and Kent. While Shropshire and Kent were soon suppressed after the rebellions of their earls, Durham was unique in that its lords were ecclesiastics, the bishops of Durham, and they did not lose their palatine jurisdiction until 1836. For background on the palatinate, see Gaillard, *The County Palatine of Durham*, 106–55. While contemporary historical accounts do mention the palatine terms of the Maryland charter, they generally do not do so in detail; nor do they draw out the political and legal impact of the charter. By contrast, late-nineteenth-century and early-twentieth-century historians paid significant attention to the palatine terms of the charter, particularly Andrews, *The Colonial Period of American History*. Those accounts, however, have favored progressive accounts of English colonialism, excluding any substantive account of cultural diversity or of colonist–indigene or intra- and inter-colonial conflict: see Andrews, *The Colonial Period of American History*, 2:98–213; Mereness, *Maryland as a Proprietary Province*, 6–11; Lippincott, *Maryland as a Palatinate*, 9–12. Recent studies include Thornton, "The Palatinate of Durham and the Maryland Charter," and Palumbo, "The Boundaries of Empire."

23. Pagden, "Law, Colonization, Legitimation, and the European Background," 10.

24. Krugler, "Our Trusty and Well Beloved Councillor." On the English colonization of Ireland, see Andrews et al., *The Westward Enterprise*.

25. Jordan, *Foundations of Representative Government in Maryland*, 1.

26. *Charter*, 1679, sec. VI.

27. The quote is from Tomlins, "The Legal Cartography of Colonization, the Legal Polyphony of Settlement," 327.

28. Jordan, *Foundations of Representative Government in Maryland*, 3. According to Jordan, "An assembly had gathered annually during the fourteenth century in Durham but sat without extensive legislative powers and possessed only limited control over taxation. Although barons and freemen had a voice in the government, the powerful bishop substantially circumscribed their role."

29. See Lapsley, *The County Palatine of Durham*, 106–55.

30. From Hall, *Narratives of Early Maryland*, 174.

31. *Charter*, 1680–81, sec. VIII.

32. Ibid., 1681, sec. IX.

33. Ibid., 1682, sec. XII. See also Jameson, *Privateering and Piracy in the Colonial Period.*

34. *Charter*, 1681, secs. IX, XII.

35. Ibid., 1679–80, sec. VII; emphasis added.

36. Ibid.

37. Ibid., 1680–81, sec. VIII.

38. See Thorpe, *The Federal and State Constitutions*, 69–76, 3810–12.

39. *Charter*, 1679–80, sec. VII.

40. Jordan, *Foundations of Representative Government in Maryland*, 2–3.

41. *Charters*, 1679–80, sec. VII.

42. See *Oxford English Dictionary*, online ed., http://www.oed.com (accessed May 20, 2009). Both Skinner and Peltonen discuss discretion and its sibling concepts, negotiation, and prudence in Peltonen, *Classical Humanism and Republicanism in English Political Thought*, 21–34, 63–64, 109; Skinner, *The Foundations of Modern Political Thought*, 44–45, 55–64, 80, 108, 217–19. Hoffer, *Law and People in Colonial America*, 8–10, also notes that William Lambarde's manual discusses discretion as a faculty to be used in keeping the peace, admitting suspects to bond, hearing evidence on local disputes, and ordering compliance with the myriad regulatory ordinances passed each year by Parliament.

43. *Charter*, 1679–81, secs. VII–VIII.

44. On the diversity of English law, see Sharpe, "The People and the Law"; Harrison, "Manor Courts and the Governance of Tudor England." On the relationship between colonial law and English law, see Hoffer, *Law and People in Colonial America*; Brown, "British Statutes in the Emergent Nations of North America: 1606–1949"; Hulsebosch, *Constituting Empire*, 29–32.

45. Konig, "Regionalism in Early American Law," 149.

46. Ibid., 150.

47. See Thorpe, *The Federal and State Constitutions*. The Massachusetts charter of 1620, which was revoked for another version in 1629, emphasized, "So always as the same be not contrary" and "as near as conveniently may be, agreeable." Robert Heath's charter of 1629 to the territory that was eventually included in the Carolina claim possessed similar phrasing.

48. See Bilder, *The Transatlantic Constitution*, 15–72; idem, "English Settlement and Local Governance."

49. Idem, "English Settlement and Local Governance," 78–79, although, as Bilder notes, "Initial proprietor ascendancy was eroded by the growth in the assembly's lawmaking authority and the Crown's desire for direct governance. Faced with these dual challenges, almost everywhere the proprietor's authority collapsed. Two proprietaries, Maryland and Pennsylvania, survived at least in name because of the intense commitment of their founding families, but the proprietors *per se* came to hold little real authority."

50. *Charter*, 1679–81, secs. VII, VIII.

51. Ibid.

52. See Ross, "Legal Communications and Imperial Governance," 105. As Ross explains, "Geographic distance and slow, irregular communications encouraged the autonomy and interpretative leeway of local elites at the expense of their nominal superiors. Opportunities to organize colonial law and politics in ways that differed meaningfully from seventeenth-century England abounded. The result was far more variety among the early legal orders of New England, New York, and Carolina, than, say, among those of Devon, Sussex, and York."

53. de Certeau, *The Practice of Everyday Life*, 115–31.

54. Bilder, "English Settlement and Local Governance," 68.

55. *Instructions*, in *Narratives Md*, 16. In this chapter, numbers in parentheses refer to page numbers in the *Instructions*, 11–23.

56. Taylor, *American Colonies*, 137. Virginia and Maryland absorbed thousands of poor laborers considered redundant and dangerous in England, and in practice the distant Crown (for Virginia) or the Lord Proprietor (for Maryland) had to share power with the wealthiest and most ambitious colonists. They refused to pay taxes unless authorized by their own elected representatives in a colonial assembly.

57. All citations in the paragraph are from "Letter from Lord Baltimore, Cecil Calvert, to Thomas Wentworth, Earl of Stafford," January 10, 1634, in Neill, *The Founders of Maryland*, 60–63.

58. Ibid.

59. Noted in Father Andrew White, *A Briefe Relation in Maryland* (1634), in *Narratives Md*, 34–37. In secondary accounts: Brugger et al., *Maryland: A Middle Temperament*, 6; Andrews, *The Founding of Maryland*, 55; Treacy, *Old Catholic Maryland and Its Early Jesuit Missionaries*, 2–14.

60. My reference to Aristotle is drawn from van Gelderen and Skinner, *Republicanism*, 22–23.

61. See Machiavelli, *The Prince and the Discourses*, which adapts Aristotle's dictum in *The Politics* with his discussion of the prince's discretion. "It is still more prudent on your part to adhere to one; for you go to the ruin of one with the help of him who ought to save him if he were wise, and if he conquers he rests at your discretion, and it is impossible that he should not conquer with your help. And here it should be noted that a prince ought never to make common cause with one more powerful than himself to injure another, unless necessity forces him to it, as before said; for if he wins you rest in his power, and princes must avoid as much as possible being under the will and pleasure of others": ibid., 84.

62. Amory and Hall, *The Colonial Book in the Atlantic World*, 59.

63. This feature is noted in White, *A Briefe Relation in Maryland*, in *Narratives Md*, 40–42.

64. Seed, "Taking Possession and Reading Texts," 183–209.

65. *A Relation in Maryland*, in *Narratives Md*, 72. Although to be sure, Maryland settlers encountered various Patomecke and Piscataway tribes, including "kings" and "emperors" as well as interpreters, and while many of these indigenes purportedly sought refuge with the Maryland colonists, others expressed fear and intimidation. Still, both the *Instructions* and White's account emphasize the assistance of the indigenes to colonists in helping "us in fishing, fouling, hunting, or what we please." And both accounts reiterated a crude view where indigenes, White commented, "excel in smell and taste, and have far sharper sight than we": White, *A Briefe Relation in Maryland*, in *Narratives Md*, 40–42, 44.

66. Fitzmaurice, *Humanism and America*, esp. 187.

67. Calloway, *New Worlds for All*, 1–23.

68. White, *A Briefe Relation in Maryland*, in *Narratives Md*, 44.

69. Rountree and Davidson, *Eastern Shore Indians of Virginia and Maryland*, 85.

70. *A Relation in Maryland*, in *Narratives Md*, 73.

71. Ibid., 72. See Fausz, "Present at the 'Creation,'" fn. 9. See also Merrell, "Cultural Continuity among the Piscataway Indians of Colonial Maryland."

72. Rountree and Davidson, *Eastern Shore Indians of Virginia and Maryland*, 84.

73. Ibid., 85.

74. Ibid., 105–6.

75. To be sure, the Nanticokes were not exclusively fur traders. Their ties to both the Iroquois and Susquehannocks involved not only trade but diplomatic and military interests.

76. Ibid., 87.

77. Calloway, *New Worlds For All*, 1–23.

78. The paragraph quotes are from "Letter of Captain Toby Yong to Sir Toby Matthew," July 1634, in *Narratives Md*, 55.

79. *Charter*, 1679–80, secs. VI, VII.

80. Jordan, *Foundations of Representative Government in Maryland*, 1. See also Falb, *Advice and Assent*; Steiner, *Maryland under the Commonwealth*.

81. *Archives Md*, 3:53.

82. "Letter of Governor Leonard Calvert to Lord Baltimore," 1637/8, in *Narratives Md*, 156.

83. "Letter from Lord Baltimore to Governor Leonard Calvert," 1637/8, in Lee, *The Calvert Papers*, 1:187.

84. *Assembly Proceedings*, February–March 1638/9, 41; emphasis added.

85. Jordan, *Foundations of Representative Government in Maryland*, 1.

86. Slavery played a highly significant role in the founding of the colony. Particularly after the early years of settlement, relationships between Marylanders, Virginians, and local indigenous tribes cannot be adequately discussed without reference to African and indentured slavery. See, for reference, Dunn, "Master, Servants, and Slaves in the Colonial Chesapeake and the Caribbean"; Hall, *Things of Darkness*, 233–36.

87. For example, in 1638/9, the assembly passed *An Act for Church liberties, An Act for Swearing Allegeance, An Act for Trade with the Indians, An Act for Treasons,* and *An Act for felonies,* among others: *Assembly Proceedings,* 40–75.

88. Hall, "The Chesapeake in the Seventeenth Century," 60–61 and fn. 18.

89. Ibid., 59–60.

90. *Assembly Proceedings,* February–March 1638/9, 42.

91. The paragraph citations are from "Letter from Thomas Copley to Lord Baltimore," April 3, 1638, endorsed by Baltimore, in *Narratives Md,* 167–68.

92. Both quotes are from "Letter from Thomas Cornwallis to Lord Baltimore," April 16, 1638, in *Narratives Md,* 176.

93. Hall, "The Chesapeake in the Seventeenth Century," 63. This tactic helped the government clarify the troublesome distinction between laws current and laws repealed or revised, a distinction that in Maryland was overlaid with the difference, arising in part from the right of the proprietor in England to approve legislation, between "perpetuall" and "temporary" statutes. Reflecting in 1676 on the situation in their colony, the members of the assembly were acutely aware of the problem of "knowing what Lawes are in force & unrepealed"; similarly, they were frank in acknowledging the confusion arose from "the multiplicity of Lawes to one and the same thing which many tymes interfer one with another."

94. Ibid., 58.

95. Ibid., 61.

96. Ibid.

97. *Charter,* 1679–80, sec. VII.

98. Jordan, *Foundations of Representative Government in Maryland,* 42–44.

99. Hall, "The Chesapeake in the Seventeenth Century," 66. See also Konig, "Regionalism in Early American Law," 157: "Rather, the selectivity apparent in the way that the founding generations drew on available English precedents reveals a far more skilled and self-conscious process, the product of experienced and practiced users of legal institutions in England. More accustomed to the convenience and affordability of local courts than to the technicalities and expense of those at Westminster, they replicated the less complicated instrumentalism of local justice, drawing on what they knew and applying it selectively to their specific regional imperatives in the New World."

100. Hall, 63.

101. Sunstein, *Designing Democracy,* 51. "In other words," Cass Sunstein writes, "well-functioning constitutional orders try to solve problems, including problems of deliberative trouble, through reaching incompletely theorized agreements. . . . When people or groups disagree or are uncertain about an abstraction . . . they can often make progress by moving to a level of greater particularity. They can attempt a conceptual descent—a descent to the lower level of abstraction. This phenomenon has an especially notable feature: It enlists silence, on certain basic questions, as a device for producing convergence despite disagreement, uncer-

tainty, limits of time and capacity, and (most important of all) heterogeneity. Incompletely theorized agreements are thus an important source of successful constitutionalism and social stability; they also provide an important way for people to demonstrate mutual respect."

102. Quoted in Peltonen, *Classical Humanism and Republicanism in English Political Thought*, 5. See also Pocock, *The Machiavellian Moment*, 334–37.

103. Peltonen, *Classical Humanism and Republicanism in English Political Thought*, 7. "This means, of course, that when the gentry increasingly sought access to education in the grammar schools as well as in the universities they received an essentially humanist education which thus became "the common possession of the whole governing class": ibid., 14.

104. See McDiarmid, *The Monarchical Republic of Early Modern England*.

105. Fitzmaurice, "American Corruption," 227.

106. See also Levy, "Not so Novus an Ordo," 20.

107. For complaints against "arbitrary" and "Popish" government, see "Virginia and Maryland, or the Lord Baltemore's Printed Case Uncased and Unanswered" and "Babylon's Fall in Maryland, " in *Narratives Md*, 181–230, 231–46. On the assembly uprising, see Jordan, "Maryland's Privy Council"; idem, "Political Stability and the Emergence of a Native Elite in Maryland."

108. "Lord Culpepper of Virginia to Lords of Trade," letter, 1681, quoted in Land, *Colonial Maryland*, 83.

109. For information on the suspension and restoration of proprietary governance, Brugger et al., *Maryland: A Middle Temperament*, 38–40.

110. Bilder, "English Settlement and Local Governance," 78–79.

3. The *Fundamental Constitutions of Carolina*

Epigraph: Machiavelli, *Discourses*, 110–11.

1. Armitage, "John Locke, Carolina, and the *Two Treatises of Government*"; idem, "That Excellent Forme of Government"; Mishra, "[All] the World was America," 219–37; Arneil, *John Locke and America*, 65–87, 118–32; Tully, *A Discourse on Property*.

2. Parekh, "Liberalism and Colonialism," 83.

3. Locke, *Two Treatises of Government*, 301. I have addressed the *Two Treatises* and Locke's colonial investments more directly in Hsueh, "Cultivating and Challenging the Common"; idem, "Unsettling Colonies."

4. Armitage, "John Locke, Carolina, and the *Two Treatises of Government*," 603.

5. Tomlins, "The Legal Cartography of Colonization, the Legal Polyphony of Settlement," 345.

6. The edition of the *Fundamental Constitutions of Carolina* referenced in this chapter is from Locke, *Locke*, 160–81. Mark Goldie's edition incorporates draft notes and revisions made to the document. In this chapter, I will generally refer to the *Fundamental Constitutions* in the plural—although when treated as a form

or document, I treat it as singular. In part, this is a nod to the historical status of the *Fundamental Constitutions*, which was referred to in both the plural and singular by period commentators. For example, at times, the Lords Proprietors referred to "these *Fundamental Constitutions*" in their correspondences; at other moments, they described the *Constitutions* as "that excellent form" or "aforesaid model." My emphasis of the plural–singular ambivalence of the *Constitutions* is also a theoretical acknowledgement of the document's conveyance of multiplicity within singularity, for its "many" constitutions—about 120 in all—differently addressed particular areas of concern within a singular form. The original *Fundamental Constitutions* contained 111 articles, but the document was amended numerous times and by 1670 there were 120 articles in the text, which also received a new numeration system.

7. The June 30, 1665, Carolina charter was the latest of a number of English patents issued for the area, such as Sir Robert Heath's *Patent*, 1629, in Thorpe, *The Federal and State Constitutions*, 1:69–76; "State of the Case of the Duke of Norfolk's Pretension to Carolina," 1663, ibid., 6–7; *Charter of Carolina*, 1663, ibid., 5:2743–53; "Concessions and Agreements of the Lords Proprietors of the Province of Carolina, 1665," ibid., 2756–61; Carolina *Charter*, 1665, ibid., 2763 (hereafter, *Charter*).

8. *Charter*, 2764–65.

9. *Fundamental Constitutions*, 161–62. The reference to the county palatine of Durham signaled the Carolina proprietary colony as a palatinate.

10. Ibid., 161–81.

11. Other scholars have made this connection as well, and my interpretation here has benefited from their accounts: see, for example, Tomlins, "The Legal Cartography of Colonization, the Legal Polyphony of Settlement"; Goldie, "The Unacknowledged Republic"; Roper, *Conceiving Carolina*, chap. 2. For the Restoration revival of the republican form, see Pocock, *The Machiavellian Moment*, 333–422. See also Pocock's introduction in Harrington, *The Collected Works of James Harrington*, 15–42.

12. The initial proprietary association was composed of five peers and three commoners: Lord Albemarle, Lord Ashley, Lord Berkeley, Lord Clarendon, Lord Craven, Sir William Berkeley, Sir George Carteret, and Sir John Colleton (later to become deputy governor of Barbados). The proprietors officially signed and issued the *Fundamental Constitutions* in March 1670, but the three ships—the *Carolina*, the *Port Royall*, and the *Albemarle*—left Ireland in late August with a copy of the document finalized by Lord Ashley and validated with the association's general permission: see Craven, "The Early Settlement."

13. In this chapter, I refer to Anthony Ashley Cooper, then Lord Ashley, the king's chancellor of the exchequer in 1666, as Ashley rather than Shaftesbury. While Charles I had granted the Carolina territory to Sir Robert Heath as far back as the fall of 1629, Heath's ventures in the area did not lead to formal or continued

English settlement. However, during Heath's tenure the Carolina area was explored by numerous surveyors and travelers, including commissions that navigated the areas later known as Charles River, Port Royall, and Hilton Head Island. Many of these exploratory expeditions offered their services to the Lords Proprietors who before 1663 were already interested in overtaking Heath's grant. For an excellent account of the geographical claims made in these disputes, see Duff, "Designing Carolina," 17–21. Meaghan Duff notes the ways in which Carolina proprietors were influenced by earlier explorers and propagandists, as she also details how the Lords Proprietors' elaborate plans in the *Fundamental Constitutions* influenced how Carolina evolved physically and socially. For a secondary account of the competing claims over Heath's grant, see Powell, "Carolana and the Incomparable Roanoke." Relevant primary documents include: "Proposealls of Severall Gentlemen of Barbadoes," 1663, in CSCHS, 10–12; *A True Relation of a Voyage upon Discovery*, 1663, ibid., 18–25.

14. Charles II's 1663 letter patent to the Lords Proprietors specifically revoked Sir Robert Heath's longstanding grant and reassigned the management of the territory to the Lords Proprietors, first in the form of a patent (1663), which was later reissued as a proprietary charter (1665): See Sir Robert Heath's *Patent*, 1629, in Thorpe, *Federal and State Constitutions*, 1:69–76; *Charter of Carolina*, 1663, ibid., 5:2743–53.

15. *Charter of Carolina*, 1663, in Thorpe, *Federal and State Constitutions*, 2763. Compare Heath's *Patent*, 1629, 1:69–76; *Charter of Carolina*, 1663, 5:2743–53; and the 1665 *Charter*, all in Thorpe, *Federal and State Constitutions*.

16. *Charter of Carolina*, 1663, in Thorpe, *Federal and State Constitutions*, 2763.

17. Ibid.

18. See Krugler, "Our Trusty and Well Beloved Councillor." See also chap. 2, n. 11, in this volume.

19. See Lee, *The CABAL*, 211; Hutton, *Charles the Second*, 254–86; Haley, *The First Earl of Shaftesbury*, 177–84, 227–65.

20. Lists and inventories of the three ships' provisions and passengers, 1669, in CSCHS, 137–52. For secondary accounts of the passage of the *Fundamental Constitutions* to Carolina, see Sirmans, *Colonial South Carolina*, 6–10.

21. *Fundamental Constitutions*, 161.

22. Ibid., 161–66.

23. Ibid., 166–74.

24. Ibid., 175–81.

25. McFarlane, *The British in the Americas*, 109–10.

26. Russell Smith, *Harrington and His Oceana*, 161.

27. See chap. 3, n. 1, in this volume.

28. Before they were signed and launched, the *Fundamental Constitutions* underwent considerable debate and revision. Some have attributed the *Fundamental Constitutions* to Ashley, while H. F. Russell Smith suggests that the document

may have been drafted in part by Clarendon, Craven, Carteret, and Albemarle: see Russell Smith, *Harrington and His Oceana*, 160. See also Gallay, *The Indian Slave Trade*, 43–44. In addition, a number of historians have noted that Locke was likely involved in the creation, dissemination, and revision of the *Fundamental Constitutions of Carolina*, 1669, the founding constitutions of the colony: See Armitage, "John Locke, Carolina, and the *Two Treatises of Government*," 607–15; Milton, "John Locke and the Fundamental Constitutions of Carolina"; McGuinness, "The Fundamental Constitutions of Carolina as a Tool for Lockean Scholarship"; Mark Goldie's introduction to *Fundamental Constitutions*, 160–61.

29. Drawn from period accounts: *A True Relation of a Voyage upon Discovery*, 1663, in CSCHS, 18–25; Robert Sandford's account of Port Royal, 1666, ibid., 56–82; *Clarendon Address*, 1666, ibid., 84–88. Both Colleton and Berkeley were involved in the Council of Foreign Plantations before the Carolina settlement. Six of the eight proprietors were to become instrumental in other colonial ventures, as well. Carteret and Berkeley became proprietors in New Jersey; the others were involved in the Royal African and Hudson's Bay companies. Jack Greene makes the more pronounced claim that, given Carolina's strong ties to Caribbean settlements, the colony was a "colony" of a "colony": Greene, "England, the Caribbean, and the Settlement of Carolina," 271.

30. McFarlane, *The British in the Americas*, 108–11.

31. *Fundamental Constitutions*, 161–62.

32. Ibid., 162.

33. See Pocock's introduction in Harrington, *The Collected Works of James Harrington*, 20–40.

34. Goldie, "The Unacknowledged Republic," 178.

35. *Fundamental Constitutions*, 162; emphasis added. As Goldie explains, within the order of hereditary nobility there were actually two types of nobility. The first were the landgraves, each with estates of 48,000 acres; the second were the caciques, with 24,000 acres each. Among the common people, lords of the manor held roughly 3,000–12,000 acres of land. Of lesser standing were freeholders who possessed 500 acres; this granted them the ability to serve in Parliament. Those who held 50 acres had no title but were granted the status of freemen, while serfs and leet-men could possess up to 10 acres but had no freedom.

36. Harrington, *The Commonwealth of Oceana* and *A System of Politics*, 77, 83, 101.

37. Machiavelli, *The Prince* and *the Discourses*, 109; emphasis added.

38. Ibid., 209.

39. Harrington, *The Commonwealth of Oceana*, 12–13; emphasis added.

40. The *Fundamental Constitutions* has no monarch, although there is still stratification along three sociopolitical types: proprietors; landgraves and caciques; and leet-men.

41. Ibid.

42. Harrington, *The Commonwealth of Oceana and a System of Politics*, 10–15, 102–11.

43. Two members of the Carolina proprietary association were heavily involved in colonial settlements in the Americas. Sir William Berkeley served as governor of Virginia, while Sir Peter Colleton was an influential planter in Barbados. Early Carolina colonists from England stopped at Barbados before continuing on to Carolina, and many Carolina settlers were recruited from Barbados and Virginia.

44. Fitzmaurice, *Humanism and America*, 102.

45. Fitzmaurice, "The Civic Solution to the Crisis of English Colonization, 1609–1625," 27.

46. On the connections between Carolina and Virginia, see Roper, *Conceiving Carolina*, 15–19; see also nn. 38–40, for background on the Lords Proprietors. On civic humanist education, see Richard, *Early Modern Civil Discourses*; Curtis, *Oxford and Cambridge in Transition*, 63–74, 70–71; Simon, *Education and Society in Tudor England*, 121–22, 165–76, 291–92, 400–402; Stone, "The Educational Revolution in England"; Rozbicki, *The Complete Colonial Gentleman*.

47. Fitzmaurice, *Humanism and America*, 46.

48. Relatedly, Johann Sommerville argues that republicanism in England was strongly mixed with other English legal and political traditions, such as English common law traditions. "Not classical humanism by itself," Sommerville argues, "but a 'meld' of humanist and Protestant influences promoted active citizenship in early modern England": Sommerville, *Politics and Ideology in England*, 14. Similarly, Ethan Shagan emphasizes that local self-governance was grounded in English custom and tradition, not humanist ideals: see McDiarmid, *The Monarchical Republic of Early Modern England*, 14–16.

49. Skinner, *Visions of Politics*, 358.

50. A similar point is made in Tomlins, "Law's Empire," 27–35.

51. In "Coppy of Instruccons Annexed to Ye Comission for Ye Governr & Councell," July 27, 1669, in CSCHS, 119.

52. The citations are from Castoriadis, *The Imaginary Institution of Society*, 117–35.

53. Cornelius Castoriadis's conception of the imaginary is further clarified in *World in Fragments*, 7–8.

54. Idem, *The Imaginary Institution of Society*, 117–35.

55. The dimensions of the colony's probable future are most precisely articulated in the document's description of the colony's eight supreme courts of law, each of which depicts component realms of action: Indian relations, colony infrastructure, crime and punishment, and foreign trade. Chief among these, the "palatine's court" designates the executive position occupied by the palatine and the seven proprietors: "This court shall have power to call parliament, to pardon all offences, to make elections of all officers in the proprietors' dispose, to nominate and appoint port towns . . . and also, shall have a negative upon all acts and orders of the constable's court and admiral's court relating to wars." Note, in particular, how the repeated formulation "shall be" cast those dimensions in specific, almost utopian terms—for instance, "high steward's court" shall "have

the care of all foreign and domestic trade, manufactures, public buildings and workhouses, highways, passages by water above the flood of the tide, drains, sewers, and banks against inundations, bridges, posts, carriers, fairs, markets, corruptions, or infections of the common air and water": *Fundamental Constitutions*, 172–74.

56. Cited in "Carolina Temporary Laws," June 21, 1672, in cschs, 403: "It is necessary for ye supply of that defect . . . till by a sufficient number of Inhabitants of all degrees ye Governmt of Carolina can be administered according to ye forme established in ye fundamental Constitutions."

57. Sirmans, *Colonial South Carolina*, 6–10.

58. For example, Mark Goldie, editor of Locke, *Locke: Political Essays*, provides the typical form of the assertion, "The *Constitutions* never made much impact on the actual government of Carolina": Locke, *Locke: Political Essays*, 160. Meaghan Duff, however, points to the promotional dimensions of the *Fundamental Constitutions*, which continued to be used in the 1680s to solicit prospective colonists in London's Carolina Coffee House: Duff, "Designing Carolina," 48–52.

59. Russell Smith, *Harrington and his Oceana*, 161. Russell Smith is referring to a later set of "Temporary Laws."

60. cschs, 401. See also June 1672 National Archives, bpro 9/48/112.

61. In addition, the "Temporary Laws" were accompanied by "Agrarian Laws or instructions," 1672: see cschs, 405.

62. *Colonial Memoranda*, November 1670, in cschs, 245, 248 (letters from the Council and T. Colleton, respectively). See also bpro, "The Shaftesbury Papers."

63. Letter from Ashley to Joseph West, 16 December 1671, in "The Shaftesbury Papers," 366. See also bpro, December 16, 1671, bundle 30/24/48/55.

64. Letter from Lord Ashley to colonist Maurice Matthews, June 20 1672, in cschs, 399.

65. *Fundamental Constitutions*, 161–62. This paternal privilege was then to be consistently maintained, according to the requirements of the *Fundamental Constitutions*. According to Article 7, the number of proprietors was to remain steady, and "if, upon the vacancy of any proprietorship, the surviving seven proprietors shall not choose a landgrave as a proprietor before the second biennial parliament after the vacancy, then the next biennial parliament but one after such vacancy shall have power to choose any landgrave to be proprietor": ibid., 163. In addition to territorial privilege, the proprietors were granted by the express words of the *Fundamental Constitutions* clear power to judge, pardon, dispose, and distribute funds: ibid., 168.

66. Goldie, "The Unacknowledged Republic," 154–55.

67. A number of recent studies have examined Locke's relationship to Carolina, looking especially at his contributions to the colony's governing documents, *The Fundamental Constitutions of Carolina*, but most assessments have not focused heavily on Locke's responsibilities as informal secretary to the proprietary

association. If the memoranda provide insights into both the practices of the colonists and the interests of the Lords Proprietors, they also help to resituate Locke not as a theorist or philosopher but, rather, as an administrative scribe. See, for example, Banner, *How the Indians Lost Their Land*, esp. chap. 1; Armitage, "John Locke, Carolina, and the *Two Treatises of Government*," 602–27; Arneil, *John Locke and America*; Tully, *Strange Multiplicity*, 58–99; Parekh, "Liberalism and Colonialism." A similar point is made, albeit with respect to Locke's influence on nineteenth-century British imperialism, in Mehta, *Liberalism and Empire*, 1–46. There have been some excellent works on Locke's other colonial administrative roles: See, for example, Farr, "So Vile and Miserable an Estate," 260–68; idem, "Locke, Natural Law, and New World Slavery."

68. Cranston, *John Locke*, 119. Also, see Woolhouse, *Locke*, 70–118.

69. Colonial Memoranda, December 26, 1670, in CSCHS, 249.

70. Extracts from letters from Carolina in Locke's hand, November 20, 1674, ibid., 263.

71. Letter ibid., 427. Indeed, Woodward did not only gain Indian assistance, he sought to position himself as an Indian elite—a cacique.

72. The memoranda describe local indigenes as Edisto, Kywaha, and Westoes, who were part of the Cusabos. However, as James Merrell has noted, tribes in the area described in the memoranda were predominantly Catawbas: see Merrell, *The Indians' New World*. The names attributed to indigenes varied and often referred to geography rather than tribal affiliation. The Kywaha, Etiwan, and Stono likely lived near Charleston harbor. The "Edisto"—Wimbee, Combahee, and Ashepoo—probably resided south of the Edisto River. The Yamasee occupied lands along the lower Savannah River, while the Catawbas, Creeks, and Cherokees—some designated "Westoes"—controlled the piedmont area to the west and northwest of Charles Town: Swanton, *The Indian Tribes of North America*, 90–104.

73. From the "Barbados Proclamation," endorsed by Locke, November 4, 1670, in CSCHS, 211. As a promotional report to encourage Caribbean settlers to come to Carolina, the Barbados Proclamation noted, "Now for the better Expedition in settling of the said province and encouragement of all manner of people that have a desire to transport themselves servants negroes or utensils the Lords proprietors of the province of Carolina hath provided the Carolina frigot aforesaid for the transportion of the said people who will be ready to depart this island."

74. Robert Sandford, *A Relation of a Voyage on the Coast of the Province of Carolina*, submitted to the Lord Proprietors, in *Narratives Ca*, 100.

75. Letter of June 28, 1673, in *Narratives Ca*, 425. See also BPRO, 1673, bundle 30/24/48/91.

76. Young, "Hybrid Democracy," 237–58.

77. Foucault, *Power/Knowledge*, 82.

78. Ibid.

79. *Fundamental Constitutions*, 168–69, 178.

80. CSCHS, 367. As David Armitage notes, the "Temporary Laws" of 1671 were in Locke's hand: Armitage, "John Locke, Carolina, and the *Two Treatises of Government*," 610.

81. Gallay, *The Indian Slave Trade*, 50–51.

82. *Fundamental Constitutions*, 180.

83. Ibid., 445–46. The first clause directly contradicts Article 112 of the *Fundamental Constitutions*.

84. Gallay, *The Indian Slave Trade*, 51. Also, Eirlys Barker traces the later impact of these relationships in "Indian Traders, Charles Town, and London's Vital Links to the Interior of North America." As she notes, elites and ordinary traders in the beginning of the eighteenth century continued to be heavily involved in trade with Cherokees, Creeks, Yamasees, Chickasaws, and Catawbas. It was only when the Indians' capital diminished as a consequence of broader developments in Indian America that the colonial government viewed Native Americans as a "barrier" to the plantation economy.

85. Gallay, *The Indian Slave Trade*, 47.

86. Ibid., 43.

87. Ibid., 50.

88. Ibid., 44.

89. Ibid.; emphasis added.

90. BPRO, April 10, 1671, bundle 30/24/48/55; emphasis added.

91. Ibid., May 13, 1671; emphasis added. Additional passages in Carolina Memoranda also make note of the proprietors' reluctance to allow the colonists to hold money, gold, and silver. Letter endorsed by Locke.

92. The problem of abandonment was familiar in Carolina and in other English settlements. For example, in an account endorsed by Locke, Carolina possessed more than its share of disloyal settlers. "For &c as of late diverse obstinate & evil disposed persons have run away from this settlement Resolved forthwith a party of men under command of Lieutenant Col. Godfrey be dispatched to follow & take the said persons": see Council Journal, September 16, 1673, in CSCHS, 428.

93. Ibid., 427–28.

94. *Fundamental Constitutions*, 168–69, 178.

95. Ibid., 180.

96. CSCHS, 211. See also Wood, *Black Majority*, 22.

97. *Fundamental Constitutions*, 179–80.

98. Ibid.

99. Wood, *Black Majority*. See also the essays by William Ramsey, Jennifer Lyle Morgan, and S. Max Edelson in Greene et al., *Money, Trade, and Power*, 166–255. For example, Max Edelson examines the implication of these relationships in the eighteenth century, arguing that slaves increasingly entered skilled professions and these developments enhanced plantation owners' power in South

Carolina society. Such transformations increased the autonomy of slaves as they also pushed white laborers out of the skilled markets: see Edelson, "Affiliation without Affinity."

100. Most recently, Edelson has explained how these instrumental and adaptive relationships fuelled the plantation economy and stakeholder vision of the Old South: Edelson, *Plantation Enterprise in Colonial South Carolina*. See also Gallay, *The Indian Slave Trade*; Fischer, *Suspect Relations*, 13–54; Hatley, *The Dividing Paths*, esp. chap. 3; Usner, *Indians, Settlers and Slaves in a Frontier Exchange Economy*, 44–76. See Blackburn, *The Making of New World Slavery*, 219–71; Wood, *The Origins of American Slavery*, 40–67; Smith, *White Servitude in Colonial South Carolina*.

101. Locke, *Two Treatises of Government*, 293. As Barbara Arneil has explained, Locke's agriculturalist argument in the *Two Treatises* bolstered a Eurocentric normativity by denigrating indigenous practices, customs, and beliefs as "wild" and "uncultivated": Arneil, *John Locke and America*, 65–87.

102. I have found no definitive evidence that Locke had read *Oceana* in detail at the time of the drafting of the *Fundamental Constitutions*, although he is known to have possessed *Oceana* in his library by the end of the century. For example, the catalogue by Peter Laslett and John Harrison lists Toland's 1700 edition of "Harrington's *Oceana* and his other works" as item 1388 in Locke's library: Laslett and Harrison, *The Library of John Locke*. At this time, I am also uncertain whether Shaftesbury acquired *Oceana*. K.H.D. Haley notes that in May 1674 Locke had compiled "A list of books which my Lord Shaftesbury carried into the country," which included Harrington's *Oceana* and *Art of Lawgiving* (perhaps, given the date, the J. Streater edition of 1656 or the Daniel Pakeman edition of 1658): see Haley, *The First Earl of Shaftesbury*, 219. Locke's early correspondence made witty reference to *Oceana* and other utopian texts: See letters 60 and 66 in de Beer, *The Correspondence of John Locke*, 85, 90.

103. Letters 275 and 279 in Goldie, *John Locke*, 37–51.

104. Armitage, "John Locke, Carolina, and the *Two Treatises of Government*," 608, 610–11, 613–15. For example, Locke often discussed the *Constitutions* with the French philosopher and theologian Nicholas Toinard, noting in a personal letter that "together we will go to Carolina to a very fine island there which they have done me the honour of naming after me, and it is there that you shall be Emperor because I can vouch that everything that is called Locke is ready to obey you and there you will establish an empire of repose and letters": letter 475 in Goldie, *John Locke*, 76. See also the following letters in de Beer, *The Correspondence of John Locke*, vol. 2; Letter 504: Henri Justel to Locke, September 1679, 105; Letter 501: Toinard to Locke, September 1679, 96; Letter 517: Toinard to Locke, November 1679, 132–41; Letter 541: Nicholas Toinard to Locke, June 1680, 183.

105. See Tully, "Placing the *Two Treatises*"; idem, *An Approach to Political Philosophy*, 9–70; Dunn, *The Political Thought of John Locke*; Pocock, "The Varieties of

Whiggism from Exclusion to Reform," in idem, *Virtue, Commerce, and History*, 215–29.

106. Foucault, *Language, Counter-Memory, Practice*, 147.

107. Ibid., 154.

4. Treaty Power in Pennsylvania

Epigraphs: Williams, *Linking Arms Together*, 1048; Derrida, *Negotiations*, 14.

1. Merrell, *Into the American Woods*, 28. As Merrell notes, the presence of interpreters and "go-betweens" tend to be omitted in nostalgic recountings of Penn's treaties.

2. Sugrue, "The Peopling and Depeopling of Early Pennsylvania," 3.

3. My account draws particularly on recent work that situates William Penn and Pennsylvania's founding in terms of trans-Atlantic, cross-colonial, and colonial-indigenous dynamics: see Harper, *Promised Land*; Pencak and Richter, *Friends and Enemies in Penn's Woods*; Pencak and Richter, *Pennsylvania*; Murphy, *Conscience and Community*, 247–94; Geiter, *William Penn*; idem, "The Restoration Crisis and the Launching of Pennsylvania"; Richter, "A Framework for Pennsylvania Indian History"; Schwartz, *"A Mixed Multitude."*

4. Pagden, "Law, Colonization, Legitimation, and the European Background," 25.

5. Ibid., 28.

6. See Tully, *Strange Multiplicity*; Young, "Hybrid Democracy," 237–58; idem, *Inclusion and Democracy*, esp. 236–75; Williams, *Linking Arms Together*; also idem, "Linking Arms Together."

7. Tully, *Strange Multiplicity*, 116–19.

8. Williams, "Linking Arms Together," 1048–49.

9. Young, "Hybrid Democracy," 246.

10. Ibid.

11. Williams, "Linking Arms Together," 1048.

12. Tully, *Strange Multiplicity*, 117–35. For the citation, see 130–31, 135. Common constitutionalism, finally, is Tully's own assemblage of both the locally situated traditions of ancient constitutionalism and the forms of mediated exchange and "intercultural common ground" in treaty constitutionalism: It holds mutual consent, intercultural mediation, and continuity of dialogue as pre-eminent: ibid., 99–116, 183–212.

13. Tully, *Strange Multiplicity*, 83; Young, "Hybrid Democracy," 240, 246–47.

14. Young, "Hybrid Democracy," 246.

15. *Some Account of the Province of Pennsylvania* (London: Benjamin Clark, 1681), reprinted in Dunn and Dunn, *The World of William Penn*, 59.

16. Ibid.

17. Spady, "Colonialism and the Discursive Antecedents of Penn's Treaty with the Indians"; Klepp, "Encounter and Experiment"; Nash, "City Planning and Political Tension in the Seventeenth Century"; Roach, "Planting of Philadelphia."

18. Letter from Thomas Holme to Penn, November 9, 1683, in Dunn et al., *The Papers of William Penn*, 2:501.

19. For primary-source reference on the early population, see *Early Census of Philadelphia County Inhabitants*, April 14, 1683, in Soderlund, *William Penn and the Founding of Pennsylvania*, 212–16. The editors of *The Papers of William Penn* have also compiled a particularly helpful list of first purchasers in Pennsylvania during 1681–85, which includes biographical information. See *First Purchasers of Pennsylvania, 1681–85*, in Dunn et al. *The Papers of William Penn*, 2:630–64. The colony's history of slavery adds yet another layer of complication to its inter-cultural relations: see Nash, "Slaves and Slaveholders in Colonial Philadelphia"; Aptheker, "The Quakers and Negro Slavery."

20. See *Charter to Pennsylvania*, March 4, 1681, in Soderlund, *William Penn and the Founding of Pennsylvania*, 42. The edition of the charter used in this chapter is from ibid., 41–49. For historical accounts of the charter in the period's colonial policy, see Haffenden, "The Crown and the Colonial Charters."

21. *Charter to Pennsylvania*, March 4, 1681, in Soderlund, *William Penn and the Founding of Pennsylvania*, 41–42. See Soderlund's introduction in *William Penn and the Founding of Pennsylvania*, 7. As Jean Soderlund flatly points out, Penn ultimately failed to achieve palatine authority, and "therefore ended up with a patent that gave the proprietor considerably less power than he desired." Par-enthetically, the charter—one that explicitly denied Penn the power to pardon treason—was signed just as preparations were heightening for the Oxford Parliament that defeated Exclusion, providing yet another example of the ways in which political events in England were transplanted and distorted in the colonies.

22. Ibid., 46.

23. Ibid., 44.

24. Ibid., 43.

25. The charter was heavily debated by the Committee of Trade and Plantations, and one of the strongest restrictions was a suggestion of Chief Justice North, who recommended that Penn was "to Transmit all such Laws to the Privy Council (or Commrs [Commissioners] for the Plantations) as soon as conveniently may be or at least within six months after the passing them and that unless his Majesty shall within two years (after they are Received) declare them null they shall be and remain in force (until repealed by the same Authority that passed them)": Chief Justice North's Memorandum on William Penn's Draft Charter, c. January 1681, in Dunn et al., *The Papers of William Penn*, 2:58. The official charter read: "To the end that the said William Penn, or his heirs, or other the planters, own-ers, or inhabitants of the said province may not, at any time hereafter (by mis-construction of the power aforesaid) through inadvertency or design, depart from that faith and due allegiance which, by the laws of this our realm of En-gland. . . . Our further will and pleasure is, that a transcript or duplicate of all

laws . . . within five years after the making thereof, be transmitted and delivered to the Privy Council for the time being, of us, our heirs and successors; and if any of the said laws, within the space of six months after that they shall be so transmitted and delivered, be declared by us, our heirs and successors, in our or their Privy Council, inconsistent with the sovereignty or lawful prerogative of us, or contrary to the faith and allegiance due to the legal government of this realm . . . that thereupon any of the said laws shall be adjudged and declared void by us": *Charter*, in Soderlund, *William Penn and the Founding of Pennsylvania*, 44. Mary Geiter's account in "The Restoration Crisis and the Launching of Pennsylvania" is particularly useful in shedding light on the political context of Penn's charter. See, for other perspectives, Webb, "The Peaceable Kingdom"; idem, "William Blathwayt, Imperial Fixer."

26. See Tomlins, "The Legal Cartography of Colonization, the Legal Polyphony of Settlement," esp. 328–47.

27. The quote is from idem, "Law's Empire," 36. See also Ross, "Legal Communications and Imperial Governance," 104–43; Greene, *Negotiated Authorities*.

28. Ross, "Legal Communications and Imperial Governance," 110.

29. Ibid.

30. On administration, see Brewer, *The Sinews of War*, 3–24. On the Privy Council and Charles II's interests, see Hutton, *Charles the Second*, 410–20; Haley, *The First Earl of Shaftesbury*, 227–65, 327–47.

31. Greene, *Negotiated Authorities*, 1–24.

32. The citations are from the preface to *Frame of Government, and Laws Agreed upon in England*, in Dunn et al., *The Papers of William Penn*, 2:212–14. My interpretation of this issue is indebted to Gary Nash's account of Penn's practical and intellectual commitments: See Nash, "The Framing of Government in Pennsylvania." See also Illick, *Colonial Pennsylvania*, 25–31; Bronner, *William Penn's "Holy Experiment,"* 33–35.

33. *Charter*, in Soderlund, *William Penn and the Founding of Pennsylvania*, 43.

34. Geiter, *William Penn*, 38–39.

35. Ibid., 35.

36. Ibid.

37. Ibid.

38. See esp. Russell Smith, *Harrington and His Oceana*, 138, 162–64. See also Dunn, "William Penn, Classical Republican." For secondary accounts of republicanism in the Americas, see Pocock, *The Machiavellian Moment*, 333–422; Shalhope, "Toward a Republican Synthesis."

39. *Frame of Government, and Laws Agreed upon in England*, in Dunn et al., *The Papers of William Penn*, 2:215.

40. Ibid.

41. Ibid., 218.

42. Ibid., 216.

43. Ibid., 213, 215.

44. Ibid., 213.

45. Ibid., 216.

46. Ibid., 215.

47. Ibid., 213–41; emphasis added.

48. See Benjamin Furly's *Criticism of the Frame of Government*, May 1682, in Dunn et al., *The Papers of William Penn*, 2:230; Sachse, "Benjamin Furly."

49. *Frame of Government, and Laws Agreed upon in England*, in Dunn et al., *The Papers of William Penn*, 2:217.

50. All citations in this paragraph from the Article 13, ibid., 217.

51. Ibid., 212–14.

52. Ibid., 217.

53. For comparison and citations, see *Fundamental Constitutions*, ibid., 144.

54. *Fundamental Constitutions* and the *Frame*, ibid., 228–37.

55. See Cranston, *John Locke*, 260–61. Locke's detailed critique of Penn's *Frame of Government*, 1682 (cf. Cranston, *John Locke*, 260–62). According to Cranston, when he examined Penn's *Frame of Government*, Locke did not object to its being undemocratic, but he questioned the *Frame*'s policies on civil order ("Matter of perpetual prosecution and animosity"), speech ("What is loosely or prophanely?"), and political structure ("inconvenient meeting of the freeman in the council . . . difficulty of choose [*sic*] 72 men of wisdom, virtue, and ability . . . difficulty of establishing boundary for provincial council in matters of moment and lesser moment"). Locke's final summation: "But the whole is so far from a frame of government that is scarce contains a part of the materials": Cranston, *John Locke*, 262.

56. Dunn et al., *The Papers of William Penn*, 2:213–14; Tully, *Strange Multiplicity*, 79.

57. Tully, *Strange Multiplicity*, 79.

58. Geiter, *William Penn*, 124.

59. *Frame of Government, and Laws Agreed upon in England*, in Dunn et al., *The Papers of William Penn*, 2:217.

60. Geiter makes the suggestion that Penn was influenced by Locke's "Proposal on Virginia." "In 1701, the final frame of government was effected as a result of Penn's refusal to acknowledge the 1696 frame and his intention to fashion a new one along the lines of Locke's proposals for Virginia. . . . Meanwhile, he did allow a motion to go forward for yet another new frame. Penn was not acting inconsistently, but in keeping with the philosophy of members of the Board of Trade, such as Somers and Locke. He was devolving more independent authority upon the assembly. Penn's connection with Locke went back to his time as a student at Oxford, but there is no substantive evidence that he was in direct contact with him at that time. However, Penn was in contact with one of Locke's close associates, Lords Somers, who was lord chancellor and president of the Board of Trade. As a member of the Board also, Locke was heavily involved in colonial affairs.

He wrote a brief on how Virginia's administration should operate." According to Geiter, "Lockean influence can be seen in other aspects of the new constitution and its partner, the frame of land settlement. The choosing of sheriffs and coroners upon good behaviour was straight out of Locke's brief on Virginia. The controversy over the surveying of land and its granting was more particularly Lockean": see Geiter, *William Penn*, 126–27.

61. See, for example, letter from Jasper Batt (a prominent Quaker preacher) to William Penn, 1683, in Dunn et al., *The Papers of William Penn*, 2:462–66. Penn had earlier defended the *Frame* to Batt in a letter of February 1683, ibid., 2:346–349.

62. As Penn wrote to the Committee of Trade on August 14, 1683, "I have exactly followed the Bishop of London's council by buying & not taking away the natives land, with whom I have Settled a very Kind Correspondence": ibid., 435. On the various indigenous tribes and nations in Pennsylvania, see Richter, "The First Pennsylvanians"; Trigger, *Handbook of North American Indians*, 366–67; Miller, "Amerindian (Native American) Cultures in Pre- and Early European Settlement Periods in Pennsylvania," 1–4; Schönenberger, *Lenape Women, Matriliny, and the Colonial Encounter*.

63. Letter from William Clarke, Commissioner, Dover River, June 21, 1683, in Dunn et al., *The Papers of William Penn*, 400–401. For example, as Commissioner William Clarke wrote to Penn, on June 21, 1683: "Lord Baltimore did the Last third day Cause A proclamation to be read publicly in somerset County Court; that all persons that would seat Land in Either the whoreKill or Jones Counties; That he would procure them Rights at one hundred pounds of Tobacco per Right, and that they should pay but one shilling for every hundred Acres of Land yearly rent, And if the Inhabitants of both these Counties would Revolt from william Penn and own him to be their proprietary and Governor that they should have the same terms; Reports were also given out that the Lord Baltimore did Intend shortly to Come with A Troop of horse to take possession of these Two Lower Counties; which Caused great fear to a Rise in the peoples minds."

64. Jordan and Kaups, *The American Backwoods Frontier*, 5. For primary accounts, see "Report of Governor John Printz [New Sweden]," 1647, in Myers, *Narratives of Early Pennsylvania, West New Jersey, and Delaware*, 117–29. See also "Report of Governor Johan Rising [New Sweden]," 1655, in Myers, *Narratives of Early Pennsylvania, West New Jersey, and Delaware*, 153–65; Mackintosh, "New Sweden, Natives, and Nature"; Hoffecker et al., *New Sweden in America*, 112–20.

65. See, for example, "Deed: Sickoneysincks to the Dutch for Swanendale," June 1, 1629, in Vaughn and Kent, *Early American Indian Documents, Treaties, and Laws*, 5; Dahlgren and Norman, *The Rise and Fall of New Sweden*, 92–116. Indian titles are referenced as they appear in the original documents.

66. Kupperman, "Scandinavian Colonists Confront the New World."

67. Ibid.

68. Becker, "Lenape Maize Sales to the Swedish Colonists." See also Williams, "Indians and Europeans in the Delaware Valley."

69. Penn was granted Pennsylvania by Charles II in March 1681. The three lower counties (now referred to as Delaware) were added, with controversy, in August 1682. See, for example, Penn's letter to Robert Turner, Anthony Sharp, and Roger Roberts in Dunn et al., *The Papers of William Penn*, 88. In 1682, even before arriving in Pennsylvania, Penn's administrators negotiated for land in the southeast of Bucks County. Penn continued to acquire deeds, first along the Delaware River and then extending westward and, by the fall of 1683, along the Schuylkill and Susquehanna rivers.

70. *Letter to the Free Society of Traders*, 1683, in Soderlund, *William Penn and the Founding of Pennsylvania*, 314.

71. Memoranda of Additional Instructions to William Markham and William Crispin and John Bezer, October 28, 1681, in Dunn et al., *The Papers of William Penn*, II, 129.

72. See, for example, *Remonstrance from the Inhabitants of Philadelphia*, July 1684, ibid., 2:573.

73. The quotes are from Bill for Lasse Cock's Services, 1682, ibid., 2: 242–43.

74. *Letter to the Free Society of Traders*, 1683, in Soderlund, *William Penn and the Founding of Pennsylvania*, 314.

75. The quotes are from Bill for Lasse Cock's Services, 1682, in Dunn et al., *The Papers of William Penn*, 2:242–43. For background, see also Becker, "Lenape Land Sales, Treaties, and Wampum Belts"; Merrell, *Into the American Woods*, 1–10.

76. The quotes are from William Penn's *Great Law Passed by His First Legislative Assembly of Pennsylvania*, December 5, 1682, cited in Myers, *William Penn's Own Account of the Lenni Lenape or Delaware Indians*, 59. Myers's account duplicates the manuscript record from the Division of Public Records, Harrisburg, Penn.

77. Mancke, "Negotiating an Empire," 248–49. "Relations among states," Mancke explains, "between the metropole and colonial peripheries, and among rival commercial interests were all negotiated over the seventeenth and eighteenth centuries, repeatedly and often simultaneously. . . . Authority in the colonies, therefore, did not trickle down from the center to the peripheries *but was negotiated between the regions*" (emphasis added).

78. Tilly, "War-Making and State-Making as Organized Crime," 170–72.

79. *Remonstrance from the Inhabitants of Philadelphia*, July 1684, in Dunn et al., *The Papers of William Penn*, II, 573.

80. Jennings, " 'Pennsylvania Indians' and the Iroquois."

81. Richter and Merrell, *Beyond the Covenant Chain*, 6. Also, as Daniel Richter argues, despite the increase in ethno-historical and "middle ground" historical accounts of indigeneous–colonial relationships, Penn's treaties with the Lenni Lenape, Susquehannocks, and Iroquois continue to be susceptible to idealized interpretations: Richter, "A Framework for Pennsylvania Indian History." Francis

Jennings also addresses both Penn's enthusiasm for economic concerns and his interest in managing the welter of competing claims to land title in the area. See also Spady, "Colonialism and the Discursive Antecedents of *Penn's Treaty with the Indians*"; Jennings, "Brother Miquon."

82. Salisbury, "Toward the Covenant Chain."
83. Richter and Merrell, *Beyond the Covenant Chain*, 21.
84. Ibid., 21.
85. Sugrue, "The Peopling and Depeopling of Early Pennsylvania," 9–11.
86. Ibid.
87. Miller, "Amerindian (Native American) Cultures in Pre- and Early European Settlement Periods in Pennsylvania," 1–4; Schönenberger, *Lenape Women, Matriliny, and the Colonial Encounter*; Williams, "Indians and Europeans in the Delaware Valley," 112–20.
88. Jennings, "'Pennsylvania Indians' and the Iroquois," 81.
89. Richter, "A Framework for Pennsylvania Indian History," 239.
90. Ibid., 245.
91. Jennings, "'Pennsylvania Indians' and the Iroquois," 80–84.
92. Richter, "A Framework for Pennsylvania Indian History."
93. Foucault, *Power/Knowledge*, 88.
94. See, for example, Cronon, *Changes in the Land*.
95. Sugrue, "The Peopling and Depeopling of Early Pennsylvania," 22.
96. Spady, "Colonialism and Antecedents of *Penn's Treaty*," 36.
97. Jennings, "'Pennsylvania Indians' and the Iroquois," 75–92; Sugrue, "The Peopling and Depeopling of Early Pennsylvania," 3–30.
98. Becker, "Lenape Land Sales, Treaties, and Wampum Belts."
99. Merrell, *Into the American Woods*, 1–10.
100. Ibid., 80.
101. Ibid., 56; emphasis added.
102. Derrida, *Negotiations*, 12.
103. Ibid., 13.
104. Ibid.
105. Hoffer, *Law and People in Colonial America*, 69.
106. Tully, "The Agonic Freedom of Citizens."

5. Plurality and Power

Epigraphs: *Johnson and Graham's Lessee* v. *William M'Intosh*. 21 U.S. 543 (1823); Knapp, *Literary Interest*, 106.

1. Honig, "Declarations of Independence."
2. Wittgenstein, *The Blue and Brown Books*, 17–20. for an account of the language game, see also Wittgenstein, *Philosophical Investigations*, 85, 122, 201.
3. *Oxford English Dictionary*, online ed., s.v. "provocation," http://www.oed.com (accessed May 20, 2009).

4. Tully, *Strange Multiplicity*, 97.

5. Mahoney, *Legacies of Liberalism*, 1–5.

6. Muldoon, *Empire and Order*, 114–38.

7. Alexandrowicz, *An Introduction to the History of the Law of Nations in the East Indies*, 224. See also Stern, "One Body Corporate and Politick."

8. Bilder, *The Transatlantic Constitution*.

9. Hulsebosch, *Constituting Empire*, 5.

10. Konig, "Regionalism in Early American Law," 145.

11. Levy, "Not so Novus an Ordo."

12. Ross, "Legal Communications and Imperial Governance," 164–65.

13. Konig, "Regionalism in Early American Law," 165.

14. Fraser and Gordon, "A Genealogy of 'Dependency,'" 122.

15. Foucault, *Language, Counter-Memory, Practice*, 146.

16. Ibid.

17. See, for example, Williams, *The American Indian in Western Legal Thought*, 227–80.

18. Konig, "Regionalism in Early American Law," 146.

19. Ibid., 147.

20. Ibid.

21. *Johnson and Graham's Lessee v. William M'Intosh*, 21 U.S. 543 (1823); *Cherokee Nation v. Georgia*, 30 U.S. 1 (1831).

22. *Johnson and Graham's Lessee v. William M' In tosh*, 21 U.S. 543 (1823).

23. Ibid.

24. In fact, as James Muldoon and others indicate, many of the English writers that asserted a hierarchy between Indians and colonists primarily sought to defend title to native lands that had been acquired by English treaty and purchase against the counter-claims of other Europeans: See, for example, Muldoon, "Discovery, Grant, Charter, Conquest, or Purchase."

25. McHugh, *Aboriginal Societies and the Common Law*, 119. P. G. McHugh observes, "Once the tribes had been physically vanquished in the great mid-century wars and dispossessions, all jurisdictions set about erecting legal regimes for the dissolution of the tribalism that both impeded the progress of settler society and challenged its constitutional authority": ibid., 118. Also, See Anghie, *Imperialism, Sovereignty and the Making of International Law*.

26. *Worcester v. Georgia*, 31 U.S. (6 Pet.) 515 (1832).

27. Ibid.

28. Levy, "Not so Novus an Ordo," 27.

29. Ibid., 25.

30. Benton, *Law and Colonial Cultures*. For comparable accounts in political economy and constitutionalism, see Sassen, *Territory, Authority, Rights*; Hirschl, *Towards Juristocracy*.

31. Benton, "Colonial Law and Cultural Difference," 564.

32. Ibid., 564.

33. Ibid.

34. Ibid., 586.

35. Ibid., 565.

36. Skinner, *Liberty before Liberalism*, 117.

37. Webber, "Beyond Regret," 60. See also Bartlett, "Native Title in Australia."

38. Fitzmaurice, "The Genealogy of *Terra Nullius*," 14.

39. Attwood, "The Law of the Land or the Law of the Land?," 9.

40. Fitzmaurice, "The Genealogy of *Terra Nullius*," 14.

41. Attwood, "The Law of the Land or the Law of the Land?," 19.

42. Ibid., 18.

43. Brown, *Who Owns Native Culture?* 46. See also Bartlett, "Native Title in Australia."

44. Ibid., 65.

45. Webber, "Beyond Regret," 65.

46. Ibid., 87.

47. Byrnes, *The Waitangi Tribunal and New Zealand History*. See also Pocock, "Waitangi as Mystery of State"; Maaka and Fleras, "Engaging with Indigeneity"; Brownlie, *Treaties and Indigenous Peoples*.

48. As Newbury, "Review," 1469–71, notes, "In the face of Pakeha disquiet anxious ministers through Parliament can assert ultimate sovereignty to undo the recommendations of the Tribunal—as happened in 2004 in a Bill which reasserted Crown rights over foreshore and seabed, contrary to earlier Tribunal findings."

49. Byrnes, *The Waitangi Tribunal and New Zealand History*, 210–45.

50. Brown, *Who Owns Native Culture?* 206–12.

51. Ibid., 226–27.

52. Johansen, "The New York Oneidas," 98. See also Harvard Project on American Indian Economic Development, *The State of the Native Nations*, chap. 1; Coin, "Judge Refuses to Revisit Ruling on Land Trust"; Belson, "Judge Says Oneida Indians Deserve a Chance for Redress."

53. Johansen, "The New York Oneidas," 99.

54. Ibid., 111.

55. Ibid.

56. Ibid., 112.

57. Alfred, *Peace, Power, Righteousness*, 76. See also idem, "Deconstructing the British Columbia Treaty Process."

58. Beatty, "Natives Lose Court Bid to Block B[ritish] C[olumbia] Referendum on Treaties."

59. Alfred, *Peace, Power, Righteousness*, 76.

Primary Sources

A Relation of Maryland; Together with a Map of the Countrey, the Conditions of Planta-tion, His Majesties Charter to the Lord Baltemore. Promotional tract, M. William Peasley, Esq., London, September 8, 1635.

Cherokee Nation v. Georgia. 30 U.S. 1. 1831.

Cheves, L., ed. *Collections of the South Carolina Historical Society*, vol. 5., rev. ed. Charleston: South Carolina Historical Society, 2000.

de Beer, E. S., ed. *The Correspondence of John Locke*, 8 vols. Oxford: Clarendon Press, 1976.

Dunn, Mary Maples, Richard S. Dunn, Richard Ryerson, Edwin B. Bronner, D. Fraser, and Scott M. Wilds, eds. *The Papers of William Penn*, 5 volumes. Philadelphia: University of Pennsylvania Press, 1981–87.

Goldie, Mark, ed. *John Locke: Selected Correspondence.* Oxford: Oxford University Press, 2002.

Hall, Clayton Colman, ed. *Narratives of Early Maryland, 1633–1684.* New York: Charles Scribner's Sons, 1910.

Harrington, James. *The Collected Works of James Harrington.* Edited by J. G. A. Po-cock. Cambridge: Cambridge University Press, 1977.

———. *The Commonwealth of Oceana and a System of Politics*, 2d ed. Edited and translated by J. G. A. Pocock. Cambridge: Cambridge University Press, 1996.

Hobbes, Thomas. *Leviathan, or the Matter, Forme, and Power of a Commonwealth Ecclesiastical and Civil.* Edited by Richard Flathman and David Johnston. New York: W. W. Norton, 1997.

Johnson and Graham's Lessee v. *William M'Intosh.* 21 U.S. 543. 1823.

Lee, Johns Wesley, ed. *The Calvert Papers*, nos. 1–3. Baltimore: John Murphy, 1889–99.

Locke, John. *Locke: Political Essays.* Edited by Mark Goldie. Cambridge: Cambridge University Press, 1997.

———. *Two Treatises of Government.* Edited by Peter Laslett. Cambridge: Cambridge University Press, 1965.

Machiavelli, Niccolò. *The Prince and the Discourses*. Edited by Max Lerner. New York: Modern Library, 1950.

Myers, Albert Cook, ed. *William Penn's Own Account of the Lenni Lenape or Delaware Indians*. Somerset, N.J.: Middle Atlantic Press, 1981.

————. *Narratives of Early Pennsylvania, West New Jersey, and Delaware, 1603–1707*. New York: Charles Scribner's Sons, 1912.

Neill, Edward D., ed. *The Founders of Maryland as Portrayed in Manuscripts, Provincial Records and Early Documents*. Albany, N.Y.: J. Munsell, 1876.

Salley, Alexander S., Jr., ed. *Narratives of Early Carolina, 1650–1708*. New York: Charles Scribner's Sons, 1911.

"The Shaftesbury Papers." British Public Records Office (c. 1663–c. 1700), London, bundle 30/24/48.

Stevens, S. K., Donald H. Kent, and Autumn L. Leonard, eds. *The Papers of Col. Henry Bouquet*. Harrisburg: Pennsylvania Historical Museum Commission, 1940–.

Thorpe, Francis Newton, ed. *The Federal and State Constitutions, Colonial Charters, and Other Organic Laws of the States, Territories, and Colonies Now or Heretofore Forming the United States of America Compiled and Edited under the Act of Congress of June 30, 1906*, 7 volumes. Washington, D.C.: Government Printing Office, 1909.

Thucydides. *The History of the Peloponnesian War*, trans. Thomas Hobbes. Edited by David Greene. Chicago: University of Chicago Press, 1989.

Vaughn, Alden T., and Donald H. Kent, eds. *Early American Indian Documents, Treaties, and Laws, 1607–1789: Pennsylvania and Delaware Treaties, 1629–1737*. Washington, D.C.: University Publications of America, 1979.

White, Father Andrew. *Relatio itineris in Marilandiam*. Translated and edited by Barbara Lawatsch-Boomgar. Wauconda, Ill.: Bolchaz-Carducci Publishers, 1995.

Worcester v. Georgia. 31 U.S. (6 Pet.) 515. 1832.

Secondary Sources

Alexandrowicz, C. H. *An Introduction to the History of the Law of Nations in the East Indies: 16th, 17th, and 18th Centuries*. Oxford: Clarendon Press, Oxford, 1967.

Alfred, Taiaiake. "Deconstructing the British Columbia Treaty Process." In *Dispatches from the Cold Seas: Indigenous Views on Self-Government, Ecology, and Identity*. Edited by C. Rattray and T. Mustonen. Tampere, Finland: Tampere Polytechnic, 2001.

————. *Peace, Power, Righteousness: An Indigenous Manifesto*. Don Mills, Ont.: Oxford University Press, 1999.

————. *Wasase: Indigenous Pathways of Action and Freedom*. Peterborough, Ont.: Broadview Press, 2005.

Amory, Hugh, and David D. Hall, eds. *The Colonial Book in the Atlantic World*. Cambridge: Cambridge University Press, 2000.

Anderson, Benedict. *Imagined Communities: Reflections on the Origin and Spread of Nationalism*, rev. ed. London: Verso, 1991.

Andrews, Charles McLean, *The Colonial Period of American History*, 4 vols. New Haven, Conn.: Yale University Press, 1934–38.

———. *Our Earliest Colonial Settlements, Their Diversities of Origin and Later Characteristics*. New York: New York University Press, 1933.

Andrews, K. R., N. P. Canny, and P. E. H. Hair, eds. *The Westward Enterprise: English Activities in Ireland, the Atlantic, and America, 1480–1650*. Detroit: Wayne State University Press, 1979.

Andrews, Matthew Page. *The Founding of Maryland*. New York: D. Appleton-Century Co., 1933.

Anghie, Antony, *Imperialism, Sovereignty and the Making of International Law*. Cambridge: Cambridge University Press, 2007.

Appleby, Joyce. *Liberalism and Republicanism in the Historical Imagination*. Cambridge, Mass.: Harvard University Press, 1992.

Aptheker, Herbert. "The Quakers and Negro Slavery." *Journal of Negro History* 25, no. 3 (1940): 331–62.

Arendt, Hannah. *The Human Condition*. Chicago: University of Chicago Press, 1958.

Armitage, David. "The Cromwellian Protectorate and the Languages of Empire." *Historical Journal* 35, no. 3 (September 1992): 531–55.

———. *The Ideological Origins of the British Empire*. Cambridge: Cambridge University Press, 2000.

———. "John Locke, Carolina, and the *Two Treatises of Government*." *Political Theory* 32, no. 5 (2004): 602–27.

———. "That Excellent Forme of Government." *Times Literary Supplement*, October 22, 2004, 14–15.

Arneil, Barbara. *John Locke and America: The Defence of English Colonialism*. Oxford: Clarendon Press, 1996.

Attwood, Bain. "The Law of the Land or the Law of the Land? History, Law, and Narrative in a Settler Society." *History Compass* 2 (2004): 1–30.

Axtell, James. "The Ethnohistory of Early America: A Review Essay." *William and Mary Quarterly* 35 (1978): 110–44.

———. *The European and the Indian: Essays in the Ethnohistory of Colonial North America*. New York: Oxford University Press, 1981.

———. *The Invasion Within: The Contest of Cultures in Colonial North America*. New York: Oxford University Press, 1986.

Bagehot, Walter. *The English Constitution*, 2d ed. Oxford: Oxford University Press, 1872.

Baldwin, William E., ed. *Bouvier's Law Dictionary*. New York: Banks Law Publishing, 1928.

Banner, Stuart. *How the Indians Lost Their Land: Law and Power on the Frontier*. Cambridge, Mass.: Harvard University Press, 2005.

Barker, Eirlys. "Indian Traders, Charles Town, and London's Vital Links to the Interior of North America, 1717–1785." Pp. 141–65 in *Money, Trade, and Power: The Evolu-*

tion of Colonial South Carolina's Plantation Society. Edited by Jack P. Greene, Rosemary Brana-Shute, and Randy J. Sparks. Columbia: University of South Carolina Press, 2001.

Barry, Brian. *Culture and Equality*. Cambridge, Mass.: Harvard University Press, 2001.

Bartlett, Richard H. "Native Title in Australia: Denial, Recognition, and Dispossession." Pp. 408–27 in *Indigenous Peoples' Rights in Australia, Canada, and New Zealand*. Edited by Paul Havemann. New York: Oxford University Press, 1999.

Beatty, Jim. "Natives Lose Court Bid to Block B[ritish] C[olumbia] Referendum on Treaties." *Vancouver Sun*, March 28, 2002, A3.

Becker, Marshall. "Lenape Land Sales, Treaties, and Wampum Belts." *Pennsylvania Magazine of History and Biography* 108 (July 1984): 351–56.

———. "Lenape Maize Sales to the Swedish Colonists: Cultural Stability during the Early Colonial Period." Pp. 120–35 in *New Sweden in America*. Edited by Carol E. Hoffecker et al. Newark: University of Delaware Press, 1995.

Belson, Ken. "Judge Says Oneida Indians Deserve a Chance for Redress." *New York Times*, May 22, 2007, B4.

Benton, Lauren. "Colonial Law and Cultural Difference: Jurisdictional Politics and the Formation of the Colonial State." *Comparative Studies in Society and History* 41 (1999): 563–88.

———. *Law and Colonial Cultures: Legal Regimes in World History, 1400–1900*. Cambridge: Cambridge University Press, 2002.

Bergmann, Mathias D. "Being the Other: Catholicism, Anglicanism, and Constructs of Britishness in Colonial Maryland." Ph.D. diss., Washington State University, Pullman, 2004.

Bhabha, Homi. "Of Mimicry and Man: The Ambivalence of Colonial Discourse." *October* 28 (1984): 125–33.

———. "Signs Taken for Wonder: Questions of Ambivalence and Authority under a Tree Outside Delhi, May 1817." Pp. 102–22 in Homi Bhabha, *The Location of Culture*. New York: Routledge, 1994.

Bilder, Mary Sarah. "English Settlement and Local Governance." Pp. 63–103 in *The Cambridge History of Law in America*. Edited by Michael Grossberg and Christopher L. Tomlins. Cambridge: Cambridge University Press, 2008.

———. *The Transatlantic Constitution: Colonial Legal Culture and the Empire*. Cambridge, Mass.: Harvard University Press, 2004.

Blackburn, Robin. *The Making of New World Slavery: From the Baroque to the Modern, 1492–1800*. London: Verso, 1997.

Bliss, Robert M. *Revolution and Empire: English Politics and the American Colonies in the Seventeenth Century*. Manchester: Manchester University Press, 1990.

Bodle, Wayne. "Themes and Directions in Middle Colonies Historiography, 1980–1994." *William and Mary Quarterly* 51 (1994): 355–88.

Bonomi, Patricia. *Under the Cope of Heaven: Religion, Society, and Politics in Colonial America*. New York: Oxford University Press, 1986.

Bossy, John. "Reluctant Colonists: The English Catholics Confront the Atlantic." Pp. 149–66 in *Early Maryland in a Wider World*. Edited by David B. Quinn. Detroit: Wayne State University Press, 1982.

Breen, T. H. "Creative Adaptations: Peoples and Cultures." Pp. 195–232 in *Colonial British America: Essays in the New History of the Early Modern Era*. Edited by Jack P. Greene and J. R. Pole. Baltimore: John Hopkins University Press, 1984.

Brett, Annabel. "The Development of the Idea of Citizens' Rights." Pp. 97–114 in *States and Citizens: History, Theory, Prospects*. Edited by Quentin Skinner and Bo Stråth. Cambridge: Cambridge University Press, 2003.

Brewer, John. *The Sinews of War: War, Money, and the English State, 1688–1783*. New York: Alfred A. Knopf, 1988.

Bronner, Edwin B. *William Penn's "Holy Experiment."* Philadelphia: Temple University Press, 1962.

Brown, Elizabeth Gaspar. "British Statutes in the Emergent Nations of North America: 1606–1949." *American Journal of Legal History* 7 (1963): 95–135.

Brown, Michael. *Who Owns Native Culture?* Cambridge, Mass.: Harvard University Press, 2003.

Browne, William Hand. *George Calvert and Cecilius Calvert, Barons Baltimore of Baltimore*. New York: Dodd, Mead, 1890.

Brownlie, Ian. *Treaties and Indigenous Peoples*. New York: Oxford University Press, 1992.

Brugger, Robert J., with Cynthia Horsburgh Requardt, Robert I. Cotton Jr., and Mary Ellen Hayward. *Maryland: A Middle Temperament, 1635–1980*, 2d ed. Baltimore: Johns Hopkins University Press, 1989.

Buranelli, Vincent. *The King and the Quaker: A Study of William Penn and James II*. Philadelphia: University of Pennsylvania Press, 1962.

Burgess, Glenn. *The Politics of the Ancient Constitution: An Introduction to English Political Thought, 1603–1642*. University Park: Pennsylvania State University Press, 1993.

Burke, Edmund, and William Burke. *An Account of the European Settlements in America*, 2d ed., 2 vols, London, 1758. New York: Research Reprints, 1970.

Byrnes, Giselle Byrnes. *The Waitangi Tribunal and New Zealand History*. Oxford: Oxford University Press, 2004.

Calloway, Colin. *New Worlds for All*. Baltimore: Johns Hopkins University Press, 1999.

Canny, Nicholas. "Writing Atlantic History; or, Reconfiguring the History of Colonial British America." *Journal of American History* 86 (2000): 1093–1114.

Canny, Nicholas, ed. *The Oxford History of the British Empire*, vol. 1. Oxford: Oxford University Press, 1998.

Carr, Lois Green. "Emigration and the Standard of Living: The Seventeenth Century Chesapeake." *Journal of Economic History* 52, no. 2 (1992): 271–91.

Carr, Lois Green, and David William Jordan. *Maryland's Revolution of Government, 1689–1692*. Ithaca, N.Y.: Cornell University Press, 1974.

Carr, Lois Green, Philip D. Morgan, and Jean B. Russo, eds. *Colonial Chesapeake Society*. Chapel Hill: University of North Carolina Press, 1988.

Carroll, Kenneth L. "Persecution of Quakers in Early Maryland (1658–1661)." *Quaker History* 53 (1964): 67–80.

Castoriadis, Cornelius. *The Imaginary Institution of Society*. Cambridge, Mass.: Harvard University Press, 1987.

———. *World in Fragments: Writings on Politics, Society, Psychoanalysts, and the Imagination*. Stanford, Calif.: Stanford University Press, 1997.

Chaplin, Joyce. *Subject Matter: Technology, the Body, and Science on the Anglo-American Frontier, 1500–1676*. Cambridge, Mass.: Harvard University Press, 2001.

Chapman, James Milling. *Red Carolinians*. Chapel Hill: University of North Carolina Press, 1940.

Clifford, James. *The Predicament of Culture*. Cambridge, Mass.: Harvard University Press, 1988.

Coakley, Thomas D. "George Calvert and Newfoundland: The Sad Face of Winter." *Maryland Historical Magazine* 71 (1976): 1–19.

Coin, Glenn. "Judge Refuses to Revisit Ruling on Land Trust." *Post-Standard* (Syracuse, N.Y.), September 12, 2007, B1.

Collinson, Patrick. "Afterword." Pp. 245–60 in *The Monarchical Republic of Early Modern England*. Edited by John F. McDiarmid. Aldershot: Ashgate Press, 2007.

———. "De Republica Anglorum: Or, History with the Politics Put Back." Pp. 14–27 in Patrick Collinson, *Elizabethan Essays*. London: Hambledon Press, 1994.

Connolly, William E. "The Liberal Image of the Nation." Pp. 183–99 in *Political Theory and the Rights of Indigenous Peoples*. Edited by Duncan Ivison et al. Cambridge: Cambridge University Press, 2000.

Cranston, Maurice. *John Locke, a Biography*. London: Longman, 1957.

Craven, Wesley Frank. "The Early Settlement." Pp. 15–19 in *Perspectives in South Carolina History: The First 300 Years*. Edited by Ernest M. Lander Jr. and Robert K. Ackerman. Columbia: University of South Carolina Press, 1973.

Cronon, William. *Changes in the Land: Indians, Colonists, and the Ecology of New England*. New York: Hill and Wang, 1983.

Cross, Geoffrey, and G. D. G. Hall. *The English Legal System*, 4th ed. London: Butterworths, 1964.

Curry, Steven. *Indigenous Sovereignty and the Democratic Project*. Aldershot: Ashgate, 2004.

Curtis, Mark. *Oxford and Cambridge in Transition, 1558–1642: An Essay on Changing Relations between the English Universities and English Society*. Oxford: Clarendon Press, 1959.

Dahlgren, Stellan, and Hans Norman. *The Rise and Fall of New Sweden*. Stockholm: Almquist and Wiksell, 1988.

Daniels, Christine, and Michael V. Kennedy, eds. *Negotiated Empires: Centers and Peripheries in the Americas, 1500–1820*. New York: Routledge, 2002.

de Certeau, Michel. *The Practice of Everyday Life*. Translated by Steven Rendall. Berkeley: University of California Press, 1984.

——. *The Writing of History*. Translated by Tom Conley. New York: Columbia University Press, 1988.

Derrida, Jacques. *Negotiations: Interventions and Interviews, 1971–2001*, ed. and trans. by Elizabeth Rottenberg. Stanford, Calif.: Stanford University Press, 2002.

de Tocqueville, Alexis. *Democracy in America*, ed. and trans. by Harvey C. Mansfield and Delba Winthrop. Chicago: University of Chicago Press, 2000.

Deveaux, Monique. *Cultural Pluralism and the Dilemmas of Justice*. Ithaca, N.Y.: Cornell University Press, 2000.

Duff, Meaghan N. "Designing Carolina: The Construction of an Early American Social and Geographical Landscape, 1670–1719." Ph.D. diss., College of William and Mary, Williamsburg, Va., 1998.

Dunn, John. *The Political Thought of John Locke*. Cambridge: Cambridge University Press, 1969.

Dunn, Mary Maples. "William Penn, Classical Republican." *Pennsylvania Magazine of History and Biography* 81 (1957): 138–56.

——. *William Penn, Politics and Conscience*. Princeton: Princeton University Press, 1967.

Dunn, Richard S. "Master, Servants, and Slaves in the Colonial Chesapeake and the Caribbean." Pp. 242–66 in *Early Maryland in a Wider World*. Edited by David B. Quinn. Detroit: Wayne State University Press, 1982.

Edelson, S. Max. "Affiliation without Affinity." Pp. 217–55 in *Money, Trade, and Power: The Evolution of Colonial South Carolina's Plantation Society*. Edited by Jack P. Greene, Rosemary Brana-Shute, and Randy J. Sparks. Columbia: University of South Carolina Press, 2001.

——. *Plantation Enterprise in Colonial South Carolina*. Cambridge, Mass.: Harvard University Press, 2006.

Edwards, Philip. *The Making of the Modern English State, 1460–1660*. New York: St. Martin's Press, 2000.

Elton, G. R. "Contentment and Discontent on the Eve of Colonization." Pp. 105–18 in *Early Maryland in a Wider World*. Edited by David B. Quinn. Detroit: Wayne State University Press, 1982.

Endy, Melvin B. *William Penn and Early Quakerism*. Princeton: Princeton University Press, 1973.

Fagg, Daniel W. "Sleeping Not with the King's Grant: A Rereading of Some Proprietary Documents." *North Carolina Historical Review* 41 (1971): 171–86.

Falb, Susan Rosenfeld. *Advice and Assent: The Development of the Maryland Assembly, 1635–1689*. New York: Garland Publishing, 1986.

Farr, James. "Locke, Natural Law, and New World Slavery." *Political Theory* 36 (August 2008): 495–522.

———. " 'So Vile and Miserable an Estate': The Problem of Slavery in Locke's Political Thought." *Political Theory* 14 (1986): 263–89.

Fausz, J. Frederick. "Merging and Emerging Worlds: Anglo-Indian Interest Groups and the Development of the Seventeenth-Century Chesapeake." Pp. 47–98 in *Colonial Chesapeake Society*. Edited by Lois Green Carr, Philip D. Morgan, and Jean B. Russo. Chapel Hill: University of North Carolina Press, 1988.

———. "Present at the 'Creation': The Chesapeake World that Greeted the Maryland Colonists." *Maryland Historical Magazine* 79 (1984): 7–20.

Ferguson, Alice L. L. *Moyaone and the Piscataway Indians*. Washington, D.C.: National Capitol Press, 1937.

Fischer, Kirsten. *Suspect Relations: Sex, Race, and Resistance in Colonial North Carolina*. Ithaca, N.Y.: Cornell University Press, 2002.

Fitzmaurice, Andrew. "American Corruption." Pp. 217–32 in *The Monarchical Republic of Early Modern England*. Edited by John F. McDiarmid. Aldershot: Aldgate, 2007.

———. "The Civic Solution to the Crisis of English Colonization, 1609–1625," *Historical Journal* 42, no. 1 (March 1999): 25–51.

———. "Classical Rhetoric and the Promotion of the New World." *Journal of the History of Ideas* 58, no. 2 (April 1997): 221–43.

———. "The Genealogy of *Terra Nullius*." *Australian Historical Studies* 38, no. 129 (April 2007): 1–15.

———. *Humanism and America: An Intellectual History of English Colonisation, 1500–1625*. Cambridge: Cambridge University Press, 2003.

Foucault, Michel. *Language, Counter-Memory, Practice: Selected Essays and Interviews*. Edited by Donald F. Bouchards. Translated by Donald F. Bouchard and Sherry Simon. Ithaca, N.Y.: Cornell University Press, 1977.

———. *Power/Knowledge: Selected Interviews and Other Writings, 1972–1977*. Edited and translated by Colin Gordon. New York: Pantheon Books, 1980.

Fraser, Nancy, and Linda Gordon. "A Genealogy of 'Dependency': Tracing a Keyword of the U.S. Welfare State." Pp. 121–150 in *Justice Interruptus: Critical Reflections on the "Postsocialist" Condition*. New York: Routledge, 1997.

Gallay, Alan. *The Indian Slave Trade: The Rise of the English Empire in the American South, 1670–1717*. New Haven, Conn.: Yale University Press, 2003.

Garrison, Hazel S. "Cartography of Pennsylvania before 1800." *Pennsylvania Magazine of History and Biography* 59 (1935): 259–63.

Geiter, Mary K. "London Merchants and the Launching of Pennsylvania." *Pennsylvania Magazine of History and Biography* 121 (1997): 101–22.

———. "The Restoration Crisis and the Launching of Pennsylvania, 1679–81." *English Historical Review* 112 (1997): 313–24.

———. *William Penn*. London: Longman, 2000.

Geiter, Mary K., and W. A. Speck. *A Dictionary of British America, 1584–1783*. Basing-stoke: Palgrave Macmillan, 2007.

Goldie, Mark. "The Unacknowledged Republic: Political Participation in Early Modern England." Pp. 153–94 in *The Politics of the Excluded, c. 1500–1850*. Edited by T. Harris. New York: Palgrave, 2001.

———. *The Reception of Locke's Politics*, 6 vols. London: Pickering and Chatto, 1999.

Gough, J. W. *Fundamental Law in English Constitutional History*. Oxford: Clarendon Press, 1961.

Gray, Edward G. *New World Babel: Languages and Nations in Early America*. Princeton: Princeton University Press, 1999.

Greenberg, Douglas. "The Middle Colonies in Recent American Historiography." *William and Mary Quarterly* 36 (1979): 396–427.

Greene, Jack P. "England, the Caribbean, and the Settlement of Carolina." *Journal of American Studies* 9 (1975): 260–75.

———. *Imperatives, Behaviors, and Identities: Essays in Early American Cultural History*. Charlottesville: University Press of Virginia, 1992.

———. *Interpreting Early America: Historiographical Essays*. Charlottesville: University Press of Virginia, 1996.

———. *Negotiated Authorities: Essays in Colonial Political and Constitutional History*. Charlottesville: University Press of Virginia, 1994.

———. *Peripheries and Center: Constitutional Development in the Extended Polities of the British Empire and the United States, 1607–1788*. Athens: University of Georgia Press, 1986.

———. *Pursuits of Happiness: The Social Development of Early Modern British Colonies and the Formation of American Culture*. Chapel Hill: University of North Carolina Press, 1988.

Greene, Jack P., ed. *Great Britain and the American Colonies, 1606–1763*. Columbia: University of South Carolina Press, 1970.

Greene, Jack P., Rosemary Brana-Shute, and Randy J. Sparks, eds. *Money, Trade, and Power: The Evolution of Colonial South Carolina's Plantation Society*. Columbia: University of South Carolina Press, 2001.

Grossberg, Michael, and Christopher L. Tomlins, eds. *The Cambridge History of Law in America*. Cambridge: Cambridge University Press, 2008.

Gutmann, Amy, ed. *Multiculturalism and "The Politics of Recognition."* Princeton: Princeton University Press, 1992.

Hadfield, Andrew. *Amazons, Savages, and Machiavels: Travel and Colonial Writing in English, 1550–1630*. Oxford: Oxford University Press, 2001.

Haffenden, Philip S. "The Crown and the Colonial Charters, 1675–1688." *William and Mary Quarterly* 15 (1958): 297–311.

Haley, K. H. D. *The First Earl of Shaftesbury*. Oxford: Clarendon Press, 1968.

Hall, Clayton Colman, *The Lords Baltimore and the Maryland Palatinate*, 2d ed. Baltimore: Nunn, 1904.

Hall, David. "The Chesapeake in the Seventeenth Century." Pp. 55–82 in *A History of the Book in America*, vol. 1. Edited by Hugh Amory and David D. Hall. Cambridge: Cambridge University Press, 1999.

Hall, Kim F. *Things of Darkness: Economies of Race and Gender in Early Modern England.* Ithaca, N.Y.: Cornell University Press, 1995.

Harper, Steven Craig. *Promised Land: Penn's Holy Experiment, the Walking Purchase, and the Dispossession of Delawares, 1600–1763.* Bethlehem, Penn.: Lehigh University Press, 2006.

Harrison, Christopher. "Manor Courts and the Governance of Tudor England." Pp. 43–60 in *Communities and Courts in Britain, 1150–1900.* Edited by Christopher Brooks and Michael Lobban. London: Continuum International Publishing Group, 1997.

Harvard Project on American Indian Economic Development, comp. *The State of the Native Nations: Conditions under U.S. Policies of Self-Determination.* New York: Oxford University Press, 2008.

Hatley, Thomas M. *The Dividing Paths: Cherokees and South Carolinians through the Era of Revolution.* New York: Oxford University Press, 1993.

Helgerson, Richard. "The Land Speaks: Cartography, Chorography, and Subversion in Renaissance England." *Representations* 16 (1986): 50–85.

Hendrix, Burke A. "Moral Error, Power, and Insult." *Political Theory* 35, no. 5 (2007): 550–73.

Hewitt, Gary. "The State in the Planters' Service." Pp. 59–70 in *Money, Trade, and Power: The Evolution of Colonial South Carolina's Plantation Society.* Edited by Jack P. Greene, Rosemary Brana-Shute, and Randy J. Sparks. Columbia: University of South Carolina Press, 2001.

Hindess, Barry. "Divide and Rule: The International Character of Modern Citizenship." *European Journal of Social Theory* 1, no. 1 (1998): 57–70.

Hirschl, Ran. *Towards Juristocracy: The Origins and Consequences of the New Constitutionalism.* Cambridge, Mass.: Harvard University Press, 2004.

Hoffecker, Carol E., et al., eds. *New Sweden in America.* Newark, Del.: University of Delaware Press, 1995.

Hoffer, Peter Charles. *Law and People in Colonial America.* Baltimore: Johns Hopkins University Press, 1998.

Honig, Bonnie. "Declarations of Independence: Arendt and Derrida on the Problem of Founding a Republic." *American Political Science Review* 85, no. 1 (March 1991): 97–113.

———. *Democracy and the Foreigner.* Princeton: Princeton University Press, 2001.

Hont, Istvan. *Jealousy of Trade: International Competition and the Nation-State in Historical Perspective.* Cambridge, Mass.: Harvard University Press, 2005.

Houston, Alan Craig. *Algernon Sidney and the Republican Heritage in England and America.* Princeton: Princeton University Press, 1991.

Hsueh, Vicki. "Cultivating and Challenging the Common: Lockean Property, Indigenous Traditionalisms, and the Problem of Exclusion." *Contemporary Political Theory* 5 (2006): 193–214.

———. "Giving Orders: Theory and Practice in the *Fundamental Constitutions of Carolina*." *Journal of the History of Ideas* 63: 3 (2002): 425–46.

———. "Unsettling Colonies: Locke, Carolina, and 'Atlantis.'" *History of Political Thought* 29 (2008): 295–319.

Hulsebosch, Daniel J. *Constituting Empire: New York and the Transformation of Constitutionalism in the Atlantic World, 1664–1830*. Chapel Hill: University of North Carolina Press, 2005.

Hutton, Ronald. *Charles the Second, King of England, Scotland, and Ireland*. Oxford: Oxford University Press, 1989.

Illick, Joseph E. *Colonial Pennsylvania: A History*. New York: Charles Scribner's Sons, 1976.

———. "The Pennsylvania Grant: A Re-evaluation." *Pennsylvania Magazine of History and Biography* 86 (1962): 375–96.

Ingle, Edward. *Captain Richard Ingle, the Maryland "Pirate and Rebel," 1642–1653*. Baltimore: J. Murphy & Co., 1884.

Ivison, Duncan. *Postcolonial Liberalism*. Cambridge: Cambridge University Press, 2002.

Ivison, Duncan, et al., eds. *Political Theory and the Rights of Indigenous Peoples*. Cambridge: Cambridge University Press, 2000.

Jameson, John Franklin. *Privateering and Piracy in the Colonial Period*. New York, A. M. Kelley, 1970.

Jennings, Francis. "Brother Miquon: Good Lord!" Pp. 195–210 in *The World of William Penn*. Edited by Richard S. Dunn and Mary Maples Dunn. Philadelphia: University of Pennsylvania Press, 1986.

———. "Indians and Frontiers in Seventeenth-Century Maryland." Pp. 216–41 in *Early Maryland in a Wider World*. Edited by David B. Quinn. Detroit: Wayne State University Press, 1982.

———. *The Invasion of America: Indians, Colonialism, and the Cant of Conquest*. New York: W. W. Norton, 1975.

———. "'Pennsylvania Indians' and the Iroquois." Pp. 75–92 in *Beyond the Covenant Chain: The Iroquois and Their Neighbors in Indian North America, 1600–1800*. Edited by Daniel K. Richter and James H. Merrell. Syracuse, N.Y.: Syracuse University Press, 1987.

Johansen, Bruce E. "The New York Oneidas: A Business Called a Nation." Pp. 95–134 in *Enduring Legacies: North American Treaties and Contemporary Controversies*. Edited by Bruce Johansen. Westport, Conn.: Praeger, 2004.

Jordan, David W. *Foundations of Representative Government in Maryland, 1632–1715*. Cambridge: Cambridge University Press, 1987.

———. "Maryland's Privy Council, 1637–1715." Pp. 65–87 in *Law, Society, and Politics in Early Maryland*. Edited by Aubrey C. Land, Lois Green Carr, and Edward C. Papenfuse. Baltimore: Johns Hopkins University Press, 1977.

———. "Political Stability and the Emergence of a Native Elite in Maryland." Pp. 243–73 in *The Chesapeake in the Seventeenth Century: Essays on Anglo-American Society*. Edited by Thad W. Tate and David L. Ammerman. New York: W. W. Norton, 1979.

Jordan, Terry G., and Matti Kaups. *The American Backwoods Frontier: An Ethnic and Ecological Interpretation*. Baltimore: Johns Hopkins University Press, 1989.

Juricek, John. "English Territorial Claims in North America under Elizabeth and the Early Stuarts." *Terrae Incognitae* 7 (1975): 7–22.

Keal, Paul. *European Conquest and the Rights of Indigenous Peoples*. New York: Cambridge University Press, 2003.

Kirkby, Diane, and Catherine Colebourne, eds. *The Reach of Empire: Law, History, Colonialism*. Manchester: Manchester University Press, 2001.

Klein, William. "The Ancient Constitution Revisited." Pp. 23–44 in *Political Discourse in Early Modern Britain*. Edited by Nicholas Phillipson and Quentin Skinner. Cambridge: Cambridge University Press, 1993.

Klepp, Susan. "Encounter and Experiment: The Colonial Period." Pp. 47–100 in *Pennsylvania: A History of the Commonwealth*. Edited by William A. Pencak and Randall M. Miller. University Park: Pennsylvania State University Press and Harrisburg: Pennsylvania Historical and Museum Commission, 2002.

Knapp, Steven. *Literary Interest: The Limits of Literary Formalism*. Cambridge, Mass.: Harvard University Press, 1993.

Konig, David. "Regionalism in Early American Law." Pp. 144–77 in *The Cambridge History of Law in America*. Edited by Michael Grossberg and Christopher L. Tomlins. Cambridge: Cambridge University Press, 2008.

Krugler, John D. "The Calvert Family, Catholicism and Court Politics in Early Seventeenth Century England." *Historian* 43 (1981): 378–92.

———. "Lord Baltimore, Roman Catholics, and Toleration: Religious Policy in Maryland during the Early Catholic Years, 1634–1649." *Catholic Historical Review* 65 (1979): 49–75.

———. "'Our Trusty and Well Beloved Councillor': The Parliamentary Career of Sir George Calvert, 1609–24." *Maryland Historical Magazine* 72 (1977): 470–91.

Kupperman, Karen Ordahl. *Indians and English: Facing Off in Early America*. Ithaca, N.Y.: Cornell University Press, 2000.

———. "Scandinavian Colonists Confront the New World." Pp. 89–111 in *New Sweden in America*. Edited by Carol E. Hoffecker et al. Newark: University of Delaware Press, 1995.

———. *Settling with the Indians: The Meeting of English and Indian Cultures in America, 1580–1640*. Totowa, N.J.: Rowman and Littlefield, 1980.

Land, Aubrey C. *Colonial Maryland, a History*. Millwood, N.Y.: KTO Press, 1981.

Lapsley, Gaillard Thomas. *The County Palatine of Durham: A Study in Constitutional History*. New York: Longmans, Green, 1900.

Laslett, Peter, and John Harrison. *The Library of John Locke*. Oxford: Oxford University Press, 1965.

Lee, Maurice. *The CABAL*. Urbana: University of Illinois Press, 1965.

Levy, Jacob T. "Not so Novus an Ordo: Constitutions without Social Contracts." *Political Theory*, forthcoming.

Lippincott, Constance. *Maryland as a Palatinate*. Philadelphia: J. B. Lippincott, 1902.

Lucas, Samuel. *Charters of the Old English Colonies in America*. London: J. W. Parker, 1850.

Maaka, Roger, and Augie Fleras. "Engaging with Indigeneity: *Tino Rangatiratanga* in Aotearoa." Pp. 89–112 in *Political Theory and the Rights of Indigenous Peoples*. Edited by Duncan Ivison et al. Cambridge: Cambridge University Press, 2000.

Mackintosh, Michael Dean. "New Sweden, Natives, and Nature." Pp. 3–17 in *Friends and Enemies in Penn's Woods: Indians, Colonists, and the Racial Construction of Pennsylvania*. University Park: Pennsylvania State University Press, 2004.

MacMillan, Kenneth. "Common and Civil Law? Taking Possession of the English Empire in America, 1575–1630." *Canadian Journal of History* 38, no. 3 (2003): 409–24.

————. *Sovereignty and Possession in the English New World: The Legal Foundations of Empire, 1576–1640*. Cambridge: Cambridge University Press, 2006.

Mahoney, James. *Legacies of Liberalism: Path Dependence and Political Regimes in Central America*. Baltimore: Johns Hopkins University Press, 2001.

Mancke, Elizabeth. "Negotiating an Empire: Britain and its Overseas Population, c. 1550–1780." Pp. 235–66 in *Negotiated Empires: Centers and Peripheries in the Americas, 1500–1820*. Edited by Christine Daniels and Michael V. Kennedy. New York: Routledge, 2002.

Marshall, P. J., ed. *Cambridge Illustrated History of the British Empire*. Cambridge: Cambridge University Press, 2001.

McClure, Kirstie M. "Cato's Retreat: *Fabula, Historia*, and the Question of Constitutionalism in Mr. Locke's Anonymous Essay on Government." In *Writing Readers in Early Modern England*. Edited by Steven Zwicker and Kevin Sharpe. Cambridge: Cambridge University Press, forthcoming.

McDiarmid, John F., ed. *The Monarchical Republic of Early Modern England*. Aldershot: Ashgate Press, 2007.

McFarlane, Anthony. *The British in the Americas, 1480–1815*. London: Longman, 1992.

McGuinness, Celia. "The Fundamental Constitutions of Carolina as a Tool for Lockean Scholarship." *Interpretation* 17, no. 1 (1990): 127–43.

McHugh, P. G. *Aboriginal Societies and the Common Law: A History of Sovereignty, Status, and Self-Determination*. Oxford: Oxford University Press, 2004.

McIlwain, Charles H. *Constitutionalism: Ancient and Modern*, rev. ed. Ithaca, N.Y.: Great Seal Books, 1947.

Mehta, Uday Singh. *Liberalism and Empire: A Study in Nineteenth-Century British Liberal Thought*. Chicago: University of Chicago Press, 1999.

Menard, Russell R., and Lois Green Carr. "The Lords Baltimore and the Colonization of Maryland." Pp. 172–85 in *Early Maryland in a Wider World*. Edited by David B. Quinn. Detroit: Wayne State University Press, 1982.

Mereness, Newton Dennison. *Maryland as a Proprietary Province* (1901), reprint. ed. Cos Cob, Conn.: J. E. Edwards, 1968.

Merrell, James H. "Cultural Continuity among the Piscataway Indians of Colonial Maryland." *William and Mary Quarterly* 36 (1979): 548–70.

———. *The Indians' New World: Catawbas and Their Neighbors from European Contact through the Era of Removal*. Chapel Hill: Institute of Early American History and Culture, Williamsburg, Va., by University of North Carolina Press, 1989.

———. "The Indian's New World: The Catawba Experience." *William and Mary Quarterly* 41, no. 4 (1984): 537–565.

———. *Into the American Woods: Negotiators on the Pennsylvania Frontier*. New York: W. W. Norton, 1999.

Merritt, Jane T. *At the Crossroads: Indians and Empires on a Mid-Atlantic Frontier*. Chapel Hill: Omohundro Institute of Early American History and Culture, Williamsburg, Va., by University of North Carolina Press, 2003.

Miller, Randall. "Amerindian (Native American) Cultures in Pre- and Early European Settlement Periods in Pennsylvania." *Pennsylvania Ethnic Studies Newsletter*, 1989, 1–4.

Mills, Charles W. *The Racial Contract*. Ithaca, N.Y.: Cornell University Press, 1997.

Milton, J. R. "John Locke and the Fundamental Constitutions of Carolina." *Locke Newsletter* 21 (1990): 111–33.

Mishra, Pramod. "'[All] the World Was America': The Transatlantic (Post)Coloniality of John Locke, William Bartram, and the Declaration of Independence." *New Centennial Review* 2 (2002): 224–37.

Muldoon, James. "Discovery, Grant, Charter, Conquest, or Purchase: John Adams on the Legal Basis for English Possession of North America." Pp. 25–46 in *The Many Legalities of Early America*. Edited by Christopher L. Tomlins and Bruce H. Mann. Chapel Hill: Omohundro Institute of Early American History and Culture, Williamsburg, Va., by University of North Carolina Press, 2001.

———. *Empire and Order: The Concept of Empire, 800–1800*. New York: St. Martin's Press, 1999.

Murphy, Andrew R. *Conscience and Community: Revisiting Toleration and Religious Dissent in Early Modern England and America*. University Park: Pennsylvania State University Press, 2001.

Murray, David. *Forked Tongues: Speech, Writing, and Representation in North American Native Texts*. Bloomington: Indiana University Press, 1991.

Nash, Gary B. "City Planning and Political Tension in the Seventeenth Century: The Case of Philadelphia." *Proceedings of the American Philosophical Society* 112 (1968): 54–73.

———. "The Framing of Government in Pennsylvania: Ideas in Conflict with Reality." *William and Mary Quarterly* 23 (1966): 183–209.

———. *Red, White, and Black: The Peoples of Early North America*, rev. ed. Englewood Cliffs, N.J.: Prentice-Hall, 1992.

———. "Slaves and Slaveholders in Colonial Philadelphia." *William and Mary Quarterly* 30, no. 2 (1973): 223–56.

Newbury, Colin. "Review: The Waitangi Tribunal and New Zealand History." *English Historical Review* 120, no. 489 (December 2005): 1469–71.

Pagden, Anthony. *The Languages of Political Theory in Early-Modern Europe*. New York: Cambridge University Press, 1987.

———. "Law, Colonization, Legitimation, and the European Background." Pp. 1–31 in *The Cambridge History of Law in America*. Edited by Michael Grossberg and Christopher L. Tomlins. Cambridge: Cambridge University Press, 2008.

Palumbo, Rina. "The Boundaries of Empire: Writing, Authority, and the Feudal Imaginary: Forging the British Atlantic Community, c. 1580–1670." Ph.D. diss., Johns Hopkins University, Baltimore, 2001.

Parekh, Bhikhu. "Liberalism and Colonialism: A Critique of Locke and Mill." Pp. 81–98 in *The Decolonization of Imagination: Culture, Knowledge, and Power*. Edited by Jan N. Pieterse and Bhikhu Parekh. London: Zed Books, 1995.

———. *Rethinking Multiculturalism: Cultural Diversity and Political Theory*. Houndmills: Macmillan, 2000.

Peltonen, Markku. *Classical Humanism and Republicanism in English Political Thought, 1570–1640*. Cambridge: Cambridge University Press, 1995.

Pencak, William A., and Randall M. Miller, eds. *Pennsylvania: A History of the Commonwealth*. University Park: Pennsylvania State University Press, and Harrisburg: Pennsylvania Historical and Museum Commission, 2002.

Pencak, William A., and Daniel K. Richter, eds. *Friends and Enemies in Penn's Woods: Indians, Colonists, and the Racial Construction of Pennsylvania*. University Park: Pennsylvania State University Press, 2004.

Phillipson, Nicholas, and Quentin Skinner. *Political Discourse in Early Modern Britain*. Cambridge: Cambridge University Press, 1993.

Pocock, J. G. A. *The Ancient Constitution and the Feudal Law: A Study of English Historical Thought in the Seventeenth Century, a Reissue with a Retrospect*. Cambridge: Cambridge University Press, 1987.

———. "The Concept of a Language and the *Métier d'Historien*: Some Considerations on Practice." Pp. 19–40 in *The Languages of Political Theory in Early-Modern Europe*. Edited by Anthony Pagden. New York: Cambridge University Press, 1987.

———. *The Machiavellian Moment: Florentine Political Thought and the Atlantic Republican Tradition*. Princeton: Princeton University Press, 1975.

—————. *Virtue, Commerce, and History*. Cambridge: Cambridge University Press, 1985.

—————. "Waitangi as Mystery of State: Consequence of the Ascription of Federative Capacity to the Maori." Pp. 25–35 in *Political Theory and the Rights of Indigenous Peoples*. Edited by Duncan Ivison et al. Cambridge: Cambridge University Press, 2000.

Pocock, J. G. A., ed. *Three British Revolutions, 1641, 1688, 1776*. Princeton: Princeton University Press, 1980.

Powell, William S. "Carolana and the Incomparable Roanoke: Explorations and Attempted Settlements, 1620–1663." *North Carolina Historical Review* 59 (1974): 12–21.

Quinn, David B., ed. *Early Maryland in a Wider World*. Detroit: Wayne State University Press, 1982.

Richard, Jennifer, ed. *Early Modern Civil Discourses*. Basingstoke: Palgrave Macmillan, 2003.

Richter, Daniel K. "A Framework for Pennsylvania Indian History." *Pennsylvania History* 57 (1990): 236–61.

—————. "The First Pennsylvanians." Pp. 3–46 in *Pennsylvania: A History of the Commonwealth*. Edited by William A. Pencak and Randall M. Miller. University Park: Pennsylvania State University Press, and Harrisburg: Pennsylvania Historical and Museum Commission, 2002.

Richter, Daniel K., and James H. Merrell, eds. *Beyond the Covenant Chain: The Iroquois and Their Neighbors in Indian North America, 1600–1800*. Syracuse, N.Y.: Syracuse University Press, 1987.

Ritchie, Robert C. *The Duke's Province: A Study of New York Politics and Society*. Chapel Hill: University of North Carolina Press, 1977.

Ritter, David. "The 'Rejection of Terra Nullius' in *Mabo*: A Critical Analysis." *Sydney Law Review* 18 (1996): 5–34.

Roach, Hannah. "Planting of Philadelphia: A Seventeenth Century Real Estate Development." *Pennsylvania Magazine of History and Biography* 92 (1968): 185–89.

Roper, Louis H. *Conceiving Carolina: Proprietors, Planters, and Plots, 1662–1729*. New York: Palgrave, 2004.

Roper, Louis H., and B. van Ruymbeke, eds. *Constructing Early Modern Empires: Proprietary Ventures in the Atlantic World, 1500–1750*. Leiden: Brill, 2007.

Ross, Richard J. "Legal Communications and Imperial Governance: British North America and Spanish America Compared." Pp. 104–43 in *The Cambridge History of Law in America*. Edited by Michael Grossberg and Christopher L. Tomlins. Cambridge: Cambridge University Press, 2008.

Rountree, Helen C., and Thomas E. Davidson. *Eastern Shore Indians of Virginia and Maryland*. Charlottesville: University Press of Virginia, 1997.

Rousseau, Jean-Jacques. *The Social Contract*, trans. and edited by Frederick Watkins. Madison: University of Wisconsin Press, 1986.

Rozbicki, Michal J. *The Complete Colonial Gentleman: Cultural Legitimacy in Plantation America*. Charlottesville: University Press of Virginia, 1998.

Russell Smith, H. F. *Harrington and His Oceana: A Story of a 17th Century Utopia and Its Influence in America*. New York: Octagon Books, 1971.

Sachse, Julius F. "Benjamin Furly." *Pennsylvania Magazine of History and Biography* 19 (1895): 297–306.

Salisbury, Neal. "Toward the Covenant Chain: Iroquois and Southern New England Algonquians, 1637–1684." Pp. 61–74 in *Beyond the Covenant Chain: The Iroquois and Their Neighbors in Indian North America, 1600–1800*. Edited by Daniel K. Richter and James H. Merrell. Syracuse, N.Y.: Syracuse University Press, 1987.

Sassen, Saskia. *Territory, Authority, Rights: From Medieval to Global Assemblages*. Princeton: Princeton University Press, 2006.

Scaife, Walter B. "The Boundary Dispute between Maryland and Pennsylvania." *Pennsylvania Magazine of History and Biography* 9 (1885): 264–68.

Scharf, John Thomas. *History of Maryland from Earliest Times to the Present Day*, vol. 1. Baltimore: J. B. Piet, 1879.

Schönenberger, Regula Trenkwalder. *Lenape Women, Matriliny, and the Colonial Encounter: Resistance and Erosion of Power*. Bern: Peter Lang, 1991.

Schwartz, Sally. *"A Mixed Multitude": The Struggle for Toleration in Colonial Pennsylvania*. New York: New York University Press, 1987.

Seed, Patricia. *Ceremonies of Possession in Europe's Conquest of the New World, 1492–1640*. Cambridge: Cambridge University Press, 1995.

———. "Taking Possession and Reading Texts: Establishing the Authority of an Overseas Empire." *William and Mary Quarterly* 49 (1992): 183–209.

Shalhope, Robert E. "Toward a Republican Synthesis: The Emergence of an Understanding of Republicanism in American Historiography." *William and Mary Quarterly* 29 (1972): 49–80.

Sharpe, James. "The People and the Law." Pp. 244–70 in *Popular Culture in Seventeenth Century England*. Edited by Barry Reay. New York: St. Martin's Press, 1985.

Simon, Joan. *Education and Society in Tudor England*. Cambridge: Cambridge University Press, 1966.

Sirmans, Eugene. *Colonial South Carolina: A Political History, 1663–1776*. Chapel Hill: University of North Carolina Press, 1966.

Skinner, Quentin. *The Foundations of Modern Political Thought*, vol. 1. Cambridge: Cambridge University Press, 1978.

———. *Liberty before Liberalism*. Cambridge: Cambridge University Press, 1998.

———. "Meaning and Understanding in the History of Ideas." Pp. 55–63 in *Meaning and Context: Quentin Skinner and His Critics*. Edited by James Tully. Princeton: Princeton University Press, 1989.

———. *Reason and Rhetoric in the Philosophy of Hobbes*. Cambridge: Cambridge University Press, 1996.

————. *Visions of Politics*, Volume 2: *Renaissance Virtues*. Cambridge: Cambridge University Press, 2004.

Smith, Warren B. *White Servitude in Colonial South Carolina*. Columbia: University of South Carolina Press, 1961.

Soderlund, Jean, ed. *William Penn and the Founding of Pennsylvania, 1680–1684: A Documentary History*. Philadelphia: University of Pennsylvania Press, 1983.

Sommerville, Johann P. "The Ancient Constitution Reassessed: The Common Law, the Court, and the Languages of Politics in Early Modern England." Pp. 39–63 in *The Stuart Court and Europe: Essays in Politics and Political Culture*. Edited by R. Malcolm Smuts. Cambridge: Cambridge University Press, 1996.

————. *Politics and Ideology in England, 1603–1640*. London: Longman, 1986.

Spady, James O'Neil. "Colonialism and the Discursive Antecedents of *Penn's Treaty with the Indians.*" Pp. 18–40 in *Friends and Enemies in Penn's Woods: Indians, Colonists, and the Racial Construction of Pennsylvania*. University Park: Pennsylvania State University Press, 2004.

Spivak, Gayatri Chakravorty. *A Critique of Postcolonial Reason: Toward a History of the Vanishing Present*. Cambridge, Mass.: Harvard University Press, 1999.

Steiner, Bernard Christian. *Beginnings of Maryland, 1631–1639*. Baltimore: Johns Hopkins University Press, 1903.

————. *Maryland under the Commonwealth: A Chronicle of the Years 1649–1658*. New York: AMS Press, 1971.

Stern, Philip J. "'One Body Corporate and Politick': The English East India Company-State in the Late Seventeenth Century." Ph.D diss., Columbia University, New York, 2004.

Stone, Lawrence. "The Educational Revolution in England, 1560–1649." *Past and Present*, no. 28 (1964): 41–80.

Sugrue, Thomas J. "The Peopling and Depeopling of Early Pennsylvania: Indians and Colonists, 1680–1720." *Pennsylvania Magazine of History and Biography* 116, no. 1 (1992): 3–31.

Sunstein, Cass. *Designing Democracy: What Constitutions Do*. Oxford: Oxford University Press, 2001.

Swanton, John R. *The Indian Tribes of North America*, reprint. ed. Washington, D.C.: Smithsonian Institution Press, 1952.

Taylor, Alan. *American Colonies*. New York: Viking, 2001.

Thornton, Tim. "The Palatinate of Durham and the Maryland Charter." *American Journal of Legal History* 45, no. 3 (July 2001): 235–55.

Tilly, Charles. "War-Making and State-Making as Organized Crime." Pp. 169–91 in *Bringing the State Back In*. Edited by Peter B. Evans, Dietrich Rueschemeyer, and Theda Skocpol. Cambridge: Cambridge University Press, 1985.

Tomlins, Christopher L. *In a Wilderness of Tigers: The Culture of Violence, the Discourse of English Colonizing, and the Refusals of American History*. Chicago: American Bar Foundation, 2002.

———. "Law's Empire: Chartering English Colonies on the American Mainland in the Seventeenth Century." Pp. 26–45 in *Law, History, Colonialism*. Edited by Diane Kirkby and Catherine Colebourne. Manchester: Manchester University Press, 2001

———. *The Legal Cartography of Colonization: English Intrusions on the American Mainland in the Seventeenth Century*. Chicago: American Bar Foundation, 1998.

———. "The Legal Cartography of Colonization, the Legal Polyphony of Settlement: English Intrusions on the American Mainland in the Seventeenth Century." *Law and Social Inquiry* 26, no. 2 (Spring 2001): 315–72.

Tomlins, Christopher L., and Bruce H. Mann, eds. *The Many Legalities of Early America*. Chapel Hill: University of North Carolina Press, 2001.

Treacy, William. *Old Catholic Maryland and Its Early Jesuit Missionaries*. Swedesboro, N.J.: St. Joseph's Rectory, 1889.

Trigger, Bruce G., ed. *Handbook of North American Indians*, vol. 15. Washington, D.C.: Smithsonian Institution, 1978.

Tubbs, J. W. *The Common Law Mind: Medieval and Early Modern Conceptions*. Baltimore: Johns Hopkins University Press, 2000.

Tully, James. "Aboriginal Peoples: Negotiating Reconciliation," *Canadian Politics*, 3d ed. Edited by James Bickerton and Alain-G. Gagnon. Toronto: University of Toronto Press, 1999.

———. "The Agonic Freedom of Citizens." *Economy and Society* 28 (1999): 161–82.

———. *An Approach to Political Philosophy: Locke in Contexts*. Cambridge: Cambridge University Press, 1993.

———. *A Discourse on Property: John Locke and His Adversaries*. Cambridge: Cambridge University Press, 1980.

———. "Placing the *Two Treatises*." Pp. 253–82 in *Political Discourse in Early Modern Britain: Essays in Honour of John Pocock*. Edited by Nicholas Philipson and Quentin Skinner. Cambridge: Cambridge University Press, 1993.

———. "Rediscovering America: The *Two Treatises* and Aboriginal Rights." Pp. 137–76 in *An Approach to Political Philosophy: Locke in Contexts* by James Tully. Cambridge: Cambridge University Press, 1993.

———. *Strange Multiplicity: Constitutionalism in an Age of Diversity*. Cambridge: Cambridge University Press, 1995.

Tully, James, ed., *Meaning and Context: Quentin Skinner and His Critics*. Princeton: Princeton University Press, 1989.

Turner, Dale. *This Is Not a Peace Pipe: Towards a Critical Indigenous Philosophy*. Toronto: University of Toronto Press, 2006.

Usner, Daniel H. *Indians, Settlers and Slaves in a Frontier Exchange Economy: The Lower Mississippi Valley before 1783*. Chapel Hill: Institute of Early American History and Culture, Williamsburg, Va., by University of North Carolina Press, 1992.

van Gelderen, Martin, and Quentin Skinner. *Republicanism: A Shared Heritage*. Cambridge: Cambridge University Press, 2002.

Walzer, Michael. *On Toleration*. New Haven, Conn.: Yale University Press, 1997.

Webb, Stephen Saunders. "'The Peaceable Kingdom': Quaker Pennsylvania in the Stuart Empire." Pp. 173–94 in *The World of William Penn*. Edited by Richard S. Dunn and Mary Maples Dunn. Philadelphia: University of Pennsylvania Press, 1986.

———. "William Blathwayt, Imperial Fixer: From Popish Plot to Glorious Revolution." *William and Mary Quarterly* 25 (1968): 3–21.

Webber, Jeremy. "Beyond Regret: Mabo's Implications for Australian Constitutionalism." Pp. 60–88 in *Political Theory and the Rights of Indigenous Peoples*. Edited by Duncan Ivison et al. Cambridge: Cambridge University Press, 2000.

Weir, Robert. *Colonial South Carolina—A History*. Millwood, N.Y.: KTO Press, 1983.

White, Richard. *The Middle Ground: Indians, Empires, and Republics in the Great Lakes Region, 1650–1815*. Cambridge: Cambridge University Press, 1991.

Williams, Lorraine E. "Indians and Europeans in the Delaware Valley, 1620–1655." Pp. 112–20 in *New Sweden in America*. Edited by Carol E. Hoffecker et al. Newark: University of Delaware Press, 1995.

Williams, Robert A. *The American Indian in Western Legal Thought*. New York: Oxford University Press, 1990.

———. *Linking Arms Together: American Indian Treaty Visions of Law and Peace 1600–1800*. London: Routledge, 1998.

———. "Linking Arms Together: Multicultural Constitutionalism in a North American Indigenous Vision of Law and Peace." *California Law Review* 82, no. 981 (1994): 981–1052.

Wittgenstein, Ludwig. *The Blue and Brown Books: Preliminary Studies for the "Philosophical Investigations."* Oxford: Basil Blackwell, 1972.

———. *Philosophical Investigations*, 3d ed. Translated by G. E. M. Anscombe. New York: Macmillan, 1958.

Wood, Betty. *The Origins of American Slavery: Freedom and Bondage in the English Colonies*. New York: Hill and Wang, 1997.

Wood, Peter. *Black Majority: Negroes in Colonial South Carolina from 1670 through the Stono Rebellion*. New York: W. W. Norton, 1975.

Woolhouse, Roger. *Locke: A Biography*. Cambridge: Cambridge University Press, 2007.

Young, Iris Marion. "Hybrid Democracy: Iroquois Federalism and the Postcolonial Project." Pp. 237–58 in *Political Theory and the Rights of Indigenous Peoples*. Edited by Duncan Ivison et al. Cambridge: Cambridge University Press, 2000.

———. *Inclusion and Democracy*. Oxford: Oxford University Press, 2001.

autonomy (*cont.*)
    51; self-sufficiency in Carolina and,
    67–68, 71–72
Avalon colony, Newfoundland, 28, 31,
    33, 47
Axtell, James, 14

Bagehot, Walter, 2
Baltimore, Lord. *See* Calvert, Cecilius,
    Baron Baltimore; Calvert, George,
    Baron Baltimore
Barbados, 149n43
Barbados Proclamation, 71, 78, 150n73
Barker, Eirlys, 152n84
Benton, Lauren, 124–25
Berkeley, John, Baron Berkeley of
    Stratton, 58, 64, 148n29
Berkeley, William, Sir, 58, 148n29, 149n43
Bhabha, Homi, 17
bicameral legislature, in Pennsylvania,
    92–93
Bilder, Mary Sarah: on collapse of
    proprietorship, 141n49; on delegation
    of authority, 2; on Maryland, 54; on
    nonproprietary colonies, 118; on plu-
    rality of documents, 38; on proprietary
    colonialism, 1–2; on repugnancy, 36,
    137n22
border ambiguity, in Pennsylvania, 97
Botein, Stephen, 90
British Columbia, 132–33
Brown, Michael, 128, 130
Bulkley, John, 120
Burke, Edmund, 1, 119
Burke, Wilson, 1
Byrnes, Giselle, 129

caciques, 63, 148nn35, 40
Calloway, Colin, 42, 44
Calvert, Cecilius, Baron Baltimore:
    Assembly and challenges to, 46–47;
    Carolina and, 58; Copley's complaints

to, 49; fur trade and, 44; *Instructions*,
    38–45; Penn and, 88, 91; privilege,
    insecurity, and, 33; promotional tract
    by, 29; proprietary charter to, 25–26,
    45–46. *See also* Maryland colony
Calvert, George, Baron Baltimore, 26, 31,
    42, 47
Calvert, Leonard, 38, 40
Canada, 132–33
Caribbean slaves, 79
Carolina and the *Fundamental Consti-
    tutions*, 59–60; creation and author-
    ship of, 147n28; earlier charters and,
    58, 146n13; Harrington's *Oceana* and,
    61–65; imaginaries and, 65–66; inter-
    pretations of, 79–82; Locke's mem-
    oranda and, 69–72, 80, 150n67; Lord
    Proprietors and charter, 57–58, 148n28;
    Maryland charter compared to, 56–57,
    58–59; native knowledge and adap-
    tation, 69–79; number of proprie-
    tors, 150n65; overview of, 55–57;
    Penn's *Frame* compared to, 94–95;
    plural-singular ambivalence and,
    146n6; preamble paragraph of, 60–61;
    settlers from Barbados and Virginia
    and, 149n43; slavery and, 78–79;
    supreme courts of law under, 149n55;
    temporary laws and grounded prac-
    tices, 66–69
Carteret, George, 58, 148n29
Castoriadis, Cornelius, 65–66
Catholics vs. Protestants, in Maryland,
    28–29, 38–39
Charles I, 28, 146n13
Charles II, 57, 59, 87, 92, 147n14
Charter of Pennsylvania, 88
charters: assemblies and, 47; of Carolina
    (1629 and 1663), 58; for English
    boroughs, 2; Hobbes on meaning of,
    26–27; incomplete theorizing in, 51;
    legal hybridity and, 9; of Massachusetts

Bay, 36; of Pennsylvania, 86–90;
performance of, 13, 41; proprietary, 2;
as starting points, 19; Virginia, 36. *See
also* Carolina and the *Fundamental
Constitutions*; Maryland charter

chorographical discourse, 29

civic humanism. *See* republicanism and
civic humanism

Claiborne, William, 26, 45, 48, 53–54

Clarendon, Lord. *See* Hyde, Edward, Earl
of Clarendon

Clarke, William, 158n63

Cocke, Lars Parsson (Lasse), 98, 107

Colleton, John, 58, 148n29

Colleton, Peter, 67, 149n43

Colleton, Thomas, 67

colonialism: contemporary theory on,
7–8; cultural negotiation and, 15;
English shift to consolidating Crown's
interest and, 89–90; genealogies
of, 81–82; imperial administration,
unified system of, 119; Locke and, 81;
proprietary form of, 1–2, 30, 89, 141n49

colonists. *See under names of specific
colonies*

Committee of Trade and Plantations, 87,
89–90, 155n25

commodity, land as, 106–7

common constitutionalism, 154n12

Commonwealth of Oceana, The
(Harrington), 60, 61–65, 92, 153n102

composite monarchies, 117–18

confirmatory treaties, 107

conflicts: Carolina and prospect of, 69;
center-periphery relationship, 53;
distance and intracolonial, 37; fur trade
and, 44; intertribal, 105; in Maryland
Assembly, 48. *See also* power, privilege,
and authority

Connolly, William, 22

constitutionalism. *See* English constitutionalism; hybrid constitutionalism;

modern constitutionalism; proprietary
constitutionalism

contemporary theory of colonialism, 7–8

contractarian theories, 51–52, 123

conversion of indigenes, goal of, 74

Copley, Thomas, 49

Cornwallis, Thomas, 40, 46, 49

Council of Foreign Plantations, 148n29

courts, in Carolina's *Fundamental Constitutions*, 149n55

Covenant Chain confederation, 86, 103–5

Cranston, Maurice, 55, 70, 157n55

Craven, William, Earl of Craven, 58

Culpeper, Thomas, Lord Culpeper, 54

cultural hybridity, 14–18, 22

cultural kaleidoscope, 44–45

culture: cultural contact and negotiation
of, 14–15; humanist or rhetorical, 64;
situated understanding of, 22; as skill
set, 109; stadial histories, 7–8, 74, 115,
122. *See also* insertion; negotiation

customary law, 9, 11, 35, 123

Davidson, Thomas E., 43, 44

de-centered power, 101–6

deception in treaty making, 110–11

de Certeau, Michel, 37

Delaware tribes, trade with, 44. *See also*
Pennsylvania and treaty negotiation
with Lenape and Susquehannocks

Deleuze, Gilles, 20

democratic expression, Maryland Assembly as, 46

Derrida, Jacques, 15–16, 83, 109, 138n39

dialogic aspects of treaty negotiation, 107

discretion: in Carolina, 69; conflict
and, 44; cultural hybridity and, 14;
Machiavelli on, 142n61; in Maryland,
26, 34–35, 40–46, 51; meaning of, 35,
141n42; negotiation and, 36; in Pennsylvania, 88–89; religious tolerance and,
51; tacticality of, 41, 42

and periphery, 21; indeterminacy of outcome in, 110; insertion and, 116; negotiation and, 85; relation of, to power, 86, 111; variable power in, 105–6

hybridity: of colonial texts, 17; beyond proprietary constitutionalism, 114–15, 117–19; types of, 9–18. *See also* legal and political hybridity; *and subentries under names of specific colonies*

Hyde, Edward, Earl of Clarendon, 58, 64

imaginaries, 65–66; charter as founding narrative, 37; indigenous knowledge and, 73; republican and civic humanist motifs, influence of, 52

imperial administration, unified system of, 119

imperium in imperio, 2, 36, 37

India, 125

indigenes: African slaves vs., 78; alcohol and, 99; assistance to colonists by, 70–71, 143n65; Australian Aborigines, 126–28; conversion of, as goal, 74; crisscrossing relationships with, in Maryland, 44–45; knowledge from, in Carolina, 69–73; land rights of, 121–23, 161n24; law and social normativity and, 128–29; local guide and exchange in Maryland, 41–42; Locke's denigration of practices of, 153n101; Māori in New Zealand, 129–30; in Maryland charter territory, 26; names attributed to, 150n72; stadial narratives of, 7–8, 74, 115, 122; toleration in Maryland and, 40; trade and insertion in Maryland and, 42–44, 49; trade and proprietary power in Carolina and, 74–77, 152n84; violence against, 77–78. *See also* Pennsylvania and treaty negotiation with Lenape and Susquehannocks;

treaty negotiation; *and under names of specific Native American tribes*

Ingle, Richard, 53–54

insecurity: ambition and, 114, 117; hybrid constitutionalisms and, 21; palatine privilege and, 32–33; pursuit of profit and, 80; variable power and, 105

insertion: in Carolina, 77; in Maryland, 42–44; in Pennsylvania, 87

Instructions (Calvert), 38–45

Iroquois Confederacy, 44, 101–5, 108

Jefferson, Thomas, 120–21

Jennings, Francis, 104

Jesuits, in Maryland colony, 39

Johansen, Bruce, 130, 131

Johnson and Graham's Lessee v. William M'Intosh, 113, 121–22

joint-stock vs. proprietary ventures, 30

Jordan, David, 30, 46, 47, 140n28

Jordan, Terry, 97

judicial decisions, U.S., 121–23

jurisdictio, 52, 136n21

jurisdictionalism, and jurisdictional conflicts, 122–25

Kant, Immanuel, 5

Kaups, Matti, 97

Knapp, Steven, 113

knowledge: agricultural, of slaves, 79; cross-cultural, as relational power, 108–9; humanist culture and contingency of, 64; local, in Maryland, 41–43; of natives, and adaptation in Carolina, 69–73, 80–81; subjugated, 73

Konig, David, 2, 35, 51, 120–21, 144n99

Kupperman, Karen, 97

Lambarde, William, 141n42

land, division of: in Carolina's *Fundamental Constitutions* and Harrington's

land, division of (*cont.*)
Oceana, 62, 148n35; in Pennsylvania,
87
land as commodity vs. usufruct, 106–7
landgraves, 63, 148nn35, 40
land tenure: indigenous, Proprietor view
of, 74; in *Johnson and Graham's Lessee
v. William M'Intosh*, 121–22; land
held in free and common socage vs.
in capite, 29, 88; in *Mabo v. Queensland*, 126–28; New York Oneida and,
130–32; terra nullius doctrine and,
127–28
languages, 43; translation and, 42, 108
Latin America, 125
laziness, 67–68
leet-men, 63, 148nn35, 40
legal and political hybridity: affirmative
and negative locutions, 36; in Carolina,
58; center-periphery relationship and,
53; confusion over, with revisions
and repeals, 50, 144n93; in English
constitutionalism, 2–3, 38, 51–52;
Hulsebosch on power centers and,
118; incomplete theorizing and constitutional silence, 51, 144n101; in
Maryland charter, 29–30, 33–38; in
nonproprietary settlements, 118; overview of, 3–4, 9–11; in Pennsylvania,
90, 95; power struggles in Maryland
and, 45–53; republican, feudal, and
authoritative rule and, 65, 68–69
legal development, American, 121–23
legal regimes, 124
Lenape: trade and, 44; treaty negotiation
as de-centered power and, 103–5; treaty
negotiation as monopolistic power
and, 96–101. *See also* Pennsylvania and
treaty negotiation with Lenape and
Susquehannocks
Letter to the Free Society of Traders
(Penn), 99

Levy, Jacob, 53, 119, 123–24
liberalism, reassessment of, 80–81
locale, locality: acquisition of knowledge
of, in Maryland, 41–43; cultural
hybridity and, 14–15; subjugated
knowledges and, 73
Locke, John: creation of Carolina's
Fundamental Constitutions and,
148n28; Harrington's *Oceana* and,
153n102; memoranda of, 69–72, 80,
150n67; on Penn's *Frame*, 95, 157n55;
"Proposal on Virginia," 157n60; as
secretary to Lord Proprietors of Carolina, 69–70, 80; on social compact,
137n27; Toinard and, 153n104; *Two
Treatises of Government*, 55–56, 59–60,
80–81, 153n101
Logan, James, 107–8

Mabo v. Queensland (Australia), 126–28
Machiavelli, Niccolò, 55, 62–63, 142n61
Madison, James, 123
magistrate judgments, in Maryland,
50–51
Mahoney, James, 116
Mancke, Elizabeth, 159n77
Māori, 129–30
Marshall, John, 121–22
Maryland Assembly, 46–54
Maryland charter: Assembly and, 46;
Carolina's *Fundamental Constitutions*
compared to, 56–59; discretion in,
34–35, 51; legal hybridity in, 29–30;
palatinate model and, 25–26, 30–33;
poor laborers in, 142n56; territorial
language in, 28–30
Maryland colony: Calvert's *Instructions*
and discretion in, 38–45; legal
hybridity and discretion in, 33–38;
legal hybridity and power struggles
in, 45–54; overtures of, to Pennsylvania colonists, 97, 101; overview of,

25–28; palatinate model and, 30–33; "perpetuall" vs. temporary statutes in, 144n93; relocations from Virginia to, 38–39; suspension and restoration of proprietary government in, 54; territorial disputes and, 30. *See also* Maryland Assembly; Maryland charter

Massachusetts Bay colony, 36

Massachusetts charter (1620), 141n42

Matthews, Maurice, 77

McFarlane, Anthony, 59

McHugh, P. G., 122, 161n25

McIlwain, Charles, 136n21

mediation: cultural hybridity and, 14; by indigenes, 45; limits of cross-cultural, 129; treaties and, 105

Memorandum of Additional Instructions to William Markham and William Crispin and John Bezer (Penn), 98

Merrell, James, 84, 101–2, 108, 150n72, 159n81

mines, alleged discovery of, 76–77

modern constitutionalism: Aboriginal people and, 95; Levy on, 123; Tully on, 6–7, 53, 115

modernity, 13–14, 116, 120–26

Monck, George, Duke of Albemarle, 57, 91

monopolistic power, treaty negotiation as, 96–101

moral discourse, in Penn's treaty making, 99, 100

More, Thomas, Sir, 81

Muldoon, James, 117–18, 161n24

Nanticokes, 44

Native Americans. *See* indigenes

Navigation Acts, 89

ne exeat regno, right of, 84

negotiation: adjudication and, 126–33; cross-cultural knowledge and, 108–9; cultural hybridity and, 14, 15, 22; Derrida on "shuttling" and, 15–16, 83, 109, 138n39; discretion and, 36; of English empire, 90; Maryland colony and, 42, 49; of power between regions, 159n77; vulnerabilities in, 111. *See also* treaty negotiation

Neville, Henry, 81

New Netherlands, 97

New Sweden, 87

New York, 118

New York Oneida, 130–32

New Zealand, 129–30

nobility, hereditary, 148n35

non-contractarian forms, 123–24

oaths, 39

Oceana (Harrington), 60–65, 92, 153n102

Oneida, 130–32

opportunism, constitutionalism of, 79

pacification, and treaty negotiation, 100, 105

Pagden, Anthony, 31, 84

palatine model: in Carolina, 58, 61; in England, 140n22; in Maryland, 25–26, 30–33; origins of, 140n22; overview of, 2; Penn and denial of, 84–85, 155n21; republicanism mixed with, 68

pamphlets. *See* promotional pamphlets

Parekh, Bhikhu, 6, 55–56

Pataki, George, 131

paternalism, 4, 64–65, 68–69, 150n65

path dependence, and path development, 116–17

Peltonen, Markku, 51–52, 145n103

Penn, William: background of, 91; charter and restricted proprietary power of, 84–85, 87–89, 155n21; *Frame of the Government of the Province*, 90–96, 157n55; *Letter to the Free Society of Traders*, 99; *Memorandum*

Penn, William (*cont.*)
    *of Additional Instructions to William
    Markham and William Crispin and
    John Bezer*, 98; palatine authority and,
    2; *Remonstrance for the Inhabitants of
    Philadelphia*, 101; romantic image of,
    83–84; *Some Account of the Province
    of Pennsylvania*, 86–87; treaty
    negotiation by, 83, 96–101, 105, 107
Pennsylvania and treaty negotiation
    with Lenape and Susquehannocks:
    addition of territory to, 159n69;
    bicameral legislature and, 92–93;
    Carolina's *Fundamental Constitutions*
    compared to, 94–95; charter and
    curtailed proprietary power of, 86–90,
    155n21; contemporary theory in,
    85–86; English political context and,
    91–92; *Frame of the Government of
    the Province* and, 90–96; indigenous
    motivations and de-centered power
    of, 101–6; monopolistic power and,
    96–101; overview of, 83–85; relational
    power and, 106–11; territorial
    ambiguity and, 97
Pennsylvania Assembly, 88–89, 92–93
performative recitation of charters, 13, 41
Piscataways, 42
place. *See* locale, locality
Pocock, J. G. A., 9, 11–12, 18–20, 30,
    51–52
political hybridity. *See* legal and political
    hybridity
polyvalent authority, 10, 118
polyvocality of English constitution, 10
power, privilege, and authority: absent
    proprietors and, 10–11; agrarian law
    for stabilization of, 63; Carolina
    temporary laws and balance of,
    67, 69; Carolina trade and, 74–76;
    collapse of proprietorship and, 141n49;

complex intercultural tensions and,
    79; contextual and operational effects
    of constitutionalism and, 117; cultural
    hybridity and, 14; dual authority and
    imperium in imperio, 2, 36, 37; Foucault
    on, 106; legal hybridity and power
    struggles in Maryland, 45–53; Mary-
    land charter and, 29, 31–33; as negoti-
    ated between regions, 159n77; open-
    ended, 9; in palatinate model, 30–32;
    Penn and restricted proprietary power,
    84–85, 87–89, 98–100; practices
    of founding vs. claims of, 81; relin-
    quishing of, in Carolina, 80; treaty
    negotiation and contemporary theory
    on, 86; treaty negotiation and de-
    centered power, 101–6; treaty negotia-
    tion and monopolistic power, 96–101;
    treaty negotiation as relational power,
    106–11; variable power in hybrid
    constitutionalism, 105–6; vulner-
    abilities in negotiating and, 111. *See also*
    palatine model
printing revolution, 137n32
privilege. *See* power, privilege, and
    authority
Privy Council, 88–90, 99–100
proclamations, 48
promotional pamphlets, 12–13, 29, 64
"Proposal on Virginia" (Locke), 157n60
proprietary charters. *See* charters
proprietary constitutionalism: extension
    of hybridity beyond, 114–15, 117–19;
    locality, discretion, and limits of
    power, 45; path dependence and path
    development, 116–17; as plural, local,
    and elastic, 109; theory and practice
    blurred in, 19–20. *See also* charters
proprietary form of colonization: collapse
    of, 141n49; eclipse of, 89; joint-stock
    ventures vs., 30; overview of, 1–2. *See*

also subentries under names of specific
    colonies
proprietors, 9–11. *See also under names of*
    specific colonies and proprietors
protectionism, treaty making and, 100
Protestants, Protestantism: influences
    of, in English republicanism, 149n48;
    Maryland and Catholics vs., 28–29,
    38–39
Provincial Council (Pennsylvania), 92–93
provisions, settler requests for, 68–69,
    72–73
provocation, historical, 115

realist power, and Penn, 100
reciprocity, 85, 103, 108
referenda, in British Columbia, 132–33
relational power, 106–11
religion: Catholics vs. Protestants in
    Maryland, 28–29, 38–39; conversion
    of indigenes and, 74; Penn's *Frame*
    and, 95–96; Protestant influences in
    English republicanism, 149n48
Remonstrance for the Inhabitants of
    Philadelphia (Penn), 101
republicanism and civic humanism,
    12–13, 51–52, 64–65; Carolina
    adaptation and, 57, 60–65; English mix
    of Protestant and humanist influ-
    ences and, 149n48; Harrington's
    Oceana and, 61–65, 92; imaginary of,
    in Carolina, 66; indigenous knowledge
    and, 73–74; Machiavelli and, 63; Penn-
    sylvania charter and, 92–93
repugnancy standard, 9, 36, 58, 137n22
Restoration politics, 59, 60
Reynolds, Henry, 128
Rhode Island, 118
Richter, Daniel, 84, 101–4, 159n81
Ritter, David, 127
Ross, Richard, 89, 90, 119, 142n52

Rountree, Helen C., 43, 44
Rousseau, Jean-Jacques, 11
rum, 99

Sandford, Robert, 71
Sayle, William, 67, 76
Seed, Patricia, 41
self-sufficiency in Carolina, 67–68, 71–72
serfs, 148n35
Shaftesbury, Earl of. *See* Ashley Cooper,
    Anthony, Baron Ashley and Earl of
    Shaftesbury
Shenandoah, Maisie, 131
silence, constitutional, 51, 144n101
simultaneity, 13–14
Skinner, Quentin, 12, 18, 65, 126
slavery, 78–79, 143n86
Smith, Adam, 95
Smith, H. F. Russell, 59, 66–67, 147n28
Soderlund, Jean, 155n21
Some Account of the Province of Pennsyl-
    vania (Penn), 86–87
Sommerville, Johann, 149n48
South Africa, 125
sovereignty: dual, 53, 57; indigenous, in
    Australia, 127, 128; legal regimes and,
    124–25; performances of, 13; popular,
    6; symbolized in recitations of char-
    ters, 13
space, colonial, 12–13
Spady, James, 107
stadial histories, 7–8, 74, 115, 122
state development, 125–26
state making, as "organized crime," 100
statute law: common law vs., 9; Mary-
    land Assembly and, 48, 50; Maryland
    charter and, 35, 47. *See also* legal and
    political hybridity
Strange Multiplicity (Tully), 6–7
Sugrue, Thomas, 83, 103, 106–7
Sunstein, Cass, 51, 144n101

Susquehannocks, 44, 96–101, 103–5. *See also* Pennsylvania and treaty negotiation with Lenape and Susquehannocks

Swedish settlers: trade and, 103–4; treaties and, 84, 97, 107

Taylor, Alan, 38

temporal hybridity, 11–14

temporary laws and order: Calvert's *Instructions*, 38–45; in Carolina, 66–68; from Maryland Assembly, 48–49; "perpetuall" laws vs., 144n93

terra nullius, 127–28

Tilly, Charles, 100

Tocqueville, Alexis de, 25

Toinard, Nicholas, 153n104

toleration, 40, 51, 62, 88, 95–96

Tomlins, Christopher, 1–2, 56, 89

trade: Carolina and, 74–77, 152n84; cross-cultural knowledge and, 108–9; in Delaware River area, 104–5; Maryland and, 42–44, 49; translation and, 43

translation, 42, 43, 108

treaty constitutionalism, 86

treaty negotiation: agonism and deception in, 110–11; British Columbia and referenda on, 132–33; Carolina and restrictions on, 74; confirmatory treaties, 107; as constitutional power, 106–11; in East Indies, 118; exclusion and opportunism in, 110; impartiality of, 78; indigenous participation and de-centered power, 101–6; interactive and multicultural model of adjudication, 86; *Mabo v. Queensland*, 126–28; modern, 110; as monopolistic power, 96–101; provisions and gifts offered in, 98–99; for trade (Maryland), 44; Waitangi Tribunal and, 129–30

treaty rights, 122–23

triumphalist narratives, 7, 24, 82, 117, 126

Tully, James: on common constitutionalism, 154n12; on cultural diversity, 22; on "empire of uniformity," 6, 95; influence of, 136n12; on modern constitutionalism, 6–7, 53, 115; on treaties, 85–86, 110

Turning Stone Casino (New York), 130–31

Two Treatises of Government (Locke), 55–56, 59–60, 80–81, 153n101

United States, 121–23, 130–32

usufruct conception of land, 106–7

utopian literature, 81, 153n102

violence against indigenes, 77–78

Virginia: charters, 36; poor laborers in, 142n56; relocations to Carolina from, 149n43; relocations to Maryland from, 38–39

Virginia Company, 64–65

"virtue," cultivation of, 93–94

Waitangi Tribunal, New Zealand, 129–30

"walls," constitutional, 5

Webber, Jeremy, 126–29

West, Benjamin, 83

West, Joseph, 67–68, 72

Wharton, Samuel, 120

White, Andrew, 39, 41–43

Williams, Robert, 83, 85–86, 101, 103

Wittgenstein, Ludwig, 114

Wood, Peter, 79

Woodward, Henry, 71, 75, 76

Woolhouse, Roger, 70

Worcester v. Georgia, 122–23

Young, Iris Marion, 6, 22, 85–86

Young, Toby, 45

VICKI HSUEH is an associate professor of political science
at Western Washington University.

Library of Congress Cataloging-in-Publication Data
Hsueh, Vicki.
Hybrid constitutions : challenging legacies of law, privilege,
and culture in colonial America / Vicki Hsueh.
p. cm.
Includes bibliographical references and index.
ISBN 978-0-8223-4618-0 (cloth : alk. paper)
ISBN 978-0-8223-4632-6 (pbk. : alk. paper)
1. Constitutional history—United States—States.
2. Constitutional history—Great Britain—Colonies.
I. Title.
KF 4541.H78 2010
342.7302'9—dc22   2009039111